Praise for *Design Patterns Explained, Second Edition:*

The explanation of fundamental object-oriented concepts throughout is exceptional. I have struggled to teach similar concepts to beginners in my classes and I definitely plan to borrow some of the authors' approaches (and recommend the book, of course)!

—CLIF NOCK

Well-written, thought-provoking, and very enlightening. A must-read for anyone interested in design patterns and object-oriented development.

—JAMES HUDDLESTON

Design Patterns
Explained

The Software Patterns Series

Series Editor: John M. Vlissides

The Software Patterns Series (SPS) comprises pattern literature of lasting significance to software developers. Software patterns document general solutions to recurring problems in all software-related spheres, from the technology itself, to the organizations that develop and distribute it, to the people who use it. Books in the series distill experience from one or more of these areas into a form that software professionals can apply immediately.

Relevance and *impact* are the tenets of the SPS. Relevance means each book presents patterns that solve real problems. Patterns worthy of the name are intrinsically relevant; they are borne of practitioners' experiences, not theory or speculation. Patterns have impact when they change how people work for the better. A book becomes a part of the series not just because it embraces these tenets, but because it has demonstrated it fulfills them for its audience.

Titles in the series:

For more information, check out the series web site at www.awprofessional.com/series/swpatterns

Design Patterns Explained

A New Perspective on Object-Oriented Design
Second Edition

Alan Shalloway

James R. Trott

✦ Addison-Wesley

Boston • San Francisco • New York • Toronto • Montreal
London • Munich • Paris • Madrid
Capetown • Sydney • Tokyo • Singapore • Mexico City

Publisher: John Wait
Acquisitions Editor: John Neidhart
Executive Editor: Stephane Nakib
Editorial Assistant: Ebony Haight
Marketing Manager: Curt Johnson
Publicity: Joan Murray
Managing Editor: Gina Kanouse
Senior Project Editor: Sarah Kearns
Production Editor: Kerry Reardon
Manufacturing Buyer: Dan Uhrig

The publisher offers discounts on this book when ordered in quantity for bulk purchases and special sales. For more information, please contact:

U.S. Corporate and Government Sales
(800) 382-3419
corpsales@pearsoned.com

For sales outside of the U.S., please contact:

International Sales
international@pearsoned.com

Visit Addison-Wesley on the Web: www.awprofessional.com

Library of Congress Cataloging-in-Publication Data

LOC 2004108740

ISBN 0-321-24714-0

Text printed on recycled paper

3 4 5 6 7 8 9 10—MA—0605

Third printing, April, 2005

To Leigh, Bryan, Lisa, Michael, and Steven
for their love, support,
encouragement, and sacrifice.

—Alan Shalloway

To Jill, Erika, Lorien, Mikaela, and Geneva,
the roses in the garden of my life.
sola gloria Dei

—James R. Trott

Contents

PART V
Toward a New Paradigm of Design _____251

Chapter 14
The Principles and Strategies of Design
Patterns _____253

Chapter 15
Commonality and Variability Analysis_____269

Chapter 16
The Analysis Matrix _____279

Chapter 17
The Decorator Pattern _____297

PART VI
Other Values of Patterns _____313

Chapter 18
The Observer Pattern _____315

Preface

Should You Buy the Second Edition If You Already Own the First?

The answer, of course, is yes! Here's why.

Since the first edition was written, we have learned so much more about design patterns, including the following:

- How to use commonality and variability analysis to design application architectures

- How design patterns relate to and actually facilitate eXtreme programming (XP) and agile development.

- How testing is a first principle of quality coding.

- Why the use of factories to instantiate and manage objects is critical

- Which set of patterns are essential for students to help them learn how to think in patterns

This book covers all of these topics. We have deepened and clarified what we had before and have added some new content that you will find very helpful, including the following:

- Chapter 15: Commonality and Variability Analysis

- Chapter 20: Lessons from Design Patterns: Factories

- Chapter 21: The Object-Pool Pattern (a pattern not covered by the Gang of Four)

- Chapter 22: Factories Summarized

We have changed the order in which we present some of the patterns. This sequence is more helpful for the students in our courses as they learn the ideas behind patterns.

We have touched every chapter, incorporating the feedback we have received from our many readers over these past three years.

And, to help students, we have created study questions for each chapter (with answers on the book's companion Web site).

We can honestly say this is one of the few second editions that is definitely worth buying — even if you have the first one.

We would love to hear what you think.

—Alan and Jim

Design patterns and object-oriented programming. They hold such promise to make your life as a software designer and developer easier. Their terminology is bandied about every day in the technical and even the popular press. It can be hard to learn them, however, to become proficient with them, to understand what is really going on.

Perhaps you have been using an object-oriented or object-based language for years. Have you learned that the true power of objects is not inheritance, but is in "encapsulating behaviors"? Perhaps you are curious about design patterns and have found the literature a bit too esoteric and high-falutin. If so, this book is for you.

It is based on years of teaching this material to software developers, both experienced and new to object orientation. It is based upon the belief—and our experience—that when you understand the basic principles and motivations that underlie these concepts, why they are doing what they do, your learning curve will be incredibly shorter. And in our discussion of design patterns, you will understand the true mindset of object orientation, which is a necessity before you can become proficient.

As you read this book, you will gain a solid understanding of 12 core design patterns and a pattern used in analysis. You will learn that design patterns do not exist in isolation, but work in concert with other design patterns to help you create more robust applications. You will gain enough of a foundation that you will be able to read the design pattern literature, if you want to, and possibly discover patterns on your own. Most importantly, you will be better equipped to create flexible and complete software that is easier to maintain.

Although the 12 patterns we teach here are not all of the patterns you should learn, an understanding of these will enable you to learn the others on your own more easily. Instead of giving you more patterns than you need to get started, we have included pattern-related issues that will be more useful.

From Object Orientation to Patterns to True Object Orientation

In many ways, this book is a retelling of my personal experience learning design patterns. This started with learning the patterns themselves and then learning the principles behind them. I expanded this understanding into the realms of analysis and testing as well as learning how patterns relate to agile coding methods. This second edition of this book includes many additional insights I have had since publication of the first edition. Prior to studying design patterns, I considered myself to be reasonably expert in object-oriented analysis and design. My track record had included several fairly impressive designs and implementations in many industries. I knew C++ and was beginning to learn Java. The objects in my code were well-formed and tightly encapsulated. I could design excellent data abstractions for inheritance hierarchies. I thought I knew object orientation.

Now, looking back, I see that I really did not understand the full capabilities of object-oriented design, even though I was doing things the way most experts advised. It wasn't until I began to learn design patterns that my object-oriented design abilities expanded and deepened. Knowing design patterns has made me a better designer, even when I don't use these patterns directly.

I began studying design patterns in 1996. I was a C++/object-oriented design mentor at a large aerospace company in the Northwest. Several people asked me to lead a design pattern study group. That's where I met my coauthor, Jim Trott. In the study group, several interesting things happened. First, I grew fascinated with design patterns. I loved being able to compare my designs with the designs of others who had more experience than I. And second, I discovered that I was not taking full advantage of designing to interfaces and that I didn't always concern myself with seeing whether I could have an object use another object without knowing the used object's type. I also noticed that beginners in object-oriented design—those who would normally be deemed as learning design patterns too early— were benefiting as much from the study group as the experts were. The patterns presented examples of excellent object-oriented designs and illustrated basic object-oriented principles, which helped to mature their designs more quickly. By the end of the study sessions, I was convinced that design patterns were the greatest thing to happen to software design since the invention of object-oriented design.

When I looked at my work at the time, however, I saw that I was not incorporating *any* design patterns into my code. Or, at least, not consciously. Later, after learning patterns, I realized I had incorporated many design patterns into my code just out of being a good coder. However, now that I understand patterns better, I am able to use them better.

I just figured I didn't know enough design patterns yet and needed to learn more. At the time, I only knew about six of them. Then I had an epiphany. I was working as a mentor in object-oriented design for a project and was asked to create the project's high-level design. The leader of the project was extremely sharp, but was fairly new to object-oriented design.

The problem itself wasn't that difficult, but it required a great deal of attention to make sure the code was going to be easy to maintain. Literally, after about two minutes of looking at the problem, I had developed a design based on my normal approach of data abstraction. Unfortunately, it was also clear to me this was not going to be a good design. Data abstraction alone had failed me. I had to find something better.

Two hours later, after applying every design technique I knew, I was no better off. My design was essentially the same. What was most frustrating was that I knew there was a better design. I just couldn't see it. Ironically, I also knew of four design patterns that "lived" in my problem, but I couldn't see how to use them. Here I was—a supposed expert in object-oriented design—baffled by a simple problem!

Feeling very frustrated, I took a break and started walking down the hall to clear my head, telling myself I would not think of the problem for at least 10 minutes. Well, 30 seconds later, I was thinking about it again! But I had gotten an insight that changed my view of design patterns: rather than using patterns as individual items, I should use the design patterns together.

Patterns are supposed to be sewn together to solve a problem.

I had heard this before, but hadn't really understood it. Because patterns in software have been introduced as *design* patterns, I had always labored under the assumption that they had mostly to do with design. My thoughts were that in the design world, the patterns came as pretty much well-formed relationships between classes. Then I read Christopher Alexander's amazing book, *The Timeless Way of Building* (Oxford University Press, 1979). I learned that patterns existed at all levels—analysis, design, and implementation. Alexander discusses using patterns to help in the understanding of the problem domain (even in describing it), not just using them to create the design after the problem domain is understood.

My mistake had been in trying to create the classes in my problem domain and then stitch them together to make a final system, a process that Alexander calls a particularly bad idea. I had never asked whether I had the right classes because they just seemed so right, so obvious; they were the classes that immediately came to mind as I started my analysis, the "nouns" in the description of the system that we had been taught to look for. But I had struggled trying to piece them together.

When I stepped back and used design patterns and Alexander's approach to guide me in the creation of my classes, a far superior solution unfolded in only a matter of minutes. It was a good design, and we put it into production. I was excited—excited to have designed a good solution and excited about the power of design patterns. It was then that I started incorporating design patterns into my development work and my teaching.

I began to discover that programmers who were new to object-oriented design could learn design patterns, and in doing so, develop a basic set of object-oriented design skills. It was true for me, and it was true for the students whom I was teaching.

Imagine my surprise! The design pattern books I had been reading and the design pattern experts I had been talking to were saying that you really needed to have a good grounding in object-oriented design before embarking on a study of design patterns. Nevertheless, I saw, with my own eyes, students who learned object-oriented design concurrently with design patterns learned object-oriented design faster than those just studying object-oriented design. They even seemed to learn design patterns at almost the same rate as experienced object-oriented practitioners.

I began to use design patterns as a basis for my teaching. I began to call my classes *Pattern-Oriented Design: Design Patterns from Analysis to Implementation*.

I wanted my students to understand these patterns and began to discover that using an exploratory approach was the best way to foster this understanding. For instance, I found that it was better to present the Bridge pattern by presenting a problem and then have my students try to design a solution to the problem using a few guiding principles and strategies that I had found were present in most of the patterns. In their exploration, the students discovered the solution—essentially the Bridge pattern—and remembered it.

Design Patterns and Agile/XP

The guiding principles and strategies underlying design patterns seem very clear to me now. Certainly, they are stated in the "Gang of Four's" design patterns book, but too succinctly to be of value to me when I first read it. I believe the Gang of Four were writing for the Smalltalk community, which was very grounded in these principles and therefore needed little background. It took me a long time to understand them because of limitations in my own understanding of the object-oriented paradigm. It was only after integrating in my own mind the work of the Gang of Four with Alexander's work, Jim Coplien's work on commonality and variability analysis, and Martin Fowler's work in methodologies and analysis patterns that these principles became clear enough to me so that I was able to talk about them to others. It helped that I was making my livelihood explaining things to others—so I couldn't get away with making assumptions as easily as I could when I was just doing things for myself.

Since the first edition of this book appeared, I have been doing a considerable amount of agile development and have become very grounded in eXtreme Programming (XP) coding practices, test-driven development (TDD), and Scrum. Initially, I had a difficult

time reconciling design patterns with XP and TDD. However, I
quickly realized that both have great value and both are grounded in the same principles (although they take different design approaches). In fact, in our agile software development boot camps,
we make it clear that design patterns, used properly, are strong en-
ablers of agile development.

Throughout this book, I discuss many of the ways design patterns
relate to agile management and coding practices. If you are unfa-
miliar with XP, TDD, or Scrum, do not be too concerned about
these comments. However, if this is the case, I suggest the next
book you read be about one of these topics.

In any event, I found that these guiding principles and strategies
could be used to "derive" several of the design patterns. By "derive
a design pattern," I mean that if I looked at a problem that might be
solved by a design pattern, I could use the guiding principles and
strategies that I learned from patterns to come up with the solution
expressed in a pattern. I made it clear to my students that we weren't
really coming up with design patterns this way. Instead, I was just illustrating one possible thought process that the people who came up
with the original solutions, those that were eventually classified as design patterns, might have used.

My abilities to explain these few, but powerful, principles and strategies improved. As they did, I found that it became more useful to explain an increasing number of the Gang of Four patterns. In fact, I use
these principles and strategies to explain virtually all the patterns I discuss in my design patterns course.

I found that I was using these principles in my own designs both with
and without patterns. This didn't surprise me. If using these strategies resulted in a design equivalent to a design pattern when I knew
the pattern was present, that meant they were giving me a way to
derive excellent designs (because patterns are excellent designs by

definition). Why would I get any poorer designs from these techniques just because I didn't know the name of the pattern that might or might not be present anyway?

These insights helped hone my training process (and now my writing process). I had already been teaching my courses on several levels. I was teaching the fundamentals of object-oriented analysis and design. I did that by teaching design patterns and using them to illustrate good examples of object-oriented analysis and design. In addition, by using the patterns to teach the concepts of object orientation, my students were also better able to understand the principles of object orientation. And by teaching the guiding principles and strategies, my students were able to create designs of comparable quality to the patterns themselves.

I relate this story because this book follows much the same pattern as my course (pun intended). Virtually all the material in this book now is covered in one of our courses on design patterns, test-driven-development or agile development best practices.[1]

As you read this book, you will learn the patterns. Even more importantly, you will learn why they work and how they can work together, and the principles and strategies upon which they rely. It will be useful to draw on your own experiences. When I present a problem in the text, it is helpful if you imagine a similar problem that you have come across. This book isn't about new bits of information or new patterns to apply, but rather a new way of looking at object-oriented software development. I hope that your own experiences, connected with the principles of design patterns, will prove to be a powerful ally in your learning.

Alan Shalloway
December 2000
Updated October 2004

---

1. See the book's companion Web site, *http://www.netobjectives.com/dpexplained*, to see more about these courses.

From Artificial Intelligence to Patterns to True Object Orientation

My journey into design patterns had a different starting point than Alan's, but we have reached the same conclusions:

- Pattern-based analyses make you a more effective and efficient analyst because they enable you to deal with your models more abstractly and because they represent the collected experiences of many other analysts.

- Patterns help people to learn principles of object orientation. The patterns help to explain why we do what we do with objects.

I started my career in *artificial intelligence* (AI) creating rule-based expert systems. This involves listening to experts and creating models of their decision-making processes and then coding these models into rules in a knowledge-based system. As I built these systems, I began to see repeating themes: In common types of problems, experts tended to work in similar ways. For example, experts who diagnose problems with equipment tend to look for simple, quick fixes first, and then they get more systematic, breaking the problem into component parts; in their systematic diagnosis, however, they tend to try first inexpensive tests or tests that will eliminate broad classes of problems before other kinds of tests. This was true whether we were diagnosing problems in a computer or a piece of oil field equipment.

Today I would call these recurring themes patterns. Intuitively I began to look for these recurring themes as I was designing new expert systems. My mind was open and friendly to the idea of patterns, even though I did not know what they were.

Then, in 1994, I discovered that researchers in Europe had codified these patterns of expert behavior and put them into a package that they called *Knowledge Analysis and Design Support* (KADS). Dr. Karen Gardner, a most gifted analyst, modeler, mentor, and human being, began to apply KADS to her work in the United States. She extended the European's work to apply KADS to object-oriented systems. She opened my eyes to an entire world of pattern-based analysis and design that was forming in the software world, in large part due to Christopher Alexander's work. Her book *Cognitive Patterns* (Cambridge University Press, 1998) describes this work.

Suddenly I had a structure for modeling expert behaviors without getting trapped by the complexities and exceptions too early. I was able to complete my next three projects in less time, with less rework, and with greater end-user satisfaction, because

- I could design models more quickly because the patterns predicted for me what ought to be there. They told me what the essential objects were and what to pay special attention to.

- I was able to communicate much more effectively with experts because we had a more structured way to deal with the details and exceptions.

- The patterns allowed me to develop better end-user training for my system because the patterns predicted the most important features of the system.

This last point is significant. Patterns help end users understand systems because they provide the context for the system, why we are doing things in a certain way. We can use patterns to describe the guiding principles and strategies of the system. And we can use patterns to develop the best examples to help end users understand the system.

I was hooked.

So, when a design patterns study group started at my place of employment, I was eager to go. This is where I met Alan, who had reached a similar point in his work as an object-oriented designer and mentor. The result is this book.

Since writing the first edition, I have learned just how deeply this approach to analysis can get into your head. I have been involved in many different sorts of projects, many outside of software development. I look at systems of people working together, exchanging knowledge, exchanging ideas, living in remote places. The principles of patterns and object orientation have stood me well here, too. Just as in computer systems, much efficiency is to be gained by reducing the dependencies among work systems.

I hope that the principles in this book help you in your own journey to become a more effective and efficient analyst.

James R. Trott
December 2000
Updated October 2004

A Note About Conventions Used in This Book

In the writing of this book, we had to make several choices about style and convention. Some of our choices have surprised our readers. So it is worth a few comments about why we have chosen to do what we have done.

Approach	Rationale
First person voice	This book is a collaborative effort between two authors. We debated and refined our ideas to find the best ways to explain these concepts. Alan tried them out in his courses, and we refined some more. We chose to use the first person singular in the body of this book because it enables us to tell the story in what we hope is a more engaging and natural style.

Approach	Rationale
Scanning text	We have tried to make this book easy to scan so that you can get the main points even if you do not read the full body of text, or so that you can quickly find the information you need. We make significant use of tables and bulleted lists. We provide text in the outside margin that summarizes paragraphs. With the discussion of each pattern, we provide a summary table of the key features of the pattern. Our hope is that these will make the book that much more accessible.
Code examples	This book is about analysis and design more than implementation. Our intent is to help you think about crafting good designs based on the insights and best practices of the object-oriented community, as expressed in design patterns. One of the challenges for all of us programmers is to avoid going to the implementation too early, doing before thinking. Knowing this, we have purposefully tried to stay away from too much discussion on implementation. Our code examples may seem a bit lightweight and fragmentary. Specifically, we never provide error checking in the code. This is because we are trying to use the code to illustrate concepts. However, the book's companion Web site, at http://www.netobjectives.com/dpexplained, contains more complete code examples from which the fragments were extracted. Examples in C++ and C# are also present at this site.
Strategies and principles	Ours is an introductory book. It will help you be able to get up to speed quickly with design patterns. You will understand the principles and strategies that motivate design patterns. After reading this book, you can go on to a more scholarly book or a reference book. The last chapter points you to many of the references that we have found useful.
Show breadth and give a taste	We are trying give you a taste for design patterns, to expose you to the breadth of the pattern world but not go into depth in any of them (see the previous point).

Approach	Rationale
Show breadth and give a taste *(cont.)*	We are trying give you a taste for design patterns, Our thought was this: If you brought someone to the United States for a two-week visit, what would you show that person? Maybe a few sites to help him get familiar with architectures, communities, the feel of cities and the vast spaces that separate them, freeways, and coffee shops. But you would not be able to show him everything. To fill in his knowledge, you might choose to show him slide shows of many other sites and cities to give him a taste of the country. Then he could make plans for future visits. Likewise, we are showing you the major sites in design patterns, and then giving you tastes of other areas, so that you can plan your own journey into patterns.

How to Read Java Code
If You Are a C# Developer

All the code examples in this book are written in Java. If you do not have experience with Java but can read C#, here is what you need to know:

Java uses the words **extends** and **implements** to denote a class that extends another class or one that implements an interface, rather than the colon (:), which is used for both purposes in C#.

Hence, in Java, you would see

```
public class NewClass extends BaseClass
```

or

```
public class NewClass implements AnInterface
```

whereas in C#, you would see

```
public class NewClass : BaseClass
```

or

```
public class NewClass : AnInterface
```

All methods are virtual in Java, and therefore you don't specify whether they are **new** or **overridden**. There are no such keywords in Java; all subclass methods override any methods they reimplement from a base class. Although there are other differences, they won't show up in our code examples.

How to Read Java Code If You Are a C++ Developer

This is a little more difficult, but not much more. The most obvious difference is the lack of header files. But how to read the combined header-code file is self-evident. In addition to the C# differences, Java never stores objects on the stack. Java stores objects in heap storage and stores variables that hold references (pointers) to objects on the stack. Every object must be created with a **new**.

Hence, in Java you would see

```
MyClass anObject= new MyClass();
anObject.someMethod();
```

whereas in C++, you would see

```
MyClass *anObject= new MyClass();
anObject->someMethod();
```

Thus Java code looks like C++ code if you add an asterisk (*) in the declaration of every variable name that references an object and convert the period (.) to a hyphen followed by a right-angle bracket (->).

Feedback

Design patterns are a work in progress, a conversation among practitioners who discover best practices, who discover fundamental principles in object orientation.

We value your feedback on this book:

- What did we do well or poorly?
- Are there errors that need to be corrected?
- Was there something that was confusingly written?

Please visit us at the Net Objectives companion Web site for this book; the URL is http://www.netobjectives.com/dpexplained. At this site, you will find our latest research as well as a discussion group related to this book and to software development in general. Please post corrections, comments, insights, and "aha" moments to this discussion group.

New in the Second Edition

This second edition represents several changes and improvements over the first edition. It reflects what we have learned from using and teaching design patterns over the past several years as well as the generous and valuable feedback we have received from our readers.

Here is a highlight of changes:

- Chapter reordering (for instance, the Strategy pattern is described earlier in the book).
- Expanded discussion about *commonality and variability analysis* (CVA).
- A synthesis of eXtreme Programming (XP) and design patterns.

- All code examples complete rather than notional or fragments. All code is in Java. The Web site also has C# and C++ examples.

- Why the use of factories as object instantiators/managers proves extremely helpful.

- A design pattern not in the Gang of Four: the Object Pool pattern.

- A discussion of the pitfalls of patterns, including a caution to treat patterns as guides to help you think. Patterns are not truth!

- We also made numerous small corrections in grammar and style.

Acknowledgments

Almost every preface ends with a list of acknowledgments of those who helped in the development of the book. We never fully appreciated how true this was until doing a book of our own. Such an effort is truly a work of a community. The list of people to whom we are in debt is long.

The following people are especially significant to us:

- Debbie Lafferty and John Neidhart from Addison-Wesley, who never grew tired of encouraging us and keeping us on track.

- Scott Bain, our colleague who patiently reviewed this work and gave us insights. His collaboration with Alan at Net Objectives also led to many of the new insights in the second edition of this book.

- Our team of reviewers: James Huddleston, Steve Metsker, and Clifton Nock.

- And especially Leigh and Jill, our patient wives, who put up with us and encouraged us in our dream of this book.

We received fantastic comments from so many people who reviewed the first edition and the drafts of this present edition. We especially want to recognize Brian Henderson, Bruce Trask, Greg Frank, and Sudharsan Varadharajan, who shared freely and patiently their insights, suggestions, and questions.

Special thanks from Alan:

- Several of my students early on had an impact they probably never knew. Many times during my courses, I hesitated to project new ideas, thinking I should stick with the tried and true. However, their enthusiasm in my new concepts when I first started my courses encouraged me to project more and more of my own ideas into the curriculum I was putting together. Thanks to Lance Young, Peter Shirley, John Terrell, and Karen Allen. They serve as a constant reminder to me how encouragement can go a long way.

- Thanks to John Vlissides for his thoughtful comments and tough questions.

- For the second edition, I want to add thanks to Dr. Dan Rawsthorne, another colleague at Net Objectives. His approach to agile development has contributed to mine. Jeff McKenna's (another colleague) support and affirmation is also greatly appreciated. I also want to thank Kim Aue, our "director of everything" at Net Objectives. Her support in general has been extremely helpful.

- Although not implying they agree or endorse anything I say here, I also want to give special thanks to Martin Fowler, Ken Schwaber, Ward Cunningham, Robert Martin, Ron Jeffries, Kent Beck, and Bruce Eckel for conversations (sometimes via e-mail) about several of these issues.

Special thanks from Jim:

- Dr. Karen Gardner, a mentor and wise teacher in patterns of human thought.

- Dr. Marel Norwood and Arthur Murphy, my initial collaborators in KADS and pattern-based analysis.

- Brad VanBeek, who gave me the space to grow in this discipline.

- Alex Sidey, who coached me in the discipline and mysteries of technical writing.

- Sharon and Dr. Bob Foote, now teaching at West Point, who fostered in me an insatiable curiosity and an abiding interest in people. Their love and encouragement endure as patterns in me, as a person, a husband and father, and as an analyst.

- Bill Koops and Lindy Backues, of Millennium Relief and Development Services (www.mrds.org), for helping me see how pattern-based approaches may even be used to help the poor and the marginalized. They are good mates and good mentors.

PART I

An Introduction to Object-Oriented Software Development

Part Overview

This part introduces you to a method for developing object-oriented software that is based on patterns—the insights and best practices learned by designers and users over the years—and on the modeling language (UML) that supports this method.

In this part

I will not follow the approach of the 1980s, where developers were simply told to "find the nouns in the requirement statements and make them into objects." In that approach, encapsulation was defined as "data hiding," and objects were defined as "things with data and behavior used to access and manipulate those data." This was (and is) a limited view, constrained as it is by a focus on how to implement objects. It is incomplete.

This part discusses a version of the object-oriented paradigm that is based on an expanded definition of these concepts. These expanded definitions are the result of strategies and principles that arise from the study of design patterns. It reflects a more complete mindset of object orientation.

Chapter	Discusses These Topics
1	**The Object-Oriented Paradigm** An introduction to the latest understanding of objects.
2	**The UML (Unified Modeling Language)** The UML gives us the tools to describe object-oriented designs in a graphical, more readily understood manner.

CHAPTER 1

The Object-Oriented Paradigm

Overview

This chapter introduces you to the object-oriented paradigm by comparing and contrasting it with something familiar: standard structured programming.

In this chapter

The object-oriented paradigm grew out of a need to meet the challenges of past practices using standard structured programming. By being clear about these challenges, we can better see the advantages of object-oriented programming, as well as gain a better understanding of this mechanism.

This chapter will not make you an expert on object-oriented methods. It will not even introduce you to all of the basic object-oriented concepts. It will, however, prepare you for the rest of this book, which explains the proper use of object-oriented design methods as practiced by the experts.

In this chapter

- I discuss a common method of analysis, called *functional decomposition*.

- I address the problem of requirements and the need to deal with change (the scourge of programming!).

- I describe the object-oriented paradigm and show its use in action.

- I point out special object methods.

- I provide a table of important object terminology used in this chapter on pages 22–23.

Before the Object-Oriented Paradigm: Functional Decomposition

Functional decomposition is a natural way to deal with complexity

Let's start by examining a common approach to software development. If I were to give you the task of writing code to access a description of shapes that were stored in a database and then display them, it would be natural to think in terms of the steps required. For example, you might think that you would solve the problem by doing the following:

1. Locate the list of shapes in the database.

2. Open up the list of shapes.

3. Sort the list according to some rules.

4. Display the individual shapes on the monitor.

You could take any one of these steps and break it down further into the steps required to implement it. For example, you could break down Step 4. For each shape in the list, do the following:

4a. Identify the type of shape.

4b. Get the location of the shape.

4c. Call the appropriate function that will display the shape, giving it the shape's location.

This is called *functional decomposition* because the analyst breaks down (decomposes) the problem into the functional steps that compose it. You and I do this because it is easier to deal with smaller pieces than it is to deal with the problem in its entirety. It is the same approach I might use to write a recipe for making lasagna, or instructions to assemble a bicycle. We use this approach so often and so naturally that we seldom question it or ask whether other alternatives exist.

One problem with functional decomposition is that it usually leads to having one "main" program that is responsible for controlling its subprograms. It is a natural outcome of decomposing functions into smaller functions. However, it saddles the main program with too much responsibility: ensuring everything is working correctly, coordinating and sequencing functions. Often, therefore, it results in very complicated code. How much easier it would be to make some of those subfunctions responsible for their own behavior, to be able to tell the function to go do something and trust that it will know how to do it. Successful generals in the field and parents in the home have learned this lesson. Programmers are learning it as well. It is called *delegation*.

The challenge with this approach: With great power comes great responsibility

Another problem with functional decomposition is that it does not help us prepare the code for possible changes in the future, for a graceful evolution. When change is required, it is often because I want to add a new variation to an existing theme. For example, I might have to deal with new shapes or new ways to display shapes. If I have put all the logic that implements the steps into one large function or module, virtually any change to the steps will require changes to that function or module.

The challenge with this approach: Dealing with change

And change creates opportunities for mistakes and unintended consequences. Or, as I like to say,

> *Many bugs originate with changes to code.*

Verify this assertion for yourself. Think of a time when you wanted to make a change to your code, but were afraid to put it in because you knew that modifying the code in one place could break it somewhere else. Why might this happen? Must the code pay attention to all of its functions and how they might be used? How might the functions interact with one another? Were there too many details for the function to pay attention to, such as the logic it was trying to implement, the things with which it was interacting, the data it was using? Just as with people, programs trying to focus on too many things simultaneously beg for errors when anything changes. Programming is a complex, abstract, dynamic activity.

And no matter how hard you try, no matter how well you do your analysis, you can never get all of the requirements from the user. Too much is unknown about the future. Things change. They always do…

And nothing you can do will stop change. But you do not have to be overcome by it.

The Problem of Requirements

Requirements always change

Ask software developers what they know to be true about the requirements they get from users. They often answer the following:

- Requirements are incomplete.

- Requirements are usually wrong.

- Requirements (and users) are misleading.

- Requirements do not tell the whole story.

One thing you will never hear is, "Not only were our requirements complete, clear, and understandable, but they laid out all of the functionality we were going to need for the next five years!"

In my 30 years of experience writing software, the main thing I have learned about requirements is that *requirements always change*.

I have also learned that most developers think this is a bad thing. But few of them write their code to handle changing requirements well.

Requirements change for a very simple set of reasons:

- The users' view of their needs changes as a result of their discussions with developers and from seeing new possibilities for the software.

- The developers' view of the users' problem domain changes as they develop software to automate it and thus become more familiar with it.

I May Not Know What Will Change, But I Can Guess Where

Early in my career, I had a mentor who used to say, "There is always time to program it right the *second* time, so you might as well do it right the *first* time!" I have often thought about that advice. I used to think it meant trying to anticipate every change that might be made and building my code accordingly. This was overwhelming and usually disappointing because I rarely could predict every possible change that might come my way.

Finally I realized that although I could not predict what changes might occur, I could usually anticipate where the changes might occur. One of the great benefits of object orientation is that I can contain those areas of change and thus insulate my code from the effects of change more easily.

The environment in which the software is being developed changes. (Who anticipated, five years ago, Web development as it is today?)

This does not mean you and I can give up on gathering good requirements. It does mean that we must write our code to accommodate change. It also means we should stop beating ourselves up (or our customers, for that matter) for things that will naturally occur.

Change Happens! Deal With It

In all but the simplest cases, requirements will always change, no matter how well we do the initial analysis!

Rather than complaining about changing requirements, we should change the development process so that we can address change more effectively.

You can design your code so that the impact of changing requirements is much less dramatic. Your code may evolve or new code can be bolted on with little impact.

Dealing with Changes:
Using Functional Decomposition

Using modularity to isolate variation

Look a little closer at the problem of displaying shapes. How can I write the code so that it is easier to handle shifting requirements? Instead of writing one large function, I could make it more modular.

For example, in Step 4c on page 4, where I *"call the appropriate function that will display the shape, giving it the shape's location,"* I could write a module like that shown in Example 1-1.

Example 1-1   Using Modularity to Contain Variation

```
function: display shape
input: type of shape, description of shape
action:
   switch (type of shape)
      case square: put display function for square here
      case circle: put display function for circle here
```

Problems with modularity in a functional decomposition approach

Then, when I receive a requirement to be able to display a new type of shape—a triangle, for instance—I only need to change this module (hopefully!).

This approach presents some problems, however. For example, I said that the inputs to the module were the type of shape and a description of the shape. Depending upon how I am storing shapes, it may or may not be possible to have a consistent description of shapes that will work well for all shapes. What if the description of the shape is sometimes stored as an array of points and sometimes is stored another way? Would that still work?

Modularity definitely helps to make the code more understandable, and understandability makes the code easier to maintain. But modularity does not always help code deal with all the variations it might encounter.

With the approach that I have used so far, I find that I have two significant problems, which go by the terms *weak cohesion* and *tight coupling*. In his book *Code Complete* (Microsoft Press, 1993), Steve
McConnell gives an excellent description of both cohesion and coupling. He says:

*Weak cohesion, tight
coupling*

> Cohesion *refers to how "closely the operations in a routine
> are related."*[1]

I have heard other people refer to cohesion as *clarity* because the
more that operations are related in a routine (or a class), the easier
it is to understand things. Weakly cohesive classes are those that do
many, unrelated tasks. The code often appears to be a confused mass.
Taken to an extreme, these classes become entangled with most
everything in a system. I have heard some people call these *god objects*, because they do everything (or perhaps it's because only God
can understand them).

> Coupling *refers to "the strength of a connection between two
> routines. Coupling is a complement to cohesion. Cohesion de-
> scribes how strongly the internal contents of a routine are re-
> lated to each other. Coupling describes how strongly a routine
> is related to other routines. The goal is to create routines with
> internal integrity (strong cohesion) and small, direct, visible,
> and flexible relations to other routines (loose coupling)."*[2]

Most programmers have had the experience of making a change to
a function or piece of data in one area of the code that then has an
unexpected impact on other pieces of code. This type of bug is called
an *unwanted side effect*. That is because although we get the impact we

*Changing a
function, or even
data used by a
function, can wreak
havoc on other
functions*

---

1. McConnell, S. *Code Complete: A Practical Handbook of Software Construction*,
   Redmond: Microsoft Press, 1993, p. 81. (Note: McConnell did not invent these
   terms, Yourdon and Constantine did. We just happen to like his definitions best.)

2. Ibid, p. 87.

want (the change), we also get other impacts we don't want—bugs! What is worse, these bugs are often difficult to find because we usually don't notice the relationship that caused the side effects in the first place. (If we had, we wouldn't have changed it the way we did.)

In fact, bugs of this type lead me to a rather startling observation: *We really do not spend much time fixing bugs.*

I think fixing bugs takes a short period of time in the maintenance and debugging process. The overwhelming amount of time involved in maintenance and debugging is spent on *trying to discover how the code works and on finding bugs* and *taking the time to avoid unwanted side effects.* The actual fix is relatively short!

Because unwanted side effects are often the hardest bugs to find, having a function that touches many different pieces of data makes it more likely that a change in requirements will result in a problem.

The Devil Is in the Side Effects

- A focus on functions is likely to cause side effects that are difficult to find.

- Most of the time spent in maintenance and debugging is not spent on fixing bugs, but in finding them and seeing how to avoid unwanted side effects from the fix.

Functional decomposition focuses on the wrong thing

With functional decomposition, changing requirements cause my software development and maintenance efforts to thrash. I am focused primarily on the functions. Changes to one set of functions or data impact other sets of functions and other sets of data, which in turn impact other functions that must be changed. Like a snowball that picks up snow as it rolls downhill, a focus on functions leads to a cascade of changes from which it is difficult to escape.

Dealing with Changing Requirements

To figure out a way around the problem of changing requirements and to see whether there is an alternative to functional decomposition, let's look at how people do things. Suppose, for example, that you are an instructor at a conference. People in your class have another class to attend following yours, but don't know where it is located. One of your responsibilities is to make sure everyone knows how to get to the next class.

How do people do things?

If you were to follow a structured programming approach, you might do the following:

1. Get list of people in the class.

2. For each person on this list, do the following:

    a. Find the next class he or she is taking.

    b. Find the location of that class.

    c. Find the way to get from your classroom to the person's next class.

    d. Tell the person how to get to his or her next class.

To do this would require the following procedures:

1. A way of getting the list of people in the class

2. A way of getting the schedule for each person in the class

3. A program that gives someone directions from your classroom to any other classroom

4. A control program that works for each person in the class and does the required steps for each person

I doubt that you would actually follow this approach. Instead, you would probably post directions to go from this classroom to the other classrooms and then tell everyone in the class, "I have posted the

Doubtful you'd follow this approach

locations of the classes following this in the back of the room, as well as the locations of the other classrooms. Please use them to go to your next classroom." You would expect that everyone would know what his or her next class was, and that everyone could find the right classroom from the list and could then follow the directions to get to the correct classrooms.

What is the difference between these approaches?

- In the first one—giving explicit directions to everyone—you have to pay close attention to a lot of details. No one other than you is responsible for anything. You will go crazy!

- In the second case, you give general instructions and then expect that each person will figure out how to do the task individually.

Shifting responsibility from yourself to individuals…

The biggest difference is this *shift of responsibility*. In the first case, *you* are responsible for everything; in the second case, students are responsible for their *own* behavior. In both cases, the same things must be implemented, but the organization is very different.

What is the impact of this?

To see the effect of this reorganization of responsibilities, let's consider what happens when some new requirements are specified.

Suppose I am now told to give special instructions to graduate students who are assisting at the conference. Perhaps they need to collect course evaluations and take them to the conference office before they can go to the next class. In the first case, I would have to modify the control program to distinguish the graduate students from the undergraduates, and then give special instructions to the graduate students. It's possible that I would have to modify this program considerably.

…can minimize changes

However, in the second case—where people are responsible for themselves—I would just have to write an additional routine for graduate students to follow. The control program would still just say, "Go to your next class." Each person would simply follow the instructions appropriate for himself or herself.

This represents a significant shift in responsibility for the control program. In one case, every time a new category of students needs to be added, the control program itself has to be modified; the control program is responsible for telling the new category of student what to do. In the other case, the control program remains unaffected by the new category of student; the students themselves are responsible for figuring out what to do.

Why the difference?

There are three different things going on that make this happen:

What makes it happen?

- The people are responsible for their own behavior. There is not a central control program responsible for determining their behavior. (Note that to accomplish this, a person must also be aware of what type of student he or she is.)

- The control program can talk to different types of people (graduate students and regular students) as if they were exactly the same.

- The control program does not need to know about any special steps that students might need to take when moving from class to class.

To fully understand the implications of this, it's important to establish some terminology. In *UML Distilled* (Addison-Wesley, 1999), Martin Fowler describes three different perspectives in the software development process.[3] These are described in Table 1-1.

Different perspectives

---

3. Fowler, M., and Scott, K. *UML Distilled: A Brief Guide to the Standard Object Modeling Language*, Second Edition, Boston: Addison-Wesley, 1999, pp. 51–52.

Table 1-1 Perspectives in the Software Development Process

Perspective	Description
Conceptual	This perspective "represents the concepts in the domain under study…a conceptual model should be drawn with little or no regard for the software that might implement it…"It answers the question, "What am I responsible for?"
Specification	"Now we are looking at software, but we are looking at the interfaces of the software, not the implementation." It answers the question, "How am I used?"
Implementation	At this point we are at the code itself. "This is probably the most often-used perspective, but in many ways the specification perspective is often a better one to take." It answers the question, "How do I fulfill my responsibilities?"

How perspectives help

Look again at the previous example of "Go to your next class." Notice that you—as the instructor—are communicating with the people at the *conceptual level*. In other words, you are telling people *what you want*, not *how to do it*. However, the way they go to their next class is very specific. They are following specific instructions and in doing so are working at the *implementation level*.

Communicating at one level (conceptually) while performing at another level (implementation) results in the requestor (the instructor) not having to know *exactly* what is happening, only having to know in general—*conceptually*—what is happening. This can be very powerful: The requestor is insulated from changes in implementation details as long as the concept remains the same. Let's see how to take these notions and write programs that take advantage of them.

The Object-Oriented Paradigm

The object-oriented paradigm is centered on the concept of the object. Everything is focused on objects. I write code organized around objects, not functions.

Using objects shifts responsibility to a more local level

What is an object? Objects have traditionally been defined as data with *methods* (the object-oriented term for functions). Unfortunately, this is a very limiting way of looking at objects. I will look at a better definition of objects shortly (and again in Chapter 8, "Expanding Our Horizons"). When I talk about the data of an object, these can be simple things such as numbers and character strings, or they can be other objects.

The advantage of using objects is that I can define things that are responsible for themselves. (See Table 1-2.) Objects inherently know what type they are. The data in an object allows it to know what state it is in, and the code in the object allows it to function properly (that is, do what it is supposed to do).

Table 1-2 Objects and Their Responsibilities

This Object...	Is Responsible For...
Student	Knowing which classroom he or she is in
	Knowing which classroom to go to next
	Going from one classroom to the next
Instructor	Telling people to go to next classroom
Classroom	Having a location
Direction giver	Given two classrooms, giving directions from one classroom to the other

In this case, the objects were identified by looking at the entities in the problem domain. I identified the responsibilities (or methods) for each object by looking at what these entities need to do. This is consistent with the technique of finding objects by looking for the nouns in the requirements and finding methods by looking for verbs. As I get into more complex problems, you will see that this technique is quite limiting, and I will show a better way throughout this book. For now, it is a way to get us started.

How to think about objects

The best way to think about what an object is, is to think of it as something with responsibilities. A good design rule is that objects should be responsible for themselves and should have those responsibilities clearly defined. This is why I say one of the responsibilities of a student object is knowing how to go from one classroom to the next.

Or, taking Fowler's perspective

I can also look at objects using the framework of Fowler's perspectives:

- At the *conceptual level,* an object is a set of responsibilities.[4]

- At the *specification level,* an object is a set of methods (behaviors) that can be invoked by other objects or by itself.

- At the *implementation level,* an object is code and data and computational interactions between them.

Unfortunately, object-oriented design is often taught and talked about only at the implementation level—in terms of code and data—rather than at the conceptual or specification level. But there is great power in thinking about objects in these latter ways as well!

Objects have interfaces for other objects to use

Because objects have responsibilities and objects are responsible for themselves, there has to be a way to tell objects what to do. Remember that objects have data to tell the object about itself and methods to implement required functionality. Many methods of an

---

4. I am roughly paraphrasing Bertrand Meyer's work of Design by Contract as outlined in *Object-Oriented Software Construction,* Upper Saddle River, N.J.: Prentice Hall, 1997, p. 331.

object will be identified as callable by other objects. The collection of these methods is called the object's *public interface*.

For example, in the classroom example, I could write the **Student** object with the method **gotoNextClassroom()**. I would not need to pass any parameters in because each **Student** object would be re-sponsible for itself. That is, it would know:

- What it needs to be able to move

- How to get any additional information it needs to perform this task

Initially, there was only one kind of student—a regular student who goes from class to class. Note that there would be many of these "reg-ular students" in my classroom (my system). I would have an object for each student, enabling me to track the state of each student eas-ily and independently of other students. However, it seems ineffi-cient to require each **Student** object to have its own set of methods to tell it what it can do and how to do it, especially for tasks that are common to all students.

Organizing objects around the class

A more efficient approach would be to have a set of methods asso-ciated with all students that each one could use or tailor to his or her own needs. I want to define a "general student" to contain the definitions of these common methods. Then I can have all manner of specialized students, each of whom has to keep track of his or her own private information.

In object-oriented terms, this general student is called a *class*. A class is a definition of the behavior of an object. It contains a complete description of the following:

- The data elements the object contains

- The methods the object can do

- The way these data elements and methods can be accessed

Because the data elements an object contains can vary, each object of the same type may have different data but will have the same functionality (as defined in the methods).

Objects are instances of classes

To get an object, I tell the program that I want a new object of this type (that is, the class that the object belongs to). This new object is called an *instance* of the class. Creating instances of a class is called *instantiation*.

Working with objects in the example

Writing the "Go to the next classroom" example using an object-oriented approach is much simpler. The program would look like this:

1. Start the control program.

2. Instantiate the collection of students in the classroom.

3. Tell the collection to have the students go to their next class.

4. The collection tells each student to go to his or her next class.

5. Each student

   a. Finds where his next class is.

   b. Determines how to get there.

   c. Goes there.

6. Done.

The need for an abstract type

This works fine until I need to add another student type, such as a graduate student.

I have a dilemma. It appears that I must allow any type of student into the collection (either regular student or graduate student). The problem facing me is how do I want the collection to refer to its constituents? Because I am talking about implementing this in code, the collection will actually be an array or something, of some type of object. If the collection were named something like **RegularStudent**, I would not be able to put graduate students into the collection. If I say that the collection is just a group of objects, how can I be sure that I do not include the wrong type of object (that is, something that doesn't do "Go to your next class")?

The solution is straightforward. I need a general type that encompasses more than one specific type. In this case, I want a **Student** type that includes both **RegularStudent** and **GraduateStudent**. In object-oriented terms, we call **Student** an *abstract class*.[5]

Abstract classes define what other, related, classes can do. These "other" classes are classes that represent a particular type of related behavior. Such a class is often called a *concrete class* because it represents a specific, or nonchanging, implementation of a concept.

Abstract classes define what a set of classes can do

In the example, the abstract class is **Student**. There are two types of **Student** represented by the concrete classes, **RegularStudent** and **GraduateStudent**. **RegularStudent** is one kind of **Student,** and **GraduateStudent** is also a kind of **Student**.

This type of relationship is called an *is-a* relationship. An is-a relationship is an example of something we call *inheritance*. Thus, the **RegularStudent** class *inherits from* **Student**. Other ways to say this would be, the **GraduateStudent** *derives from*, *specializes*, or is *a subclass of* **Student**.

Going the other way, the **Student** class is the *base class, generalizes,* or is *the superclass of* **GraduateStudent** and of **RegularStudent**.

Abstract classes act as placeholders for other classes. I use them to define the methods their derived classes must implement. Abstract classes can also contain common methods that can be used by all derivations.[6] Whether a derived class uses the default behavior or

Abstract classes act as placeholders for other classes

---

5. Interfaces in several languages also can do this. When I refer to abstract classes in this chapter, you can pretend I've written abstract class or interface.

6. Here is one difference between abstract classes and interfaces. Interfaces just define what a set of classes can do—they cannot implement default behavior.

replaces it with its own variation is up to the derivation. (This is consistent with the mandate that objects be responsible for themselves.)

This means that I can have the controller contain **Student**s. The reference type used will be **Student**. The compiler can check that anything referred to by this **Student** reference is, in fact, a kind of **Student**. This gives the best of both worlds:

- The collection only needs to deal with **Students** (thereby allowing the instructor object just to deal with students).

- But I still get type checking (only **Students** that can "Go to their next classroom" are included).

- And each kind of **Student** is left to implement its functionality in its own way.

Abstract Classes Are More Than Classes That Do Not Get Instantiated

Abstract classes are often described as classes that do not get instantiated. This definition is accurate—at the implementation level. But that is too limited. It is more helpful to define abstract classes at the conceptual level. At the conceptual level, abstract classes are placeholders for other classes—classes that implement specifics of the concept the abstract class represents.

That is, they give us a way to assign a name to a set of related classes. This enables us to treat this set of related classes as one concept.

In the object-oriented paradigm, you must constantly think about your problem from all three levels of perspective: conceptual, specification, and implementation.

Because objects are responsible for themselves, there are many things they do not need to expose to other objects. Earlier I mentioned the concept of the *public interface*—those methods that are accessible by other objects. In object-oriented systems, the main types of accessibility are as follows:[7]

Visibility

- **Public**—Anything can see it.

- **Protected**—Only objects of this class and derived classes can see it.

- **Private**—Only objects from this class can see it.

This leads to the concept of *encapsulation*. Encapsulation has often been described simply as hiding data. Objects generally do not expose their internal data members to the outside world. (That is, their visibility is protected or private.)

Encapsulation

But encapsulation refers to more than hiding data. In general, encapsulation means *any kind of hiding*.

In the example, the instructor did not know which were the regular students and which were the graduate students. The type of student is hidden from the instructor. (I am encapsulating the "type" of the student.) In an object-oriented language, the abstract class **Student** hides the types of classes derived from it. As you will see later in the book, this is a very important concept.

Another term to learn is *polymorphism*.

Polymorphism

In object-oriented languages, we often refer to objects with one type of reference that is an abstract class type. However, what we are actually referring to are specific instances of classes derived from their abstract classes.

---

7. Different languages often have other types of accessibility. However, they are essentially variations of these three.

Thus, when I tell the objects to do something conceptually through the abstract reference, I get different behavior, depending upon the specific type of derived object I have. Polymorphism derives from *poly* (meaning many) and *morph* (meaning form). Thus, it means "many forms." This is an appropriate name because I have many different forms of behavior for the same call.

In the example, the instructor tells the students to "Go to your next classroom." However, depending upon the type of student, he or she will exhibit different behavior (hence polymorphism).

Review of Object-Oriented Terminology

Term	Description
Abstract class	Abstract classes define what a set of related classes can do.
Class	Defines the types of objects I have based on the responsibilities these objects have. Responsibilities can be divided into behavior and/or state. These can be implemented using methods and/or data, respectively.
Concrete Class	A class that implements a particular type of behavior for an abstract class. Concrete classes are specific, nonchanging implementations of a concept.
Encapsulation	Typically defined as data hiding, but better thought of as any kind of hiding (type, implementation, design, and so on).
Inheritance	A class inherits from another class when it receives some or all of the qualities of that class. The starting class is called the base, super, parent, or generalized class, whereas the inheriting class is called the derived, sub, child, or specialized class.

Term	Description
Instance	A particular example of a class. (It is always an object.) A particular instance or entity of a class. Each object has its own state. This enables me to have several objects of the same type (class).*
Instantiation	The process of creating an instance of a class.
Interface	An interface is like a class, but only provides a specification–and not an implementation–for its members. It is similar to an abstract class consisting only of abstract members. When programming, you use interfaces when you need several classes to share some characteristics that are not present in a common base class and want to be sure that each class implements the characteristic on its own (because each member is abstract).
Perspectives	There are three different perspectives for looking at objects: conceptual, specification, and implementation. These distinctions are helpful in understanding the relationship between abstract classes and their derivations. The abstract class defines how to solve things conceptually. It also gives the specification for communicating with any object derived from it. Each derivation provides the specific implementation needed.
Polymorphism	Being able to refer to different derivations of a class in the same way, but getting the behavior appropriate to the derived class being referred to.

---

* Some object-oriented analysts speak of everything as an object: Classes are objects, instances are objects. This may be technically correct, but has been the point of confusion and some controversy. For purposes of this book, an object is considered to be an instance of a class.

Object-Oriented Programming in Action

Let's reexamine the shapes example discussed at the beginning of the chapter. How would I implement it in an object-oriented manner? Remember that it has to do the following:

New example

1. Locate the list of shapes in the database.

2. Open up the list of shapes.

3. Sort the list according to some rules.

4. Display the individual shapes on the monitor.

To solve this in an object-oriented manner, I need to define the objects and the responsibilities they have.

Using objects in the Shape program

The objects I would need are listed in the following table.

Class	Responsibilities (Methods)
ShapeDataBase	*getCollection*—Gets a specified collection of shapes
Shape (an abstract class)	*display*—Defines interface for Shapes
	getX—Returns X location of Shape (used for sorting)
	getY—Returns Y location of Shape (used for sorting)
Square (derived from **Shape**)	*display*—Displays a square (represented by this object)
Circle (derived from **Shape**)	*display*—Displays a circle (represented by this object)
Collection	*display*—Tells all contained shapes to display
	sort—Sorts the collection of shapes
Display	*drawLine*—Draws a line on the screen
	drawCircle—Draws a circle on the screen

Running the program

The main program would now look like this:

1. Main program creates an instance of the database object.

2. Main program asks the database object to find the set of shapes

I am interested in and to instantiate a collection object containing all the shapes. (Actually, it will instantiate circles and squares that the collection will hold.)

3. Main program asks the collection to sort the shapes.

4. Main program asks the collection to display the shapes.

5. The collection asks each shape it contains to display itself.

6. Each shape displays itself (using the **Display** object) according to the type of shape I have.

Let's see how this helps to handle new requirements. (Remember, requirements always change.) For example, consider the following new requirements:

Why this helps—handling new requirements

- **Add new kinds of shapes (such as a triangle).** To introduce a new kind of shape, only two steps are required:

  - Create a new derivation of **Shape** that defines the shape.

  - In the new derivation, implement a version of the display method that is appropriate for that shape.

- **Change the sorting algorithm**. To change the method for sorting the shapes, only one step is required:

  - Modify the method in **Collection**. Every shape will use the new algorithm.

Bottom line: The object-oriented approach has limited the impact of changing requirements.

There are several advantages to encapsulation. The fact that it hides things from the user directly implies the following:

Encapsulation revisited

- Using things is easier because the user does not need to worry about implementation issues.

- Implementations can be changed without worrying about the caller. (Because the caller didn't know how it was implemented in the first place, there shouldn't be any dependencies. Remember that it is often the learning and keeping aware of these dependencies that take time in maintenance—more than actually adding a new function.)

- The internals of an object are unknown to other objects—they are used by the object to help implement the function specified by the object's interface.

Benefit: Reduced side effects

Finally, consider the problem of unwanted side effects that arise when functions are changed. This kind of bug is addressed effectively with encapsulation. The internals of objects are unknown to other objects. If I use encapsulation and follow the strategy that objects are responsible for themselves, the only way to affect an object will be to call a method on that object. The object's data and the way it implements its responsibilities are shielded from changes caused by other objects.

Encapsulation Saves Us

- The more I make my objects responsible for their own behaviors, the less the controlling programs have to be responsible for.

- Encapsulation makes changes to an object's internal behavior transparent to other objects.

- Encapsulation helps to prevent unwanted side effects.

It is worth noting how encapsulation relates to coupling. When I encapsulate something, I am necessarily loosely coupled to it. Hiding implementations (encapsulating them) thus promotes loose coupling.

Special Object Methods

I have talked about methods that are called by other objects or possibly used by an object itself. But what happens when objects are created? What happens when they go away? If objects are self-contained units, it would be a good idea to have methods to handle these situations.

Creating and destroying

These special methods do, in fact, exist. They are called *constructors* and *destructors* or *finalizers*.

Constructors initialize, or set up, an object

A constructor is a special procedure that is automatically called when the object is created. Its purpose is to handle starting up the object. This is part of an object's mandate to be responsible for itself. The constructor is the natural place to do initializations, set default information, set up relationships with other objects, or do anything else that is needed to make a well-defined object. All object-oriented languages look for a constructor and execute it when the object is created.

By using constructors properly, it is easier to eliminate (or at least minimize) uninitialized variables. This type of error usually occurs from carelessness on the part of the developer. By having a set, consistent place for all initializations throughout your code (that is, the constructors of your objects), it is easier to ensure that initializations take place. Errors caused by uninitialized variables are easy to fix but hard to find, so this convention (with the automatic calling of the constructor) can increase the efficiency of programmers.

Most object-oriented languages provide a way for an object to clean up after itself when the object goes out of existence; that is, when the object is destroyed. In C++ and C#, this is called a *destructor*; in Java, it is called a *finalizer*. In this book, I refer to it by the generic term *destructor*.

Destructors (finalizers) clean up an object when it is no longer needed (when it has been deleted)

All object-oriented languages look for a destructor and execute it when the object is being deleted. As with the constructor, the use of the destructor is part of the object's mandate to be responsible for itself.

Destructors are typically used for releasing resources when objects are no longer needed. Because Java has garbage collection (auto-cleanup of objects no longer in use), destructors are not as important in Java as they are in C++. In C++, it is common for an object's destructor also to destroy other objects that are used only by this object.

Summary

In this chapter

This chapter has shown how object orientation helps us minimize consequences of shifting requirements on a system and how it contrasts with functional decomposition.

I have covered a number of the essential concepts in object-oriented programming and have introduced and described the primary terminology. Table 1-3 summarizes these concepts, and Table 1-4 summarizes the primary terminology of object-oriented programming.

Table 1-3 Concepts Introduced in This Chapter

Concept	Review
Functional decomposition	Structured programmers usually approach program design with functional decomposition. Functional decomposition is the method of breaking down a problem into smaller and smaller functions. Each function is subdivided until it is manageable.
Changing requirements	Changing requirements are inherent to the development process. Rather than blaming users or ourselves about the seemingly impossible task of getting good and complete requirements, we should use development methods that deal with changing requirements more effectively.

Table 1-3 Concepts Introduced in This Chapter (cont.)

Concept	Review
Objects	Objects are defined by their responsibilities. Objects simplify the tasks of programs that use them by being responsible for themselves.
Constructors and destructors	An object has special procedures that are called when it is created and deleted. These special procedures are: <ul><li>Constructors, which initialize or set up an object.</li><li>Destructors, which clean up an object when it is deleted.</li></ul> All object-oriented languages use constructors and destructors to help manage objects.

Table 1-4 Object-Oriented Terminology

Term	Definition
Abstract class	Defines the methods and common attributes of a set of classes that are conceptually similar. Abstract classes are never instantiated.
Attribute	Data associated with an object (also called a *data member*).
Class	Blueprint of an object—defines the methods and data of an object of its type.
Constructor	Procedure that is invoked when an object is created.
Derived class	A class that is specialized from a base class. Contains all of the attributes and methods of the base class but may also contain other attributes or different method implementations.
Destructor	Procedure that is invoked when an object is deleted. (Note: In Java, this is called a *finalizer.*)
Encapsulation	Any kind of hiding. Objects encapsulate their data. Abstract classes encapsulate their derived concrete classes.
Functional decomposition	A method of analysis in which a problem is broken into smaller and smaller functions.
Inheritance	The way that a class is specialized, used to relate derived classes with their base classes.

Table 1-4 Object-Oriented Terminology (cont.)

Term	Definition
Instance	A particular object of a class.
Instantiation	The process of creating an instance of a class.
Member	Either data or a procedure of a class.
Method	Procedures that are associated with a class.
Object	An entity with responsibilities. A special, self-contained holder of both data and procedures that operate on that data. An object's data is protected from external objects.
Polymorphism	The ability of related objects to implement methods that are specialized to their type.
Superclass	A class from which other classes are derived. Contains the master definitions of data and procedures that all derived classes will use (and for procedures, possibly override).

Review Questions

Observations

1. Describe the basic approach used in functional decomposition.

2. What are three reasons that cause requirements to change?

3. I advocate thinking about responsibilities rather than functions. What is meant by this? Give an example.

4. Define coupling and cohesion. What is tight coupling?

5. What is the purpose of an interface to an object?

6. Define instance of a class.

7. A class is a complete definition of the behavior of an object. What three aspects of an object does it describe?

8. What does an abstract class do?

9. What are the three main types of accessibility that objects can have?

10. Define *encapsulation*. Give one example of encapsulation of behavior.

11. Define *polymorphism*. Give one example of polymorphism.

12. What are the three perspectives for looking at objects?

Interpretations

1. Sometimes, programmers use "modules" to isolate portions of code. Is this an effective way to deal with changes in requirements? Why or why not?

2. It is too limited to define an abstract class as a class that does not get instantiated. Why is this definition too limited? What is a better (or at least alternative) way to think about abstract classes?

3. How does encapsulation of behavior help to limit the impact of changes in requirements? How does it save programmers from unintended side effects?

4. How do interfaces help to protect objects from changes that are made to other objects?

5. A classroom is used to describe objects in a system. Describe this classroom from the conceptual perspective.

Opinions and Applications

1. Changing requirements is one of the greatest challenges faced by systems developers. Give one example from your own experience where this has been true.

2. There is a fundamental weakness in functional decomposition when it comes to changes in requirements. Do you agree? Why or why not?

3. What do you think is the best way to deal with changing requirements?

CHAPTER 2

The UML—The Unified Modeling Language

Overview

This chapter provides a brief overview of the *Unified Modeling Language* (UML), the modeling language of the object-oriented community. If you do not already know the UML, this chapter will give you the minimal understanding you need to be able to read the diagrams contained in this book.

In this chapter

This chapter

- Describes what the UML is and why to use it.
- Explains the UML diagrams essential to this book:
  - The Class diagram
  - The Interaction diagram

What Is the UML?

The Unified Modeling Language is a visual language (meaning a drawing notation with semantics) used to create models of programs. In this context, the term *models of programs* means diagrammatic representations of the programs that show the relationships among the objects in the code.

UML offers many kinds of modeling diagrams

The UML has several different diagrams—some for analysis, others for design, and still others for implementation (or more accurately, for the deployment, that is, the distribution, of the code). (See Table 2-1.) Each diagram shows the relationships among the different sets of entities, depending on the purpose of the diagram.

Table 2-1 UML Diagrams and Their Purposes

When You Are	Use the UML Diagram
In the analysis phase	Use Case diagrams, which involve entities interacting with the system (say, users and other systems) and the function points that you need to implement.
	Activity diagrams, which focus on workflow of the problem domain (the actual space where people and other agents are working, the subject area of the program) rather than the logic flow of the program.
	Note: Because this book principally focuses on design, I do not cover Use Case diagrams or Activity diagrams here.
Looking at object interactions	Interaction diagrams, which show how specific objects interact with each other. Because they deal with specific cases rather than general situations, they prove helpful both when checking requirements and when checking designs. The most popular kind of Interaction diagram is the Sequence diagram.
In the design phase	Class diagrams, which detail the relationships between the classes.
Looking at an object's *behaviors* that differ based upon the state that the object is in	State diagrams, which detail the different states an object may be in as well as the transitions between these states.
In the deployment phase	Deployment diagrams, which show how different modules will be deployed. I do not talk about these diagrams in this book .

Why Use the UML?

Principally for communication

The UML is used primarily for communication—with myself, my team members, and with my customers. Poor requirements (either incomplete or inaccurate) are ubiquitous in the field of software development. The UML gives us tools to elicit better requirements.

The UML gives a way to help determine whether my understanding of the system is the same as others'. Because systems are complex and have different types of information that must be conveyed, it offers different diagrams specializing in the different types of information.

For clarity

One easy way to see the value of the UML is to recall your last several design reviews. If you have ever been in a review where someone starts talking about his code and describes it without a modeling language such as the UML, almost certainly his talk was both confusing as well as much longer than necessary. The UML is not only a better way of describing object-oriented designs, it also forces the designer to think through the relationships between classes in his or her approach (because they must be written down).[1]

For precision

The Class Diagram

The most basic of UML diagrams is the Class diagram. It both describes classes and shows the relationships among them. The following types of relationships are possible:

The basic modeling diagram

- When one class is a "kind of" another class; the *is-a* relationship
- When there are associations between two classes
  - One class "contains" another class: the *has-a* relationship
  - One class "uses" another class: the *uses-a* relationship
  - One class "creates" another class

---

1. Some agile methodology experts believe written documentation of all sorts should be avoided unless absolutely necessary. Certainly, many developers have overused the UML and have produced documents that actually hinder rather than facilitate communication. Properly used, however, the UML can facilitate communication considerably. Even when "paired programming" is used, design concepts are typically better described at a conceptual level than at a code (implementation) level. In other words, you should strive both to do "the simplest thing possible" and to describe it in the best way possible.

There are variations on these themes. For example, to say something contains something else can mean that

- The contained item is a part of the containing item (such as an engine in a car).

- I have a collection of things that can exist on their own (such as airplanes at an airport).

The first example is called *composition*, whereas the second is called *aggregation.*[2]

Different ways of showing class information

Figure 2-1 illustrates several important things. First, each rectangle represents a class. In the UML, I can represent up to three aspects of a class:

- The name of the class

- The data members of the class

- The methods (functions) of the class

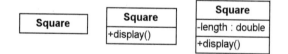

Figure 2-1 The Class diagram—its three variations.

There are three different ways of showing this information:

- The leftmost rectangle shows just the class name. I would use this type of class representation when more detailed information is not needed.

---

2. Gamma, Helm, Johnson, and Vlissides (the Gang of Four) call the first "aggregation" and the second "composition"—exactly the reverse of the UML. However, the Gang of Four book was written before the UML was finalized. The presented definition is, in fact, consistent with the UML's. This illustrates some of the motivation for the UML; before it came out there were several different modeling languages, each with its own notation and terms.

- The middle rectangle shows both the name and the methods of the class. In this case, the **Square**[3] has the method **display**. The plus sign (+) in front of **display** (the name of the method) means that this method is public—that is, objects other than objects of this class can call it.

- The rightmost rectangle shows what I had before (the name and methods of the class) as well as data members of the class. In this case, the minus sign (–) before the data member **length** (which is of type double) indicates that this data member's value is private; that is, it is unavailable to anything other than the object to which it belongs.[4]

UML Notation for Access

You can control the accessibility of class data and method members. You can use the UML to notate which accessibility you want each member to have. The three most common types of accessibility available in most object-oriented languages are as follows:

- **Public**—Notated with a plus sign (+). This means all objects can access this data or method.

- **Protected**—Notated with a pound sign (#). This means only this class and all of its derivations (including derivations from its derivations) can access this data or method.

- **Private**—Notated with a minus sign (–). This means that only methods of this class can access this data or method. (Note: Some languages further restrict this to the particular object.)

---

3. Whenever a class name is referenced in the text, it is bold (as done here).
4. In some languages, objects of the same type can share each other's private data.

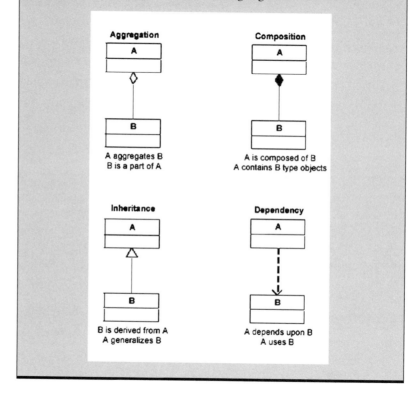

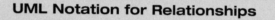

Class Diagrams also show relationships

Class diagrams can also show relationships between different classes. Figure 2-2 shows the relationship between the **Shape** class and several classes that derive from it.

Showing the is-a *relationship*

Figure 2-2 represents several things. First, the arrowhead under the **Shape** class means that those classes pointing to **Shape** derive from **Shape**. Furthermore, because Shape is *italicized*, that means it is an abstract class. An abstract class is a class that is used to define the interface for the classes that derive from it as well as being a place to put any common data and methods of these derived

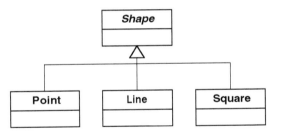

Figure 2-2 The Class diagram showing is-a relationships.

classes. An interface can be thought of as an abstract class that has no common data or methods—it merely serves as a way of defining the methods of the classes that implement it.[5]

There are actually two different kinds of *has-a* relationships. One object can have another object where the contained object is a part of the containing object—or not. In Figure 2-3, I show **Airport** "having" **Aircraft**. **Aircraft** are not part of **Airport**, but I can still say the **Airport** has them. This type of relationship is called *aggregation*.

Showing the has-a *relationship*

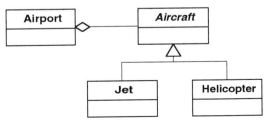

Figure 2-3 The Class diagram showing the has-a relationship.

In this diagram, I also show that an **Aircraft** is either a **Jet** or a **Helicopter**. I can see that **Aircraft** is an abstract class or an interface[6] because its name is shown in italics. That means that an **Airport**

Aggregation

---

5. I know I've used the word *interface* two times for different meanings, but don't blame me. I would have preferred using another name for the Java and C# keyword—interface.

6. For simplicity's sake, I am not going to continue to write "abstract class or interface" anymore. Just imagine that when I write "abstract class" I've written "abstract class or interface."

will have either **Jet** or **Helicopter** but can treat them the same (as **Aircraft**). The open (unfilled) diamond on the right of the **Airport** class indicates the aggregation relationship.

Composition

The other type of has-a relationship is where the containment means the contained object is a part of the containing object. This type of relationship is also called *composition*.

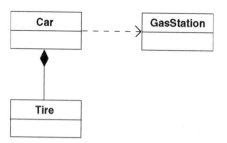

Figure 2-4 The Class diagram showing composition and the uses relationship.

Composition and uses

Figure 2-4 shows that a **Car** has **Tires** as parts (that is, the **Car** is made up of **Tires** and other things). This type of has-a relationship, called *composition*, is depicted by the solid diamond. This diagram also shows that a **Car** uses a **GasStation**. The *uses* relationship is depicted by a dashed line with an arrow. This is also called a *dependency relationship*.

Composition versus aggregation

Both composition and aggregation involve one object containing one or more objects. Composition, however, implies the contained object is a part of the containing object, whereas aggregation means the contained objects are more like a collection of things. We can consider composition to be an unshared association, with the contained object's lifetime being controlled by its containing object. The appropriate use of constructors and destructors is useful here to help facilitate object creation and destruction.

Indicating the number of things another object has

Class diagrams show the relationships among classes. With composition and aggregation, however, the relationship is more specifically about objects of that type of class. For example, it is true **Airport**s

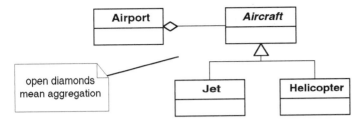

Figure 2-5 The Class diagram with a note.

Notes in the UML

Figure 2-5 contains a new symbol: the note. The box containing the message "open diamonds mean aggregation" is a note. They are meant to look like pieces of paper with the right corner folded back. You often see them with a line connecting them to a particular class, indicating they relate just to that class.

have **Aircraft**, but more specifically, specific airports have specific aircraft. A question may arise: How many aircraft does an airport have? This is called the *cardinality* of the relationship. Figures 2-6 and 2-7 show this.

Figure 2-6 tells us that when I have an **Airport**, it has from 0 to any number (represented by an asterisk here, but sometimes by the letter *n*) of **Aircraft**. The 0..1 on the **Airport** side means that when I have an **Aircraft**, it can be contained by either 0 or 1 **Airport**. (It may be in the air.)

Cardinality

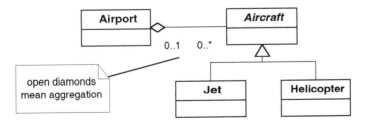

Figure 2-6 The cardinality of the Airport-Aircraft relationship.

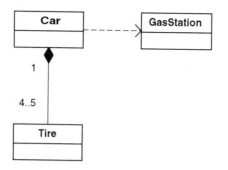

Figure 2-7 The cardinality of the Car-Tire relationship.

Cardinality continued

Figure 2-7 tells us that when I have a **Car**, it has either four or five tires. (It may or may not have a spare.) Tires are on exactly one car. I have heard some people assume no specification of cardinality assumes that there is one object. That is not correct. If cardinality is not specified, no assumption is made as to how many objects there are.

Dashes show dependence

As before, the dashed line between **Car** and **GasStation** in Figure 2-7 shows that a dependency exists between the two. The UML uses a dashed arrow to indicate semantic relationships (meanings) between two model elements.

Interaction Diagrams

Sequence Diagram

Class diagrams show static relationships between classes. In other words, they do not show us any activity. Although these are very useful, sometimes I need to show how the objects instantiated from these classes actually work together.

The UML diagrams that show how objects interact with each other are called *Interaction diagrams*. The most common type of Interaction diagram is the Sequence diagram, such as shown in Figure 2-8.

How to read Sequence diagrams

Sequence diagrams are read from top to bottom, as follows:

• Each rectangle at the top represents a particular object. Although many of the rectangles have class names in them, notice that a colon appears in front of the class name. Some of the rectangles have other names—for example, **shape1:Square**.

• The vertical lines represent the lifeline of the objects. Unfortunately, some UML drawing programs don't support this and draw the lines from the top to the bottom, leaving it unclear when an object actually comes into existence.

• I show objects sending messages[7] to each other with horizontal lines between these vertical lines.

Sometimes returned values and/or objects are explicitly shown, and sometimes it is just understood that they are returned.

For example, in Figure 2-8

• At the top I see that **Main** sends a "get shapes" message to the **ShapeDB** object (which isn't named).

• After being asked to "get shapes," the **ShapeDB**

  – Instantiates a collection.

  – Instantiates a square.

  – Adds the square to the collection.

  – Instantiates a circle.

  – Adds the circle to the collection.

  – Returns the collection to the calling routine (the **Main**).

---

7. When objects "talk" to each other, it is called *sending a message*. You are sending a request to another object to do something instead of telling the other object what to do. You allow the other object to be responsible enough to figure out what to do. Transferring responsibility is a fundamental principle of object-oriented programming. It is quite different from procedural programming, in which you retain control of what to do next, and therefore might "call a method" or "invoke an operation" in another object.

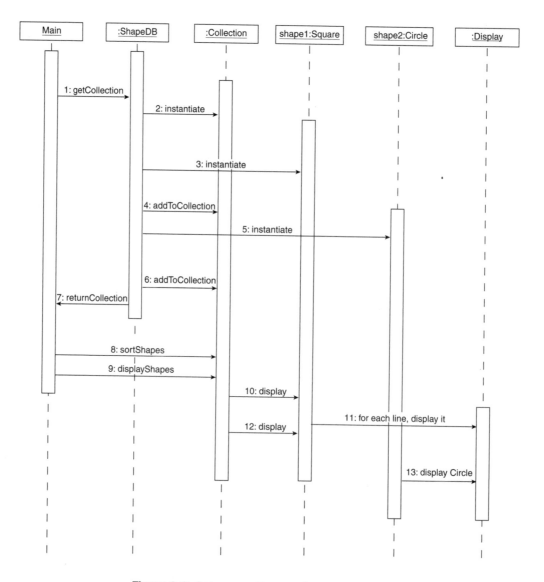

Figure 2-8 Sequence diagram for the Shapes program.

I read the rest of the diagram in this top-down fashion to see the rest of the action. This diagram is called a *Sequence diagram* because it depicts the sequence of operations.

Object:Class Notation

In some UML diagrams, you want to refer to an object with the class from which it is derived. You can do so by connecting them with a colon. In Figure 2-8, I show **shape1:Square** refers to the **shape1** object, which is instantiated from the **Square** class.

Summary

The purpose of the UML is to both flesh out your designs and to communicate them. Do not worry so much about creating diagrams the "right" way. Think about the best way to communicate the concepts in your design. In other words

In this chapter

- If you think something needs to be said, use a note to say it.

- If you aren't sure about an icon or a symbol and you have to look it up to determine its meaning, include a note to explain it; after all, others may be unclear about its meaning, too.

- Go for clarity.

Of course, this means you should not use the UML in nonstandard ways—that does not communicate properly either. Just consider what you are trying to communicate as your draw your diagrams.

Review Questions

Observations

1. What is the difference between an is-a relationship and a has-a relationship? What are the two types of "association" relationships?

2. In the Class diagram, a class is shown as a box, which can have up to three parts. Describe these three parts.

3. Define *cardinality*.

4. What is the purpose of a Sequence diagram?

Interpretations

1. Give an example of an is-a relationship and the two "association" relationships. Using these examples

    • Draw them in a Class diagram.

    • Show cardinality on this Class diagram.

2. Figure 2-8 shows a Sequence diagram. How many steps are shown in this figure? How many objects are shown and what are they?

3. When objects communicate with each other, why is it more appropriate to talk about "sending a message" than "invoking an operation"?

Opinions and Applications

1. How many steps should be shown on a Sequence diagram?

PART II

The Limitations of Traditional Object-Oriented Design

Part Overview

In this part, I solve a real-world problem using standard object-oriented methods. This was a problem I worked on when I was just beginning to learn design patterns.

In this part

Chapter	Discusses These Topics
3	**A Problem That Cries Out for Flexible Code**
	• A description of the CAD/CAM problem: Extract information from a large *computer-aided design/computer-aided manufacturing* (CAD/CAM) database to feed a complex and expensive analysis program.
	• Because the CAD/CAM system continues to evolve, the problem cries out for flexible code.
4	**A Standard Object-Oriented Solution**
	• My first solution to the CAD/CAM problem, using standard object-oriented methods.
	• At the time I actually worked on this problem, I hadn't yet learned the essence of the principles behind many design patterns. This resulted in an initial solution that over-relied on inheritance. It was easy to design and the initial solution worked, but I ended up with too many special cases.
	• My solution had significant problems—difficult maintenance and inflexibility—just the things I hoped to avoid with object-oriented design.

47

• I revisit the problem in Part 4, Chapter 13, "Solving the
   CAD/CAM Problem with Patterns." I solve the problem
   again using design patterns to orchestrate the application's architecture and its implementation details. By
   doing this, I create a solution that is much easier to
   maintain and is much more flexible.

Why read this part?   This part is important to read because it illustrates a typical problem
that results from traditional object-oriented design—taller-than-nec-
essary inheritance hierarchies that have tight coupling and low cohesion.

CHAPTER 3

A Problem That Cries Out
for Flexible Code

Overview

This chapter provides an overview of a problem we want to solve: Extract information from a large CAD/CAM[1] database to feed a complex and expensive analysis program. Because the CAD/CAM system continues to evolve, the problem cries out for flexible code.

In this chapter

This chapter examines the CAD/CAM problem, the vocabulary of the domain, and important features of the problem.

Extracting Information
from a CAD/CAM System

I am now going to review a past design of mine that got me on the road to the insights contained in this book.

The problem: Extract information for an expert system

I was supporting a design center in which engineers used a CAD/CAM system to make drawings of sheet-metal parts. Figure 3-1 shows an example of one of these parts.

My task was to write a computer tool to extract information from the CAD/CAM system so that an expert system could use it in a particular way. The expert system needed this information to control the manufacturing of the part. Because the expert system was difficult to modify and would have a longer lifespan than the current version of the CAD/CAM system, I wanted to write the information-extracting tool in such a way that it could easily be adapted to new revisions of the CAD/CAM system.

---

1. CAD: Computer Aided Drafting, CAM: Computer Aided Manufacturing.

> ## What Are Expert Systems?
>
> An *expert system* is a special computer system that uses the rules of a human expert(s) to make automated decisions. Building expert systems involves two steps. First, acquire and model the set of rules that experts use to make decisions and accomplish the task. Second, implement this set of rules in the computer system; this step often uses some sort of commercially available expert system tool. The first step is by far the more difficult assignment for the analyst.

Understand the Vocabulary

Terminology: Classifying the shapes cut from the sheet metal

The first task in analysis is to understand the vocabulary used by the users and the experts in the problem domain. The most important terms used are those that describe the dimensions and geometry of the cuts made in the sheet metal.

As shown in Figure 3-1, a piece of sheet metal is cut to a particular size and has shapes cut out inside it. Experts call these cutouts by the general name *feature*. A piece of sheet metal can be fully specified by its external dimensions and the features contained in it.

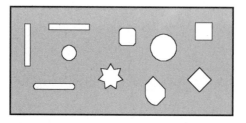

Figure 3-1 Example of a piece of sheet metal.

Table 3-1 describes the types of features that may be found in a piece of sheet metal. These are the shapes the system must address.

Table 3-1 Features Found in a Piece of Sheet Metal

Shape	Description
Slot	Straight cuts in the metal of constant width that terminate with either squared or rounded edges. Slots may be oriented to any angle. They are usually cut with a router bit. Figure 3-1 has three slots on the left side; one is oriented vertically, whereas the others are oriented horizontally.
Hole	Circles cut into the sheet metal. Typically they are cut with drill bits of varying width. Figure 3-1 has a hole toward the left surrounded by the three slots and has a larger hole toward the right of the sheet metal.
Cutout	Squares with either squared or rounded edges. These are cut by a high-powered punch hitting the metal with great impact. Figure 3-1 has three cutouts; the lower-right one is oriented at 45 degrees.
Special	Preformed shapes that are not slots, holes, or cutouts. In these cases, a special punch has been made to create these quickly. Electrical outlets are a common "special" case. The star shape in Figure 3-1 is a special shape.
Irregular	Anything else. They are formed by using a combination of tools. The five-sided object toward the bottom right of Figure 3-1 is an irregular shape.

CAD/CAM experts also use additional terminology that is important to understand, as described in Table 3-2.

Additional terminology

Table 3-2 Additional CAD/CAM Terminology

Term	Description
Geometry	The description of how a piece of sheet metal looks: the location of each of the features and their dimensions and the external shape of the sheet metal.
Part	The piece of sheet metal itself. I need to be able to store the geometry of each of the parts.

Table 3-2 Additional CAD/CAM Terminology (cont.)

Term	Description
Dataset or model	The set of records in the CAD/CAM database that stores the geometry of a part.
NC machine and NC set	Numerically controlled (NC) machine. A special manufacturing tool that cuts metal using a variety of cutting heads that are controlled by a computer program. Usually the computer program is fed the geometry of the part. This computer program is composed of commands called the NC set.

Describe the Problem

High-level description of the system's tasks

I need to design a program that will allow the expert system to open and read a model containing the geometry of a part that I want to analyze. The expert system will then generate the commands for the *numerically controlled* (NC) machine to build the piece of sheet metal.

I am concerned only about sheet-metal parts in this example. However, the CAD/CAM system can handle many other kinds of parts.

At a high level, I want the system to perform the following steps:

1. Analyze pieces of sheet metal.

2. See how they should be made, based on the features they contain.

3. Generate a set of instructions that are readable by manufacturing equipment. This set of instructions is called an NC set.

4. Give these instructions to manufacturing equipment when I want to make any of these parts

The expert system's task is not trivial

The difficulty with my programming task is that I cannot just extract the features from the dataset and generate NC set commands. The type of commands to use and the order of these commands depend on the features and their relation to other features.

Suppose, for example, that a shape is made up of several features: a cutout with two slots. One of the slots runs vertically through the cutout, whereas the other runs horizontally through it, as shown in Figure 3-2.

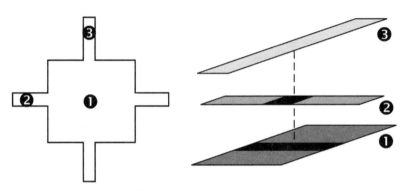

Figure 3-2 A cutout with two slots. Left: How the part looks when finished. Right: It is really composed of three features.

It is important to realize that I am actually given the three features on the right to make up the shape on the left. That is because the engineers using the CAD/CAM system typically think in terms of the features to make up more complex shapes, because they know that doing so will enable quicker manufacturing of the parts.

The problem is, I cannot just generate the NC set commands for the three features independently of one another and hope the part comes out properly—often a particular order must be used. In the example, if I do the slots first and then the cutout, as shown in Figure 3-3, when the cutout is made (remember a cutout is created by using a high-impact punch), the sheet metal will bend because the slots will have weakened the metal.

…because it must determine the order of the features

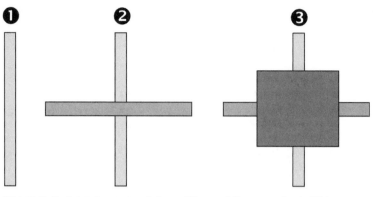

Figure 3-3 A bad approach to cutting out the openings. This sequence results in weakened, bent sheet metal.

I must create the shape shown in Figure 3-2 by punching out the cutout first, and then cutting the slots. This works because the slots are created using a router, which applies sideways pressure. Figure 3-4 shows this. Making the cutout first actually makes the job easier, not harder.

Fortunately, someone had already worked out the rules for the expert system. I did not have to worry about that. I took the time to explain these challenges so that you could understand the type of information needed by the expert system.

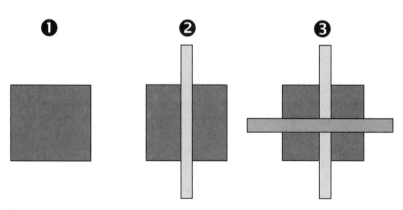

Figure 3-4 An expert's approach to cutting out the openings. This approach results in correct cutouts.

The Essential Challenges and Approaches

The CAD/CAM system is constantly evolving, changing. My real problem was to make it possible for the company to continue to use its expensive expert system while the CAD/CAM system changed. This is often the role of architecture in software: to isolate one part of the system, protecting it from another part that has a high risk of change.

Challenge: Allow the expert system to work with a constantly changing CAD/CAM system

In my situation, they were currently using one version of the CAD/CAM system, *Version 1* (V1), and a new version, *Version 2* (V2), was coming out shortly. Although one vendor made both versions, the two versions were not compatible.

For a variety of technical and administrative reasons, it was not possible to translate the models from one version to the next. Therefore the expert system needed to be able to support both versions of the CAD/CAM system.

In fact, the situation was worse than just having to accommodate two different versions of the CAD/CAM system. I knew a third version was coming out before long, but did not know when that would happen, or what its nature would be. To preserve the investment in the company's expert system, I wanted a system architecture such as the one diagrammed in Figure 3-5.

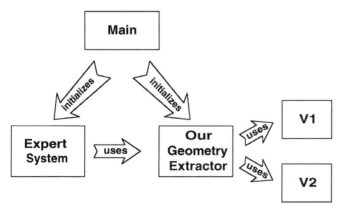

Figure 3-5 High-level view of my solution.

In other words, the application can initialize everything so that the expert system uses the appropriate CAD/CAM system. However, the expert system has to be able to use either version. Hence, I need to make V1 and V2 look the same to the expert system.

Polymorphism isn't needed at all levels

Although polymorphism is definitely needed at the geometry-extractor level, it will not be needed at the feature level. This is because the expert system needs to know what type of features it is dealing with. However, we don't want to make any changes to the expert system when Version 3 of the CAD/CAM system comes out.

High-level class diagram

A basic understanding of object-oriented design implies that I will have a high-level Class diagram similar to the one shown in Figure 3-6.

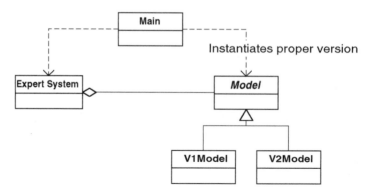

Figure 3-6 Class diagram of my solution.[2]

In other words, the expert system relates to the CAD/CAM systems through the **Model** class. The **Main** class takes care of instantiating the correct version of the **Model** (that is, **V1Model** or **V2Model**).

A more detailed look at the CAD/CAM systems

Now I describe the CAD/CAM systems and how they work. Unfortunately, the two are very different beasts.

---

2. This and all other class diagrams in this book use the Unified Modeling Language (UML) notation. See Chapter 2, "The UML—The Unified Modeling Language" for a description of UML notation.

Version 1 is essentially a collection of subroutine libraries. To get information from a model, a series of calls must be made. A typical set of queries in CAD/CAM Version 1 would be as follows:

1. Open model XYZ and return a handle to it.

2. Store this handle as H.

3. For the model referred to by H, tell me how many features are present; store as N.

4. For each feature in the model referred to by H (from 1 to N)

    a. For the model referred to by H, tell me the ID of the *i*th element and store as ID.

    b. For the model referred to by H, tell me the feature type of ID and store as T.

    c. For the model referred to by H, tell me the X coordinate of ID and store as X. (Use T to determine the proper routine to call, based on type.)

This system is painful to deal with and clearly not object-oriented. Whoever is using the system must maintain the context for every query manually. Each call about a feature must know what kind of feature it has.

CAD/CAM V1 is clearly not object-oriented

The CAD/CAM vendor realized the inherent limitations of this type of system. The primary motivation for building V2 was to make it object-oriented. The geometry in V2 is therefore stored as objects. When a system requests a model, it gets back an object that represents the model. This model object contains a set of objects, each representing a feature. Because the problem domain is based on features, it is not surprising that the classes V2 uses to represent these features correspond exactly to the ones previously mentioned: slots, holes, cutouts, specials, and irregulars.

CAD/CAM V2 is object-oriented

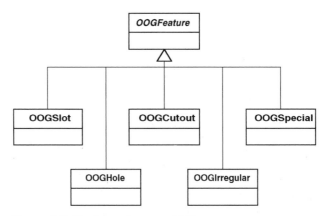

Figure 3-7 Feature classes of V2.

Therefore, in V2, I can get a set of objects that corresponds to the features that exist in the sheet metal. The UML diagram in Figure 3-7 shows the classes for the features.

The OOG stands for *object-oriented geometry*, just as a reminder that V2 is an object-oriented system.

Summary

In this chapter   This chapter described the CAD/CAM problem:

- I must extract information from different CAD/CAM systems in the same way. This will allow a system in which the company has a great investment (an expert system) to continue working without expensive modifications every time the CAD/CAM systems change.

- I have two systems implemented in completely different ways, even though they contain essentially the same information.

This task has many similarities to other problems I have run across in projects. There are different specific implementations of systems, but I want to allow other objects to communicate with these different implementations in the same way.

Review Questions

Observations

1. What five features in sheet metal will this system have to address?

2. What is the difference between the V1 system and the V2 system?

Interpretations

1. What is the essential challenge of the CAD/CAM problem?

2. Why is polymorphism needed at the geometry-extractor level but not at the feature level?

Opinions and Applications

1. I spent time defining terms related to the CAD/CAM problem.

   • Why did I do this?

   • Did you find this useful or a distraction?

   • Is it important to understand the user's terminology?

   • What is the most effective method you have found for recording user terminology?

CHAPTER 4

A Standard Object-Oriented Solution

Overview

This chapter provides an initial solution to the problem discussed in Chapter 3, "A Problem That Cries Out for Flexible Code." It is a reasonable first attempt at a solution and gets the job done quickly. However, it misses an important system requirement: flexibility as the CAD/CAM system continues to evolve.

In this chapter

This chapter describes a solution based on object orientation. It is not a great solution, but it is a solution that would work.

Note: I will show only Java code examples in the main body of this chapter. The equivalent C++ and C# code examples can be found at the book's Web site, http://www.netobjectives.com/dpexplained. Code is handled this way throughout the book.

Solving with Special Cases

Given the two different CAD/CAM systems described in Chapter 3, how do I build an information-extraction system that will look the same to a client object regardless of which CAD/CAM system that I have?

Getting to a solution: Special subclasses for each version

In thinking how to solve this problem, I reasoned that if I can solve it for slots, I can use that same solution for cutouts, holes, and so on. In thinking about slots, I saw that I could easily specialize for each case. That is, I would have a **SlotFeature** class and make a derivation from **SlotFeature** when I had the V1 system and another derivation when I had a V2 system. I show this in Figure 4-1.

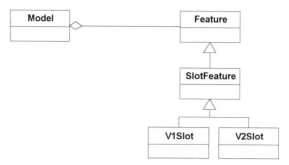

Figure 4-1 The design for slots.

Completing the solution

I complete this solution by extending it for each of the feature types, as shown in Figure 4-2.

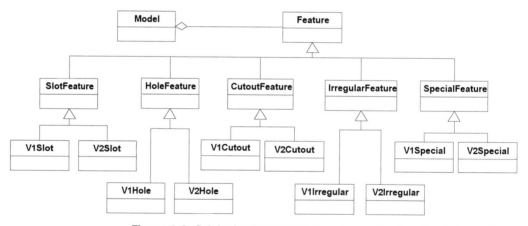

Figure 4-2 Original solution to the problem of extracting information.

Of course, Figure 4-2 is pretty high level. Each of the **V1xxx** classes would communicate with the corresponding V1 library. Each of the **V2xxx** classes would communicate with the corresponding object in the V2 model.

This is easier to visualize by looking at each class individually:

- **V1Slot** would be implemented by remembering the model it belongs to and its ID in the V1 system when it is instantiated. Then,

whenever one of the **V1Slot** methods is called to get information about it, the method would have to call a sequence of subroutine calls in V1 to get that information.

- **V2Slot** would be implemented in a similar fashion, except that,
  in this case, each **V2Slot** object would contain the **OOGSlot**
  object corresponding to it in the V2 system. Then, whenever the
  object was asked for information, it would simply pass this request on to the **OOGSlot** object and pass the response back to
  the client object that originally requested it.

Figure 4-3 is a more detailed diagram incorporating the V1 and V2
systems.

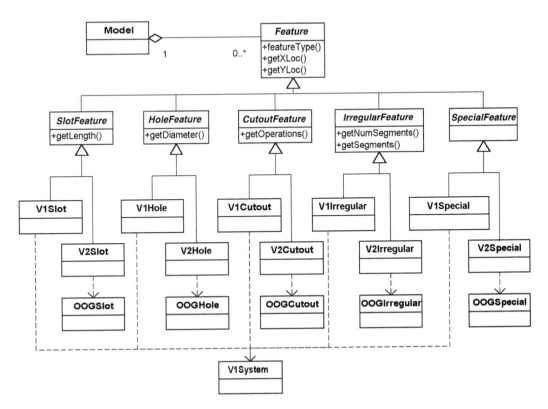

Figure 4-3 A first solution.

Code fragments help to understand the design

I am going to provide code examples for a couple of the classes in this design. These examples are just to help you understand how this design could be implemented. If you feel comfortable that you could implement this design, feel free to skip the following Java code examples. Note: The examples shown here are incomplete and are just for illustrative purposes. For complete code, see the book's Web site at http://www.netobjectives.com/dpexplained.

Example 4-1 Java Code Fragments: Instantiating the V1 Features

```java
// segment of code that instantiates the features
// no error checking provided -for illustration
// purposes only
public class V1Model extends Model {

    static public Model buildV1Model (String modelName) {
        V1Model myModel= new V1Model();
        myModel.modelNumber= myModel.openModel( modelName);
        if (myModel.modelNumber <= 0) return null;

        myModel.buildModel();
        return myModel;
    }

    private void buildModel () {
        // each feature object needs to know the model
        // number and feature ID it corresponds to in
        // order to retrieve information when requested.
        // Note how this information is passed to each
        // object's constructor

        nElements= getNumberOfElements();
        features= new Feature[ nElements];

        // do for each feature in the model
        int i;
        int ID;
        for (i= 0; i < nElements; i++) {
            // determine feature present and create
            // appropriate feature object
            ID= V1.getFeatureID( modelNumber, i);
```

```
        switch( V1.getFeatureType( modelNumber, ID)) {
           case FEATURE_SLOT:
              features[i]=new V1Slot(modelNumber, ID);
              break;

           case FEATURE_HOLE:
              features[i]=new V1Hole(modelNumber, ID);
              break;
           // Other cases
        }
      }
   }
}
```

Example 4-2 Java Code Fragments: Implementation of V1 Methods

```
// myModelNumber and myID are private members containing
// information about the model and feature (in V1) this
// feature corresponds to

public class V1Slot extends SlotFeature {
   . . .
   public double getX1 () {
      return V1.getX1forSlot( myModelNumber, myID);
   }
   public double getX2 () {
      return V1.getX2forSlot( myModelNumber, myID);
   }
}

public class V1Hole extends HoleFeature {
   . . .
   public double getXLoc () {
      return V1.getXforHole( myModelNumber, myID);
   }
}
```

Example 4-3 Java Code Fragments: Instantiating the V2 Features

```
// segment of code that instantiates the features
// no error checking provided -for illustration
```

```java
                // purposes only
                public class V2Model extends Model {

                    static public Model buildV2Model (String modelName) {
                        // open model
                        V2Model myModel= new V2Model();
                        if (!myModel.openModel( modelName)) return null;

                        myModel.buildModel();
                        return myModel;
                    }

                    private void buildModel () {
                        // each feature object needs to know the feature
                        // in the V2 system it corresponds to in order to
                        // retrieve information when requested. Note how
                        // this informationis passed into each object's
                        // constructor

                        nElements= getNumberOfElements();
                        OOGFeature oogF;

                        // do for each feature in the model
                        int i;
                        for (i= 0; i < nElements; i++) {
                            // determine feature present and create
                            // appropriate feature object
                            oogF= getElement(i);
                            switch( oogF.getType()) {
                                case OOG_SLOT:
                                    features[i]= new V2Slot( oogF);
                                    break;

                                case OOG_HOLE:
                                    features[i]= new V2Hole( oogF);
                                    break;
                                // other cases
                            }
                        }
                    }
                }
```

Example 4-4 Java Code Fragments: Implementation of V2 Methods

```java
// oogF is a reference to the feature object in V2 that
// the object containing it corresponds to

public class V2Slot extends SlotFeature {
   . . .
   public double getX1 () throws Exception {
      // call appropriate method on oogF to
      // get needed information.
      return myOogF.getX1Loc();
   }
   public double getX2 () throws Exception {
      // call appropriate method on oogF to
      // get needed information.
      return myOogF.getX2Loc();
   }
}
public class V2Hole extends HoleFeature {
   . . .
   public double getXLoc () throws Exception {
      // call appropriate method on oogF to
      // get needed information.
      return myOogF.getXLoc();
   }
}
```

In Figure 4-3, I have added a few of the methods that are needed by the features. Note how they differ depending upon the type of feature. This means I do not have polymorphism across features. This is not a problem, however, because the expert system needs to know what type of feature it has anyway. This is because the expert system needs different kinds of information from different types of features, and makes sequencing decisions based on which features are present in a given part.

This solution satisfies one goal: A common API

This brings up the point that I am not so interested in polymorphism of the features. Rather, I need the ability to plug and play different CAD/CAM systems without changing the expert system.

Keep Your Eye on the Ball

One of the fundamentals of baseball is to keep your eye on the ball. Don't let yourself get distracted by secondary details. Focus on the most important task at hand, the thing you are trying to handle now.

This is great advice for software professionals as well. Proper analysis and design requires a balancing act between competing interests. You have to decide which aspects of the problem are what you are designing to; or what sorts of changes you are trying to protect your system from. Establishing balance must be your first focus while making design decisions. Don't let other details distract you.

In this case, we expect future changes to the CAD/CAM program. Changes could have major impacts, so that is what we want to control. That is the "ball" we need to watch.

But contains many challenges

What I am trying to do—handle multiple CAD/CAM versions transparently—gives me several clues that this solution is not a good one:

- **Redundancy among methods**—I can easily imagine that the methods that are making calls to the V1 system will have many similarities among them. For example, the **V1getX** for **Slot** and **V1getX** for **Hole** will be very similar.

- **Messy**—This is not always a good predictor (and it is a very subjective measurement), but it is another factor that reinforces my discomfort with the solution.

- **Tight coupling**—This solution has tight coupling because the features are related to each other indirectly. These relationships manifest themselves as the likely need to modify all of the features if the following occurs:

  – A new CAD/CAM system is required.

  – An existing CAD/CAM system is modified.

- **Weak cohesion**—Cohesion is fairly weak because methods to perform core functions are scattered among the classes.

However, my greatest concern comes from looking into the future. Imagine what will happen when the third version of the CAD/CAM system arrives. The combinatorial explosion will kill us! Look at the third row of the class diagram in Figure 4-3:

- There are 5 types of features.
- Each type of feature has a pair of classes, one for each CAD/CAM system.
- When I get the third version, I will have groups of 3, not groups of 2.
- Instead of 10 classes, I will have 15.

This is certainly not a system I will have fun maintaining! And imagine what will happen if something else varies. Right now, I am handling two variations (what kind of feature I have, and also which system, V1 or V2, holds its data), and so the number of classes I have is the number of features times the number of systems. If I get another variation to handle, this whole approach is going to quickly get out of hand.

A Pitfall of Analysis: Too Much Attention to Details Too Early

One common problem that we analysts can have is that we dive into the details too early in the development process. It is natural because it is easy to work with these details. Solutions for the details are usually apparent, but are not necessarily the best thing to start with. Delay as long as you can before you commit to the details.

In this case, I achieved one objective: a common application programming interface (API) for feature information. Also I defined my objects from a responsibility point of view. However, I did this at the price of creating special cases for everything. When I get new special cases, I will have to implement them as such. Hence, the high maintenance costs.

...and intuition says there must be a better solution

This was my first-blush solution, and I immediately disliked it. My dislike grew more from my intuition than from the more logical reasons I gave previously. I *felt* that there were problems.

In this case, I felt strongly that a better solution existed. Yet, two hours later, this was still the best I could come up with. The problem, it turned out, was my general approach, as discussed later in this book.

Pay Attention to Your Instincts

Gut feeling is a surprisingly powerful indicator of the quality of a design. I suggest that developers learn to listen to their instincts.

By gut instinct, I mean the sensation in your stomach when you see something you do not like. I know this sounds unscientific (and it is), but my experience has shown me consistently that when I have an instinctive dislike for a design, a better one lies around the corner. Of course, there are sometimes several different corners nearby, and I'm not always sure where the solution is.

Summary

In this chapter

This chapter showed how easy it is to solve this problem by special-casing everything. The solution is straightforward. It allows me to add additional methods without changing what I already have. However, there are several disadvantages to it: high redundancy, weak cohesion, and class explosion (from future changes).

The over-reliance on inheritance will result in higher maintenance costs than should occur (or at least, than I *feel* should occur).

Review Questions

Observations

1. Identify each of the elements of the UML diagram in Figure 4-3.

   - Abstract class

   - Cardinality

   - Derivation

   - Composition

   - Public methods

2. What is the essential ability required by the CAD/CAM application?

3. The first solution exhibits four problems. What are they?

Interpretations

1. Describe the first approach to solving the CAD/CAM problem. Was it a reasonable first approach?

Opinions and Applications

1. Delay as long as possible before committing to the details. Do you agree? Why or why not?

2. One solution was rejected because "intuition told me it was not a good solution." Is it appropriate for analysts/programmers to be guided by their instinct?

PART III

Design Patterns

Part Overview

This part introduces design patterns: what they are and how to use *In this part* them. Several patterns pertinent to the CAD/CAM problem (Chapter 3, "A Problem That Cries Out for Flexible Code") are described. They are presented individually and then related to the earlier problem. Throughout the pattern-learning chapters, I emphasize the object-oriented strategies espoused by the Gang of Four (as the authors Gamma, Helm, Johnson, and Vlissides are often referred to) in their seminal work, *Design Patterns: Elements of Reusable Object-Oriented Software.*

Chapter	Discusses These Topics
5	**An Introduction to Design Patterns**
	• The concept of design patterns, their origins in architecture, and how they apply in the discipline of software design.
	• The motivations for studying design patterns.
6	**The Facade Pattern**
	• What it is, where it is used, and how it is implemented.
	• How the Facade pattern relates to the CAD/CAM problem.
7	**The Adapter Pattern**
	• What it is, where it is used, and how it is implemented.
	• Comparison between the Adapter pattern and the Facade pattern.

Objectives

At the end of this section, you will understand what design patterns are, know why they are useful, and be familiar with several specif-ic patterns. You will also see how these patterns relate to the earlier CAD/CAM problem. This information, however, may not be enough to create a better design than we arrived at by over-relying on in-heritance. However, the stage will be set for using patterns in a way more powerful than as just recurring solutions. This is different from the way many design pattern practitioners use them.

CHAPTER 5

An Introduction to Design Patterns

Overview

This chapter introduces the concept of design patterns.

This chapter

- Discusses the origins of design patterns in architecture and how they apply in the discipline of software design.
- Examines the motivations for studying design patterns.

In this chapter

Design patterns are part of the cutting edge of object-oriented technology. Object-oriented analysis tools, books, and seminars are incorporating design patterns. Study groups on design patterns abound. It is often suggested that people learn design patterns only after they have mastered basic object-oriented skills. I have found that the opposite is true: Learning design patterns early in the learning of object-oriented skills greatly helps to improve understanding of object-oriented analysis and design.

Design patterns and object-oriented design reinforce each other

Throughout the rest of the book, I discuss not only design patterns, but also how they reveal and reinforce good object-oriented principles. I hope to improve both your understanding of these principles and illustrate why the design patterns being discussed here represent good designs.

Some of this material may seem abstract or philosophical. But give it a chance! This chapter lays the foundation for your understanding of design patterns. Understanding this material will enhance your ability to understand and work with new patterns.

Give this a chance

I have taken many of my ideas from Christopher Alexander's *The Timeless Way of Building*,[1] an excellent book that presents the philosophy of patterns succinctly. I discuss these ideas throughout this book.

Design Patterns Arose from Architecture and Anthropology

Is quality objective? Years ago, an architect named Christopher Alexander asked himself, "Is quality objective?" Is beauty truly in the eye of the beholder, or would people agree that some things are beautiful and some are not? The particular form of beauty that Alexander was interested in was one of architectural quality: What makes us know when an architectural design is good? For example, if a person were going to design an entryway for a house, how would he or she know that the design was good? Can we know good design? Is there an objective basis for such a judgment? A basis for describing our common consensus?

Alexander postulates that there is such an objective basis within architectural systems. The judgment that a building is beautiful is not simply a matter of taste. We can describe beauty through a measurable objective basis.

The discipline of cultural anthropology discovered the same thing. That body of work suggests that within a culture, individuals will agree to a large extent on what is considered to be a good design, what is beautiful. Cultures make judgments on good design that transcend individual beliefs. I believe that transcending patterns serve as objective bases for judging design. A major branch of cultural anthropology looks for such patterns to describe the behaviors and values of a culture.[2]

---

1. Alexander, C., *The Timeless Way of Building*, New York: Oxford University Press, 1979.

2. The anthropologist Ruth Benedict is a pioneer in pattern-based analysis of cultures. For examples, see Benedict, R., *The Chrysanthemum and the Sword*, Boston: Houghton Mifflin, 1946.

A proposition behind design patterns is that the quality of software systems can be measured objectively.

How do you get good quality repeatedly?

If you accept the idea that it is possible to recognize and describe a good quality design, how do you go about creating one? I can imagine Alexander asking himself,

> *What is present in a good quality design that is not present in a poor quality design?*

and

> *What is present in a poor quality design that is not present in a good quality design?*

These questions spring from Alexander's belief that if quality in design is objective, we should be able to identify what makes designs good and what makes designs bad.

Alexander studied this problem by making many observations of buildings, towns, streets, and virtually every other aspect of living spaces that human beings have built for themselves. He discovered that, for a particular architectural creation, good constructs had things in common with each other.

Look for the commonalties

Architectural structures differ from each other, even if they are of the same type. Yet even though they differ, they can still be of high quality.

...especially commonality in the features of the problem to be solved

For example, two porches may appear structurally different and yet both may still be considered high quality. They might be solving different problems for different houses. One porch may be a transition from the walkway to the front door. Another porch might be a place for shade on a hot day. Or two porches might solve a common problem (transition) in different ways.

Alexander understood this. He knew that structures couldn't be separated from the problem they are trying to solve. Therefore, in his quest to identify and describe the consistency of quality in design, Alexander realized that he had to look at different structures that were designed to solve the same problem. For example, Figure 5-1 illustrates two solutions to the problem of demarking an entryway.

Figure 5-1 Structures may look different but still solve a common problem.

This led to the concept of a pattern

Alexander discovered that by narrowing his focus in this way—by looking at structures that solve similar problems—he could discern similarities between designs that were high quality. He called these similarities *patterns*.

He defined a pattern as "a solution to a problem in a context":

> *Each pattern describes a problem which occurs over and over again in our environment and then describes the core of the solution to that problem, in such a way that you can use this solution a million times over, without ever doing it the same way twice.*[3]

Let's review some of Alexander's work to illustrate this. Table 5-1 presents an excerpt from his *The Timeless Way of Building*.[4]

---

3. Alexander, C., Ishikawa, S., Silverstein, M., *A Pattern Language*, New York: Oxford University Press, 1977, p. x.

4. Alexander, C., *The Timeless Way of Building*, New York: Oxford University Press, 1979.

Table 5-1 Excerpts from The Timeless Way of Building

Alexander Says	My Comments
In the same way, a courtyard, which is properly formed, helps people come to life in it.	A pattern always has a name and has a purpose. Here, the pattern's name is Courtyard, and its purpose is to help energize people, to help them feel alive.
Consider the forces at work in a courtyard. Most fundamental of all, people seek some kind of private outdoor space, where they can sit under the sky, see the stars, enjoy the sun, perhaps plant flowers. This is obvious.	Although it might be obvious sometimes, it is important to state explicitly the problem being solved, which is the reason for having the pattern in the first place. This is what Alexander does here for Courtyard.
But there are more subtle forces too. For instance, when a courtyard is too tightly enclosed, has no view out, people feel uncomfortable, and tend to stay away …they need to see out into some larger and more distant space.	He points out a difficulty with the simplified solution and then gives us a way to solve the problem that he has just pointed out.
Or again, people are creatures of habit. If they pass in and out of the courtyard, every day, in the course of their normal lives, the courtyard becomes familiar, a natural place to go…and it is used.	Familiarity sometimes keeps us from seeing the obvious. The value of a pattern is that those with less experience can take advantage of what others have learned before them: both what must be included to have a good design, and what must be avoided to keep from a poor design.
But a courtyard with only one way in, a place you only go when you "want" to go there, is an unfamiliar place, tends to stay unused…people go more often to places which are familiar.	Although patterns are often thought of as theoretical constructs, in fact they reflect practical concerns that have arisen repeatedly in the past.
Or again, there is a certain abruptness about suddenly stepping out, from the inside, directly to the outside…it is subtle, but enough to inhibit you.	Alexander describes a force that is present (and important), but can be easily overlooked.
If there is a transitional space—a porch or a veranda, under cover, but open to the air—this is psychologically half way between indoors and outdoors, and makes it much	He proposes a solution to a possibly overlooked challenge to building a great courtyard. Also he shows that one pattern (here a courtyard) often provides the context for

Table 5-1 Excerpts from The Timeless Way of Building (cont.)

Alexander Says	My Comments
easier, more simple, to take each of the smaller steps that brings you out into the courtyard...	another pattern (here a porch or veranda). Patterns provide context for each other because recognizing a pattern helps clarify the problem itself, making other patterns easier to see.
When a courtyard has a view out to a larger space, has crossing paths from different rooms, and has a veranda or a porch, these forces can resolve themselves. The view out makes it comfortable, the crossing paths help generate a sense of habit there, the porch makes it easier to go out more often...and gradually the courtyard becomes a pleasant customary place to be.	Alexander is telling us how to build a great courtyard...and then tells us why it is great.

The four components required of every pattern description

To review, Alexander says that a description of a pattern involves four items:

- The name of the pattern

- The purpose of the pattern, the problem it solves

- How we could accomplish this

- The constraints and forces we have to consider in order to accomplish it

Patterns exist for almost any design problem

Alexander postulated that patterns can solve virtually every architectural problem that one will encounter. He further postulated that patterns could be used together to solve complex architectural problems.

...and may be combined to solve complex problems

How patterns work together is discussed later in this book. For now, I want to focus on his claim that patterns are useful to solve specialized problems.

Moving from Architectural to Software Design Patterns

What does all of this architectural stuff have to do with us software developers?

Well, in the early 1990s, some smart developers happened upon Alexander's work in patterns. They wondered whether what was true for architectural patterns would also be true for software design.[5]

Adapting Alexander for software

- Were there problems in software that occur over and over again that could be solved in somewhat the same manner?

- Was it possible to design software in terms of patterns, creating specific solutions based on these patterns only after the patterns had been identified?

The group felt the answer to both of these questions was "unequivocally yes." The next step was to identify several patterns and develop standards for cataloging new ones.

Although many people were working on design patterns in the early 1990s, the book that had the greatest influence on this fledging community was *Design Patterns: Elements of Reusable Object-Oriented Software*[6] by Gamma, Helm, Johnson, and Vlissides. In recognition of their important work, these four authors are commonly and affectionately known as the *Gang of Four*.

The Gang of Four did the early work on design patterns

This book served several purposes:

---

5. The ESPRIT consortium in Europe was doing similar work in the 1980s. ESPRIT's Project 1098 and Project 5248 developed a pattern-based design methodology called *Knowledge Analysis and Design Support* (KADS) that was focused on patterns for creating expert systems. Karen Gardner extended the KADS analysis patterns to object orientation. See Gardner, K., *Cognitive Patterns: Problem-Solving Frameworks for Object Technology*, New York: Cambridge University Press, 1998.

6. Gamma, E., Helm, R., Johnson, R., Vlissides, J., *Design Patterns: Elements of Reusable Object-Oriented Software*, Boston: Addison-Wesley, 1995.

- It applied the idea of patterns to software design—calling them *design patterns*.

- It described a structure within which to catalog and describe design patterns.

- It cataloged 23 such patterns.

- It postulated object-oriented strategies and approaches based on these design patterns.

It is important to realize that the Gang of Four did not create the patterns described in the book. Rather, they identified patterns that already existed within the software community, patterns that reflected what had been learned about high-quality designs for specific problems. (Note the similarity to Alexander's work.)

Today there are several different forms for describing design patterns. Because this is not a book about writing design patterns, I do not offer an opinion on the best structure for describing patterns; however, the following items listed in Table 5-2 need to be included in any description.

For each pattern that I present in this book, I present a one-page summary of the key features that describes that pattern.

Consequences/Forces

The term *consequences* is used in design patterns and is often misunderstood. In everyday usage, consequences usually carries a negative connotation. (You never hear someone say, "I won the lottery! As a *consequence*, I now do not have to go to work!") Within the design pattern community, on the other hand, consequences simply refers to cause and effect. That is, if you implement this pattern in such-and-such a way, this is how it will affect and be affected by the forces present.

Table 5-2 Key Features of Patterns

Item	Description
Name	All patterns have a unique name that identifies them.
Intent	The purpose of the pattern.
Problem	The problem that the pattern is trying to solve.
Solution	How the pattern provides a solution to the problem in the context in which it shows up.
Participants and collaborators	The entities involved in the pattern.
Consequences	The consequences of using the pattern. Investigates the forces at play in the pattern.
Implementation	How the pattern can be implemented. Note: Implementations are just concrete manifestations of the pattern and should not be construed as the pattern itself.
Generic structure	A standard diagram that shows a typical structure for the pattern.

Note: Unless otherwise noted, the Key Features summary is extracted from the pattern description in the GoF book.

Why Study Design Patterns?

Now that you have an idea about what design patterns are, you may still be wondering, "Why study them?" There are several reasons that are obvious and some that are not so obvious.

Design patterns help with reuse and communication

The most commonly stated reasons for studying patterns are because patterns enable us to

- **Reuse solutions**—By reusing already established designs, I get a head start on my problems and avoid *gotchas*. I get the benefit of learning from the experience of others. I do not have to reinvent solutions for commonly recurring problems.

- **Establish common terminology**—Communication and teamwork require a common base of vocabulary and a common viewpoint of the problem. Design patterns provide a common point of reference during the analysis and design phase of a project.

Design patterns give a higher perspective on analysis and design

Patterns give you a higher-level perspective on the problem and on the process of design and object orientation. This frees you from the tyranny of dealing with the details too early.

By the end of this book, I hope you will agree that this is one of the greatest reasons to study design patterns. It will shift your mindset and make you a more powerful analyst.

To illustrate this advantage, I want to relate a conversation between two carpenters about how to build the drawers for some cabinets.[7]

Example of the tyranny of details: Carpenters making a set of drawers

Consider two carpenters discussing how to build the drawers for some cabinets.

Carpenter 1: How do you think we should build these drawers?

Carpenter 2: Well, I think we should make the joint by cutting straight down into the wood, and then cut back up 45 degrees, and then going straight back down, and then back up the other way 45 degrees, and then going straight back down, and then…

---

7. This section is inspired by a talk given by Ralph Johnson and is adapted by the authors.

Now, your job is to figure out what they are talking about!

Isn't that a confusing description? What is Carpenter 2 prescribing? The details certainly get in the way! Let's try to draw out his description.

The details may confuse the solution

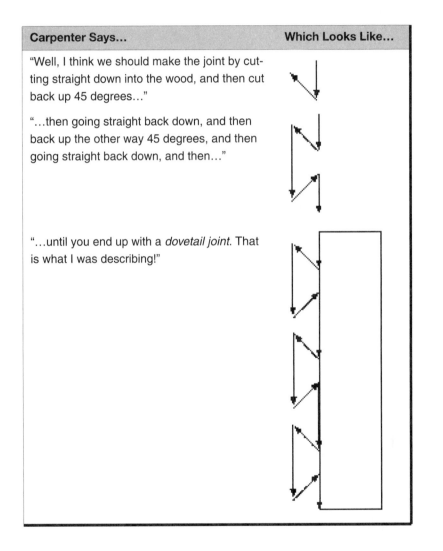

Carpenter Says...	Which Looks Like...
"Well, I think we should make the joint by cutting straight down into the wood, and then cut back up 45 degrees…"	
"…then going straight back down, and then back up the other way 45 degrees, and then going straight back down, and then…"	
"…until you end up with a *dovetail joint.* That is what I was describing!"	

Doesn't this sound like code reviews you have heard? The one where the programmer describes the code in terms such as

This sounds like so many code reviews: Details, details, details

And then, I use a WHILE LOOP here to do...followed by a series of IF statements to do...and here I use a SWITCH to handle...

You get a description of the details of the code, but you have no idea *what the program is doing and why it is doing it*!

Carpenters do not really talk at that level of detail

Of course, no self-respecting carpenter would talk like this. What would really happen is something like this:

> **Carpenter 1**: Should we use a dovetail joint or a miter joint?

Already we see a qualitative difference. The carpenters are discussing differences in the quality of solutions to a problem; their discussion is at a higher level, a more abstract level. They avoid getting bogged down in the details of a particular solution.

When the carpenter speaks of a miter joint, he or she has the following characteristics of the solution in mind:

- **It is a simpler solution**—A miter joint is a simple joint to make. You cut the edges of the joining pieces at 45 degrees, abut them, and then nail or glue them together, as shown in Figure 5-2.

Figure 5-2 A miter joint.

- **It is lightweight**—A miter joint is weaker than a dovetail. It cannot hold together under great stress.

- **It is inconspicuous**—The miter joint's single cut is much less noticeable than the dovetail joint's multiple cuts.

When the carpenter speaks of a dovetail joint, he or she has other characteristics of the solution in mind. These characteristics may not be obvious to a layman, but would be clearly understood by any carpenter:

- **It is a more complex solution**—It is more involved to make a dovetail joint. Thus, it is more expensive.

- **It is impervious to temperature and humidity**—As these change, the wood expands or contracts. However, the dovetail joint will remain solid.

- **It is independent of the fastening system**—In fact, dovetail joints do not even depend upon glue to work.

- **It is a more aesthetically pleasing joint**—It is beautiful to look at when made well.

In other words, the dovetail joint is a strong, dependable, beautiful joint that is complex (and therefore expensive) to make.

There is a meta-level conversation going on

So, when Carpenter 1 asked

Should we use a dovetail joint or a miter joint?

The real question that was being asked was

Should we use a joint that is expensive to make but is both beautiful and durable, or should we just make a quick and dirty joint that will last at least until the check clears?

We might say the carpenters' discussion really occurs at two levels: the surface level of their words, and the *real* conversation, which occurs at a higher level (a *meta-level*) that is hidden from the layman and which is much richer in meaning. This higher level is the level of "carpenter patterns" and reflects the real design issues for the carpenters.

In the first case, Carpenter 2 obscures the real issues by discussing the details of the implementations of the joints. In the second case, Carpenter 1 wants to decide which joint to use based on costs and quality of the joint.

Who is more efficient? Who would you rather work with?

Patterns help us see the forest and the trees

This is one thing I mean when I say that patterns can help raise the level of your thinking. You will learn later in the book that when you raise your level of thinking like this, new design methods become available. This is where the real power of patterns lies.

Other Advantages of Studying Design Patterns

Improve team communications and individual learning

My experience with development groups working with design patterns is that design patterns helped both individual learning and team development. This occurred because the more junior team members saw that the senior developers who knew design patterns had something of value and these junior members wanted it. This provided motivation for them to learn some of these powerful concepts.

Improved modifiability and maintainability of code

Most design patterns also make software more modifiable and maintainable. The reason for this is that they are time-tested solutions. Therefore, they have evolved into structures that can handle change more readily than what often first comes to mind as a solution. They also handle this with easier to understand code—making it easier to maintain.

Design patterns, when they are taught properly, can be used to greatly increase the understanding of basic object-oriented design principles. I have seen this countless times in the introductory
object-oriented courses I teach. In those classes, I start with a brief
introduction to the object-oriented paradigm. I then proceed to teach
design patterns, using them to illustrate the basic object-oriented
concepts (encapsulation, inheritance, and polymorphism). By the
end of the three-day course, although we've been talking mostly
about patterns, these concepts—which were just introduced to many
of the participants—feel as if they are old friends.

*Design patterns
illustrate basic
object-oriented
principles*

The Gang of Four suggests a few strategies for creating good object-
oriented designs. In particular, they suggest the following:

*Adoption of
improved
strategies—even
when patterns aren't
present*

- Design to interfaces.

- Favor aggregation over inheritance.[8]

- Find what varies and encapsulate it.

These strategies were employed in most of the design patterns discussed
in this book. Even if you do not learn a lot of design patterns, studying
a few should enable you to learn why these strategies are useful. With
that understanding comes the ability to apply them to your own design
problems even if you do not use design patterns directly.

Another advantage is that design patterns enable you or your team
to create designs for complex problems that do not require large inheritance hierarchies. Again, even if design patterns are not used directly, avoiding large inheritance hierarchies will result in improved
designs.

*Learn alternatives to
large inheritance
hierarchies*

---

8. Remember, *aggregation* means a collection of things that are not part of it (airplanes at an airport), whereas *composition* means something is a part of another
   thing (like wheels on an airplane). The distinction loses much of its importance
   in languages that have garbage collection, because you do not have to concern
   yourself with the life of the object. (When the object goes away, should its parts
   also go away?)

Summary

In this chapter

This chapter described what design patterns are. Christopher Alexander says, "Patterns are solutions to a problem in a context." They are more than a kind of template to solve one's problems. They are a way of describing the motivations by including both what we want to have happen along with the problems that are plaguing us.

This chapter examined reasons for studying design patterns. Such study helps to

- Reuse existing, high-quality solutions to commonly recurring problems.

- Establish common terminology to improve communications within teams.

- Shift the level of thinking to a higher perspective.

- Decide whether I have the right design, not just one that works.

- Improve individual learning and team learning.

- Improve the modifiability of code.

- Facilitate adoption of improved design alternatives, even when patterns are not used explicitly.

- Discover alternatives to large inheritance hierarchies.

Review Questions

Observations

1. Who is credited with the idea for design patterns?

2. Alexander discovered that by looking at structures that solve similar problems, he could discern what?

3. Define *pattern*.

4. What are the key elements in the description of a design pattern?

5. What are three reasons for studying design patterns?

6. The Gang of Four suggests a few strategies for creating good object-oriented designs. What are they?

Interpretations

1. "Familiarity sometimes keeps us from seeing the obvious." In what ways can patterns help avoid this?

2. The Gang of Four cataloged 23 patterns. Where did these patterns come from?

3. What is the relationship between "consequence" and "forces" in a pattern?

4. What do you think "find what varies and encapsulate it" means?

5. Why is it desirable to avoid large inheritance hierarchies?

Opinions and Applications

1. Think of a building or structure that felt particularly "dead." What does it not have in common with similar structures that seem to be more "alive"?

2. "The real power of patterns is the ability to raise your level of thinking." Have you had an experience in which this was true? Give an example.

CHAPTER 6

The Facade Pattern

Overview

I start the study of design patterns with a pattern that you have probably implemented in the past but may not have had a name for: the Facade pattern.

In this chapter

This chapter

- Explains what the Facade pattern is and where it is used.

- Presents the key features of the pattern.

- Presents some variations on the Facade pattern.

- Relates the Facade pattern to the CAD/CAM problem.

Introducing the Facade Pattern

According to the Gang of Four, the intent of the Facade pattern is to

Intent: A unified, high-level interface

> *Provide a unified interface to a set of interfaces in a subsystem. Facade defines a higher-level interface that makes the subsystem easier to use.*[1]

Basically, this is saying that we need to interact with a system that is easier than the current method, or we need to use the system in a particular way (such as using a 3D drawing program in a 2D way). We can build such a method of interaction because we only need to use a subset of the system in question.

---

1. Gamma, E., Helm, R., Johnson, R., Vlissides, J., *Design Patterns: Elements of Reusable Object-Oriented Software*, Boston: Addison-Wesley, 1995, p. 185.

Learning the Facade Pattern

A motivating example: Learn how to use our complex system!

Once, I worked as a contractor for a large engineering and manu-facturing company. My first day on the job, the technical lead of the project was not in. Now, this client did not want to pay me by the hour and not have anything for me to do. They wanted me to be doing something, even if it was not useful! Haven't you had days like this?

So, one of the project members found something for me to do. She said, "You are going to have to learn the CAD/CAM system we use some time, so you might as well start now. Start with these manuals over here." Then she took me to the set of documentation. I am not mak-ing this up: There were *8 feet* of manuals for me to read—each page 8.5 × 11 inches and in small print! This was one complex system!

Figure 6-1 Eight feet of manuals = one complex system!

I want to be insulated from this

Now, if you and I and say another four or five people were on a proj-ect that needed to use this system, what approach would we take? Would we all learn the system? Or would we draw straws and the *loser* would have to write routines that the rest of us would use to in-terface with the system?

This person would determine how I and others on our team were going to use the system and what *application programming interface* (API) would be best for our particular needs. She would then create a new class or classes that had the interface we required. Then I and the rest of the programming community could use this new interface without having to learn the entire complicated system (see Figure 6-2).

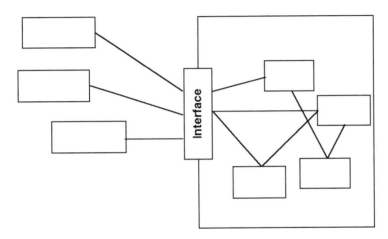

Figure 6-2 Insulating clients from the subsystem.

This approach works only when using a subset of the system's capabilities or when interacting with it in a particular way. If everything in the system needs to be used, the only way to improve the design would be if it were poor in the first place.

Works with subsets

This is the Facade pattern. It enables us to use a complex system more easily, either to use just a subset of the system or use the system in a particular way. We have a complicated system of which we need to use only a part. We end up with a simpler, easier-to-use system or one that is customized to our needs.

This is the Facade pattern

Most of the work still needs to be done by the underlying system. The Facade provides a collection of easier-to-understand methods. These methods use the underlying system to implement the newly defined functions.

The Facade Pattern: Key Features

Intent	You want to simplify how to use an existing system. You need to define your own interface.
Problem	You need to use only a subset of a complex system. Or you need to interact with the system in a particular way.
Solution	The Facade presents a new interface for the client of the existing system to use.
Participants and collaborators	It presents a simplified interface to the client that makes it easier to use.
Consequences	The Facade simplifies the use of the required subsystem. However, because the Facade is not complete, certain functionality may be unavailable to the client.
Implementation	Define a new class (or classes) that has the required interface.
	Have this new class use the existing system.

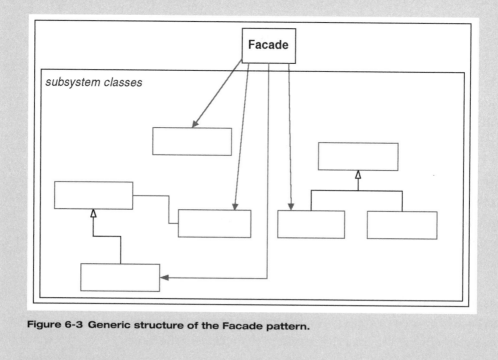

Figure 6-3 Generic structure of the Facade pattern.

Field Notes: The Facade Pattern

Facades can be used not only to create a simpler interface in terms of method calls, but also to reduce the number of objects that a client object must deal with. For example, suppose I have a **Client** object that must deal with **Database**s, **Model**s, and **Element**s. The **Client** must first open the **Database** and get a **Model**. Then it queries the **Model** to get an **Element**. Finally, it asks the **Element** for information. It might be a lot easier to create a **DatabaseFacade** that could be queried by the **Client** (see Figure 6-4).

Variations on Facade: Reduce the number of objects a client must work with

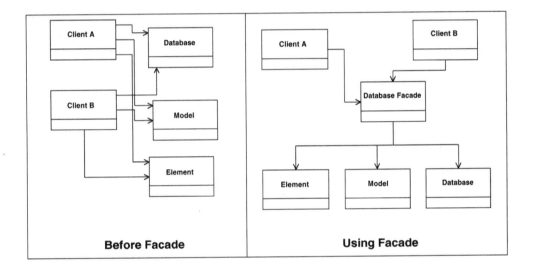

Figure 6-4 Facade reduces the number of objects for the client.

If a Facade can be made to be stateless (that is, no state is stored in it), one Facade object can be used by several other objects. Later, in Chapter 21, I show you how to do this, using the Singleton pattern and the Double-Checked Locking pattern.

Having one Facade work for many objects

Suppose that in addition to using functions that are in the system, I also need to provide some new functionality—say, record all calls to specific routines. In this case, I am going beyond a simple subset of the system.

Variations on Facade: Supplement existing functions with new routines

In this case, the methods I write for the Facade class may be supplemented by new routines for the new functionality. This is still the Facade pattern, but expanded with new functionality. I consider the primary goal one of simplification because I don't want to have to force the client routine to know that it needs to call the extra routines—the Facade does that.

The Facade pattern sets the general approach; it got me started. The Facade part of the pattern is the fact that I am creating a new interface for the client to use instead of the existing system's interface. I can do this because the Client object does not need to use all of the functions in my original system.

> ### Patterns Set a General Approach
>
> A pattern just sets the general approach. Whether or not to add new functionality depends upon the situation at hand. Patterns are blueprints to get you started; they are not carved in stone.

Variations on Facade: An "encapsulating" layer

The Facade can also be used to hide, or encapsulate, the system. The Facade could contain the system as private members of the Facade class. In this case, the original system would be linked in with the Facade class, but not presented to users of the Facade class.

There are a number of reasons to encapsulate the system, including the following:

- **Track system usage**—By forcing all accesses to the system to go through the Facade, I can easily monitor system usage.

- **Swap out systems**—I may need to switch systems in the future. By making the original system a private member of the Facade class, I can swap out the system for a new one with minimal effort. There may still be a significant amount of effort required, but at least I will only have to change the code in one place (the Facade class).

Relating the Facade Pattern to the CAD/CAM Problem

Think of the example above. The Facade pattern could be useful to help **V1Slot**s, **V1Hole**s, and so on use **V1System**. I will do just that in the solution in Chapter 13, "Solving the CAD/CAM Problem with Patterns."

Encapsulate the V1 system

Summary

The Facade pattern is so named because it puts up a new interface (a facade) in front of the original system.

In this chapter

The Facade pattern applies when

- You do not need to use all the functionality of a complex system and can create a new class that contains all the rules for accessing that system. If this is a subset of the original system, as it usually is, the API that you create for the new class should be much simpler than the original system's API.

- You want to encapsulate or hide the original system.

- You want to use the functionality of the original system and want to add some new functionality as well.

- The cost of writing this new class is less than the cost of everybody learning how to use the original system or is less than you would spend on maintenance in the future.

Review Questions

Observations

1. Define *Facade*.

2. What is the intent of the Facade pattern?

3. What are the consequences of the Facade pattern? Give an example.

4. In the Facade pattern, how do clients work with subsystems?

5. Does the Facade pattern usually give you access to the entire system?

Interpretations

1. The Gang of Four says that the intent of the Facade pattern is to "provide a unified interface to a set of interfaces in a subsystem. Facade defines a higher-level interface that makes the subsystem easier to use."

   • What does this mean?

   • Give an example.

2. Here is an example of a Facade that comes from outside of software: Pumps at gasoline stations in the United States can be very complex. There are many options on them: how to pay, the type of gas to use, watch an advertisement. One way to get a unified interface to the gas pump is to use a human gas attendant. Some states even require this.

   • What is another example from real life that illustrates a Facade?

Opinions and Applications

1. If you need to add functionality beyond what the system provides, can you still use the Facade pattern?

2. What is a reason for encapsulating an entire system using the Facade pattern?

3. Is there a case for writing a new system rather than encapsulating the old system with Facade? What is it?

4. Why do you think the Gang of Four call this pattern Facade? Is it an appropriate name for what it is doing? Why or why not?

CHAPTER 7

The Adapter Pattern

Overview

I will continue our study of design patterns with the Adapter pattern. The Adapter pattern is a very common pattern, and, as you will see, it is used with many other patterns.

In this chapter

This chapter

- Explains what the Adapter pattern is, where it is used, and how it is implemented.

- Presents the key features of the pattern.

- Uses the pattern to illustrate polymorphism.

- Illustrates how the UML can be used at different levels of detail.

- Presents some observations on the Adapter pattern from my own practice, including a comparison of the Adapter pattern and the Facade pattern.

- Relates the Adapter pattern to the CAD/CAM problem.

Introducing the Adapter Pattern

According to the Gang of Four, the intent of the Adapter pattern is to

Intent: Create a new interface

> *Convert the interface of a class into another interface that the clients expect. Adapter lets classes work together that could not otherwise because of incompatible interfaces.*[1]

---

1. Gamma, E., Helm, R., Johnson, R., Vlissides, J., *Design Patterns: Elements of Reusable Object-Oriented Software*, Boston: Addison-Wesley, 1995, p. 139.

Basically, this is saying that we need a way to create a new interface for an object that does the right stuff but has the wrong interface.

Learning the Adapter Pattern

A motivating example: Free the client object from knowing details

The easiest way to understand the intent of the Adapter pattern is to look at an example of where it is useful. Let's say I have been given the following requirements:

- Create classes for points, lines, and squares that have the behavior "display."

- The client objects should not have to know whether they actually have a point, a line, or a square. They just want to know that they have one of these shapes.

In other words, I want to encompass these specific shapes in a higher-level concept that I will call a "displayable shape."

Now, as I work through this simple example, try to imagine other situations that you have run into that are similar, such as the following:

- You have wanted to use a subroutine or a method that someone else has written because it performs some function that you need.

- You cannot incorporate the routine directly into your program.

- The interface or the way of calling the code is not exactly equivalent to the way that its related objects need to use it.

...so that it can treat details in a common way

In other words, although the system will *have* points, lines, and squares, I want the client objects to *think* I have only *shapes*.

- This allows client objects to deal with all these objects in the same way—freed from having to pay attention to their differences.

- It also enables me to add different kinds of shapes in the future without having to change the clients (see Figure 7-1).

What we have
(points, lines, squares)

What the client sees
(shapes)

Figure 7-1 The objects we have ...should all look just like "shapes."

I will make use of polymorphism; that is, I will have different objects in my system, but I want the clients of these objects to interact with them in a common way.

How to do this: Use derived classes polymorphically

In this case, the client object will simply tell a point, line, or square to do something such as display itself or undisplay itself. Each point, line, and square is then responsible for knowing the way to carry out the behavior that is appropriate to its type.

To accomplish this, I will create a **Shape** class and then derive from it the classes that represent points, lines, and squares (see Figure 7-2).

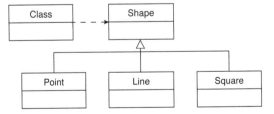

Figure 7-2 Points, Lines, and Squares are types of Shape.

How to do this:
Define the interface
and then implement
in derived classes

First I must specify the particular behavior that **Shape**s are going to provide. To accomplish this, I define an interface in the **Shape** class and then implement the behavior appropriately in each of the derived classes.

The behaviors that a **Shape** needs to have are as follows:

- Set a **Shape**'s location.

- Get a **Shape**'s location.

- Display a **Shape**.

- Fill a **Shape**.

- Set the color of a **Shape**.

- Undisplay a **Shape**.

I show these in Figure 7-3.

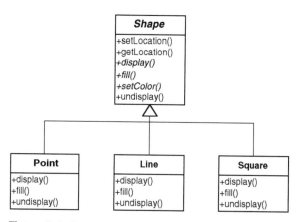

Figure 7-3 Points, Lines, and Squares showing methods.

Now, add a new
shape

Suppose I am now asked to implement a circle, a new kind of **Shape**. (Remember, requirements always change!) To do this, I will want to create a new class—**Circle**—that implements the shape "circle" and derive it from the **Shape** class so that I can still get polymorphic behavior.

Now I am faced with the task of having to code the **display**, *fill* and *undisplay* methods for **Circle**. That could be a pain.

...but use behavior from outside

Fortunately, as I scout around for an alternative (as a good coder always should), I discover that Jill down the hall has already written a class she called **XXCircle** that already handles circles (see Figure 7-4). Unfortunately, she didn't ask me what she should name the methods. She named the methods as follows:

- *displayIt*

- *fillIt*

- *undisplayIt*

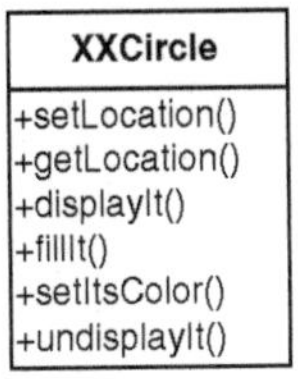

```
         XXCircle
+setLocation()
+getLocation()
+displayIt()
+fillIt()
+setItsColor()
+undisplayIt()
```

Figure 7-4 Jill's XXCircle class.

I cannot use **XXCircle** directly because I want to preserve polymorphic behavior with **Shape**. There are two reasons for this:

I cannot use XXCircle directly

- **I have different names and parameter lists**—The method names and parameter lists are different from **Shape**'s method names and parameter lists.

- **I cannot derive it**—Not only must the names be the same, but the class must be derived from **Shape** as well.

It is unlikely that Jill will be willing to let me change the names of her methods or derive **XXCircle** from **Shape**. To do so would require her to modify all the other objects that are currently using **XXCircle**. Plus, I would still be concerned about creating unanticipated side effects when I modify someone else's code.

I have what I want almost within reach, but I cannot use it and I do not want to rewrite it. What can I do?

Rather than change it, I adapt it.

I can make a new class that *does* derive from **Shape** and therefore implements **Shape**'s interface but avoids rewriting the circle implementation in **XXCircle** (see Figure 7-5):

- Class **Circle** derives from **Shape**.

- **Circle** contains **XXCircle**.

- **Circle** passes requests made to the **Circle** object through to the **XXCircle** object.

How to implement   The diamond at the end of the line between **Circle** and **XXCircle** in Figure 7-5 indicates that **Circle** contains an **XXCircle**. When a **Circle** object is instantiated, it must instantiate a corresponding **XXCircle** object. Anything the **Circle** object is told to do will get passed to the **XXCircle** object. If this is done consistently, and if the **XXCircle** object has the complete functionality the **Circle** object needs (I discuss soon what happens if this is not the case), the **Circle**

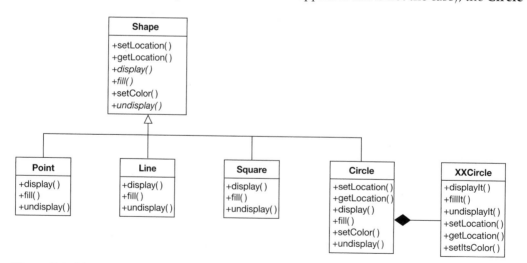

Figure 7-5 The Adapter pattern: Circle "wraps" XXCircle.

object will be able to manifest its behavior by letting the **XXCircle** object do the job.

An example of wrapping is shown in Example 7-1.

Example 7-1 Java Code Fragments: Implementing the Adapter Pattern

```
class Circle extends Shape {
  ...
  private XXCircle myXXCircle;
  ...
  public Circle () {
    myXXCircle= new XXCircle();
  }

  void public display() {
    myXXCircle.displayIt();
  }
  ...
}
```

Using the Adapter pattern enabled me to continue using polymorphism with **Shape**. In other words, the client objects of **Shape** do not know what types of shapes are actually present. This is also an example of our new thinking about encapsulation as well—the class **Shape** encapsulates the specific shapes present. The Adapter pattern is most commonly used to allow for polymorphism. As you shall see in later chapters, it is often used to allow for polymorphism required by other design patterns.

What we accomplished

Field Notes: The Adapter Pattern

Often I am in a situation similar to the one just described, but the object being adapted does not do all the things I need.

You can do more than wrapping

In this case, I can still use the Adapter pattern, but it is not such a perfect fit. In such as case

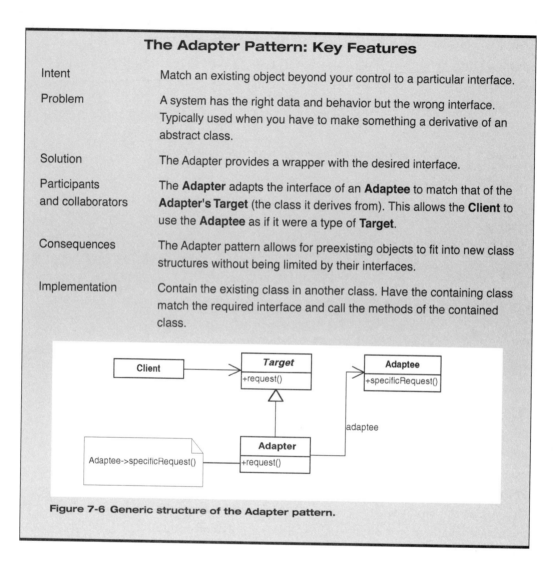

The Adapter Pattern: Key Features

Intent

Match an existing object beyond your control to a particular interface.

Problem

A system has the right data and behavior but the wrong interface. Typically used when you have to make something a derivative of an abstract class.

Solution

The Adapter provides a wrapper with the desired interface.

Participants and collaborators

The **Adapter** adapts the interface of an **Adaptee** to match that of the **Adapter's Target** (the class it derives from). This allows the **Client** to use the **Adaptee** as if it were a type of **Target**.

Consequences

The Adapter pattern allows for preexisting objects to fit into new class structures without being limited by their interfaces.

Implementation

Contain the existing class in another class. Have the containing class match the required interface and call the methods of the contained class.

Figure 7-6 Generic structure of the Adapter pattern.

- Those functions that are implemented in the existing class can be adapted.

- Those functions that are not present can be implemented in the wrapping class.

This does not give me quite the same benefit, but at least I do not have to implement all of the required functionality.

The Adapter pattern frees me from worrying about the interfaces of existing classes when I am doing a design. If I have a class that does what I need, at least conceptually, I know that I can always use the Adapter pattern to give it the correct interface.

Adapter frees you from worrying about existing interfaces

This will become more important as you learn a few more patterns. Many patterns require certain classes to derive from the same class. If there are preexisting classes, the Adapter pattern can be used to adapt it to the appropriate abstract class (as **Circle** adapted **XXCircle** to **Shape**).

There are actually two types of Adapter patterns:

Variations: Object Adapter, Class Adapter

- **Object Adapter pattern**—The Adapter pattern I have been using is called an Object Adapter because it relies on one object (the adapting object) containing another (the adapted object).

- **Class Adapter pattern**—Another way to implement the Adapter pattern is with multiple inheritance. In this case, it is called a Class Adapter pattern.

The Class Adapter works by creating a new class which

- Derives publicly from our abstract class to define its interface.

- Derives privately from our existing class to access its implementation.

Each wrapped method calls its associated, privately inherited method.

The decision of which Adapter pattern to use is based on the different forces at work in the problem domain. At a conceptual level, I may ignore the distinction; however, when it comes time to implement it, I need to consider more of the forces involved.[2]

---

2. For help in deciding between Object Adapter and Class Adapter, see pages 142–144 in the Gang of Four book.

Comparing the Adapter with the Facade

In my classes on design patterns, someone almost always states that it sounds as if both the Adapter pattern and the Facade pattern are the same. In both cases there is a preexisting class (or classes) that does not have the interface that is needed. In both cases, I create a new object that has the desired interface (see Figure 7-7).

Figure 7-7 A Client object using another, preexisting object with the wrong interface.

Both are wrappers

Wrappers and *object wrappers* are terms that you hear a lot about. It is popular to think about wrapping legacy systems with objects to make them easier to use.

At this high view, the Facade and the Adapter patterns do seem similar. They are both wrappers. But they are different kinds of wrappers. You need to understand the differences, which can be subtle. Finding and understanding these more subtle differences gives insight into a pattern's properties. It also helps when discussing and documenting a design so others know precisely what the object(s) are for. Let's look at some different forces involved with these patterns (see Table 7-1).

Table 7-1 Comparing the Facade Pattern with the Adapter Pattern

	Facade	Adapter
Are there preexisting classes?	Yes	Yes
Is there an interface we must design to?	No	Yes
Does an object need to behave polymorphically?	No	Probably
Is a simpler interface needed?	Yes	No

Table 7-1 tells us the following:

- With both the Facade and Adapter pattern, I have preexisting classes.

- With the Facade, however, I do not have an interface I must design to, as I do in the Adapter pattern.

- I am not interested in polymorphic behavior with the Facade; whereas with the Adapter, I probably am. (There are times when we just need to design to a particular interface and therefore must use an Adapter. In this case, polymorphism may not be an issue—that's why I say "probably.")

- In the case of the Facade pattern, the motivation is to simplify the interface. With the Adapter, although simpler is better, I am trying to design to an existing interface and cannot simplify things even if a simpler interface were otherwise possible.

Sometimes people draw the conclusion that another difference between the Facade and the Adapter pattern is that the Facade hides multiple classes behind it whereas the Adapter only hides one. Although this is often true, it is not part of the pattern. It is possible that a Facade could be used in front of a very complex object while an Adapter wrapped several small objects that among them implemented the desired function.

Not all differences are part of the pattern

Bottom line: A Facade *simplifies* an interface while an Adapter *converts* a preexisting interface into another interface.

Relating the Adapter Pattern to the CAD/CAM Problem

In the CAD/CAM problem (Chapter 3, "A Problem That Cries Out for Flexible Code"), the features in the V2 model will be represented by **OOGFeature** objects. Unfortunately, these objects do not have the correct interface (from my perspective) because I did not design them.

Adapter lets me communicate with OOGFeature

I cannot make them derive from the feature classes; yet, when I use the V2 system, they would do our job perfectly.

In this case, the option of writing new classes to implement this function is not even present—I must communicate with the **OOGFeature** objects. The easiest way to do this is with the Adapter pattern.

Summary

In this chapter

The Adapter pattern is a frequently used pattern that converts the interface of a class (or classes) into another interface, which we need the class to have. It is implemented by creating a new class with the desired interface and then wrapping the original class methods to effectively contain the adapted object.

Review Questions

Observations

1. Define *Adapter*.

2. What is the intent of the Adapter pattern?

3. What are the consequences of the Adapter pattern? Give an example.

4. Which object-oriented concept is being used to define the relationship between **Shape** and **Point**, **Line**, and **Square**?

5. What is the most common use for the Adapter pattern?

6. What does the Adapter pattern free you from worrying about?

7. What are the two variations of the Adapter pattern?

Interpretations

1. The Gang of Four says that the intent of the Adapter pattern is to "convert the interface of a class into another interface that the clients expect. Adapter lets classes work together that could not otherwise because of incompatible interfaces."

   • What does this mean?

   • Give an example.

2. "The Circle object wraps the **XXCircle** object." What does this mean?

3. The Facade pattern and the Adapter pattern may seem similar. What is the essential difference between the two?

4. Here is an example of an Adapter that comes from outside of software: A translator at the U.N. lets diplomats from different countries reason about and argue for the positions of their own countries in their own languages. The translator makes "dynamically equivalent" representations from one language to the other so that the concepts are communicated in the way that the recipient expects and needs to hear it.

   • What is another example from real life that illustrates an Adapter?

Opinions and Applications

1. When is it more appropriate to use the Facade pattern rather than the Adapter pattern? How about the Adapter pattern instead of Facade pattern?

2. Why do you think the Gang of Four call this pattern Adapter? Is it an appropriate name for what it is doing? Why or why not?

CHAPTER 8

Expanding Our Horizons

Overview

In previous chapters, I discussed three fundamental concepts of object-oriented design: objects, encapsulation, and abstract classes. How a designer views these concepts is important. Unfortunately, the traditional ways are very limiting.

In this chapter

In this chapter, I step back and reflect on topics discussed earlier in the book and introduce some new ones. My intent is to describe a fresh way of seeing object-oriented design, a perspective that comes from understanding design patterns. Then I describe the essential features of high-quality code. These features are emphasized by proponents of agile coding methods (such as eXtreme programming and test-driven development). Interestingly, these features are also present in design patterns and arise naturally when following the principles and approaches of design patterns. By presenting these qualities in the light of both agile coding methods and design patterns, I hope to bridge the apparent gap between these different approaches to design.

This chapter

- Compares and contrasts the traditional approach of looking at objects—as a bundle of data and methods—with the new approach—as things with responsibilities.

- Compares and contrasts the traditional way of looking at encapsulation—as hiding data—with the new way—as the ability to hide anything. Especially important is to see that encapsulation can be used to contain variation in behavior.

- Compares and contrasts different ways of handling variations in behavior.

- Compares and contrasts the traditional way of using inheritance—for specialization and reuse—with the new way—as a method of classifying objects. The new viewpoints allow for containing variation of behaviors in objects.

- Describes commonality and variability analysis.

- Shows how the conceptual, specification, and implementation perspectives relate to an abstract class and its derived classes.

- Contrasts design patterns with agile coding methods. Although these approaches initially look incompatible, they actually promote several of the same coding qualities, including redundancy, readability and testability.

Acknowledgment   Perhaps this new perspective is not all that original. I believe that this perspective is one that developers of the most common design patterns had when they developed what ended up being called a *pattern*. Certainly, it is a perspective that is consistent with the writings of Christopher Alexander, Jim Coplien (whose work I will be referring to later), and the Gang of Four.[1]

Although it may not be original, it has also not been expressed in quite the way I do in this chapter and in this book. I have had to distill this way of looking at patterns from the way design patterns behave and how they have been described by others.

When I call it a "new" perspective, what I mean is that it is most likely a new way for most developers to view object orientation. It was certainly new to me when I was learning design patterns for the first time.

---

1. Since originally writing this book, I have come to know several people from the Smalltalk community. Virtually all of these people looked at object-oriented design in a way similar to what I describe here.

Objects: The Traditional View and the New View

The traditional view of objects is that they are data with methods. Following this view, one of my teachers called them simply "smart data." They are considered just an intelligent method of handling data: "Start with data that describes the state of the problem domain, add the methods that deal with the data (the required behavior needed), and, *voilà*, you have objects!" But that is too simple, too one-dimensional. It comes from looking at objects only from an implementation perspective.

The traditional view: data with methods

A more useful definition is one based on the conceptual perspective—an object is an *entity that has responsibilities*. These responsibilities define the behavior of the object. Sometimes I also think of an object as an entity that has specific behavior.

The new view: Things with responsibilities

This is a better definition because it helps to focus on what the objects are supposed to *do*, not on how the objects are implemented. This enables me to build software in two steps:

1. Make a preliminary design without worrying about all of the details involved.

2. Implement the design.

A focus on what an object does also helps me not to worry too early about implementation details. It helps me hide those implementation details. And that helps me build software that is easier to modify in the future...if I need to.

The reason this works is that I only have to focus on the object's public interface—the communication window through which I ask the object to do something. With a good interface, I can ask the object to do anything that is within its scope of responsibility and feel confident that it will be able to do it. I do not need to know anything about what is going on *inside* the object. I do not need to know what it is going to do with the information I pass to it. I do not need to know how it will go collect other information it requires. I am free to delegate.

For example, suppose I have a **Shape** object and its responsibilities are as follows:

- To know where it is located

- To be able to draw itself on a display

- To be able to remove itself from a display

These responsibilities imply that a particular set of method calls must exist:

- *getLocation(...)*

- *drawShape(...)*

- *unDrawShape(...)*

This does not say anything about what is inside of **Shape**. I only care that **Shape** is responsible for its own behavior. It may have attributes inside it or it may have methods that calculate or even refer to other objects. Thus, **Shape** might contain attributes about its location or it might refer to another object (for example, from a database) to get its location. This gives you the flexibility you need to meet your modeling objectives (or to modify your code if your objectives change).

Not surprisingly, focusing on motivation rather than on implementation is a recurring theme in design patterns. This is because hiding implementations behind interfaces essentially decouples them from the using objects.

Look at objects this way. Make it your basic viewpoint for objects. If you do, you will have superior designs.

Encapsulation: The Traditional View and the New View

In my classes on pattern-oriented design, I often ask my students, "Who has heard encapsulation defined as 'data hiding'?" Almost everyone raises his or her hand.

My object-oriented umbrella

Then I proceed to tell a story about my umbrella. Keep in mind that I live in Seattle, which, although it has a reputation for being wetter than it is, is still a pretty wet place in the fall, winter, and spring. Here, umbrellas and hooded coats are personal friends!

Let me tell you about my great umbrella. It is large enough to get into! In fact, three or four other people can get in it with me. While we are in it, staying out of the rain, I can move it from one place to another. It has a stereo system to keep me entertained while I stay dry. Amazingly enough, it can also condition the air to make it warmer or cooler. It is one cool umbrella!

My umbrella is convenient. It sits there waiting for me. It has wheels on it so that I do not have to carry it around. I don't even have to push it because it can propel itself. Sometimes I open the top of my umbrella to let in the sun. (Why I am using my umbrella when it is sunny outside is beyond me!)

In Seattle, there are hundreds of thousands of these umbrellas and they come in all kinds of colors.

Most people call them *cars*.

But I think of mine as an umbrella because an umbrella is something I use to keep out of the rain. Many times, while I am waiting outside for someone to meet me, I sit in my "umbrella" to stay dry!

Of course, a car isn't really an umbrella. Yes, you can use it to stay out of the rain, but that is too limited a view of a car. In the same way,

Definitions can be limitations

encapsulation isn't just for hiding data. That is too limited a view of encapsulation. To think of it that way constrains my mind when I design.

How to think about
encapsulation

Encapsulation should be thought of as "any kind of hiding." In other words, it *can* hide data. But it can also hide the following:

- Implementations

- Derived classes

- Design details

- Instantiation rules

In my earlier discussion about hiding an implementation, I was essentially "encapsulating" the implementation. To take this further, consider the diagram shown in Figure 8-1, originally shown in Chapter 7, "The Adapter Pattern." Here we have **Point**s, **Line**s, **Square**s, and **Circle**s being types of **Shape**s. Furthermore, **Circle** "wraps" or contains an **XXCircle**.

Figure 8-1 shows many kinds of encapsulation:

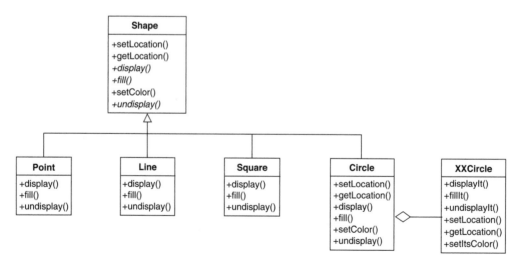

Figure 8-1 Adapting XXCircle with Circle.

- **Encapsulation of data**—The data in **Point**, **Line**, **Square**, and **Circle** are hidden from everything else.

Multiple levels of encapsulation

- **Encapsulation of methods**—For example, **Circle**'s *setLocation*.

- **Encapsulation of other objects**—Nothing but **Circle** is aware of **XXCircle**.

- **Encapsulation of type**—Clients of **Shape** do not see **Point**s, **Line**s, **Square**s, or **Circle**s.

Encapsulation of type is thus achieved when there is an abstract class with derivations (or an interface with implementations) that are used polymorphically. The client that uses this abstract class doesn't know what kind of derived class actually is present. This is the type of encapsulation that the Gang of Four typically means when they mention encapsulation.

The advantage of looking at encapsulation in this broader way is that it gives me a better way to split up (decompose) my programs. The encapsulating layers become the interfaces I design to. By encapsulating different kinds of **Shape**s, I can add new ones without changing any of the client programs using them. By encapsulating **XXCircle** behind **Circle**, I can change this implementation in the future if I choose to or need to.

The advantage of this new definition

Early promoters of the object-oriented paradigm touted reuse of classes as being one of its big benefits. This reuse was usually achieved by creating classes and then deriving new classes based on these base classes. Hence the term *specialized classes* for those subclasses that were derived from other classes (which were called *generalized classes*).

Inheritance as a concept versus inheritance for reuse

I am not arguing with this definition; rather, I am proposing what I believe to be a more powerful way of using inheritance. For example, suppose I want to work with a pentagon shape. I define a class **Pentagon**, which will contain state, draw, undraw, and so on. Later

I find the need to have a pentagon with a special border. I can take my initial **Pentagon** class and derive a new, "specialized" **Pentagon** class with a different way of drawing a border (see Figure 8-2).

This is an example of using inheritance for specialization. I have reused

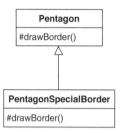

Figure 8-2 PentagonSpecialBorder derives from Pentagon

Pentagon to get me **PentagonSpecialBorder**. This approach works quite well, except for three problems, as described in Table 8-1.

Table 8-1 Problems of Using Inheritance for Specialization

Problem with the Approach	Description
Can cause weak cohesion	Consider what happens when we get lots and lots of different types of borders. **Pentagon** (and its derivations) aren't just concerned about pentagons anymore, they are also concerned about all the different borders—making these classes have to handle more issues. I also may get other things about **Pentagon**s that vary (e.g., the pattern inside them).
Reduces possibility of reuse	As I write code for different borders and include it in the **Pentagon** family, how can I reuse this code for other shapes? This may be very difficult because the context changes every time as well as because the code that handles this function is in **Pentagon** and not likely very accessible elsewhere.
Does not scale well with variation	The technique of specialization for reuse works great in the classroom because you can show it and move on before anyone asks "what happens if something else starts to vary?" For example, what if I get two different kinds of shading? To handle all of these options, I would need to specialize (and therefore partially duplicate) the **Pentagon** class repeatedly.

Another way to use inheritance is to classify classes as things that behave the same way. I discuss this further very soon.

Find What Is Varying and Encapsulate It

In *Design Patterns: Elements of Reusable Object-Oriented Software*, the Gang of Four suggests the following:

Design patterns use inheritance to classify variations in behaviors

> Consider what should be variable in your design. *This approach is the opposite of focusing on the cause of redesign. Instead of considering what might* force *a change to a design, consider what you want to be* able *to change without redesign. The focus here is* on encapsulating the concept that varies, *a theme of many design patterns.*[2]

Or, as I like to rephrase it, "Find what varies and encapsulate it."

These statements may seem odd if you only think about encapsulation as data hiding. They are much more sensible when you think of encapsulation as hiding classes with an abstract class or interface—"type encapsulation."[3] Containing a reference of this abstract class or interface type (aggregation) hides these derived classes that represent variations in behavior. In other words, the using class has a reference to an abstract class or interface that has more than one specialized derivation. These derivations are hidden (encapsulated) from the using class.

In effect, many design patterns use encapsulation to create layers between objects. This enables the designer to change things on different sides of the layer without adversely affecting the other side. This promotes loose coupling between the sides.

---

2. Gamma, E., Helm, R., Johnson, R., Vlissides, J., *Design Patterns: Elements of Reusable Object-Oriented Software*, Boston: Addison-Wesley, 1995, p. 29.

3. Generally speaking, type encapsulation is what the Gang of Four means most often when they just say "encapsulation."

Containing variation in data versus containing variation in behavior

This way of thinking is very important in the Bridge pattern, which is discussed in Chapter 10, "The Bridge Pattern." However, before proceeding, I want to show a bias in design that many developers have.

Suppose I am working on a project that models different characteristics of animals. My requirements are the following:

- Each type of animal can have a different number of legs.

- Animal objects must be able to remember and retrieve this information.

- Each type of animal can have a different type of movement.

- Animal objects must be able to return how long it will take to move from one place to another given a specified type of terrain.

A typical approach to handling the variation in the number of legs would be to have a data member containing this value and having methods to set and get it. However, one typically takes a different approach to handling variation in behavior.

Suppose there are two different methods for moving: walking and flying. These requirements need two different pieces of code: one to handle walking, and one to handle flying; a simple variable won't work for the entire solution (although it can be used to say which type of movement is present). Given that I have two different methods, I seem to be faced with a choice of approach:

- Have a data member that tells me what type of movement my object has.

- Have two different types of **Animal**s (both derived from the base **Animal** class)—one for walking and one for flying.

Unfortunately, both of these approaches fail as the problem becomes more complex. Although either one works fine when this is the only variation present (mode of travel), what happens when many variations are present? For example, what if we have eagles (carnivores that fly) and lions (carnivores that walk) and sparrows (vegetarians that fly) and cows (vegetarians that walk)? Using a switch on the type of animal couples movement with eating habits—something that doesn't really appear related. Using inheritance for each special case results in a plethora of classes. Also what happens if animals sometimes exhibit one type of behavior and a different behavior at other times (most birds can walk and fly)?

A further problem can occur. As a class handles more and more different variations (say with switches), the code can become weakly cohesive. That is, it handles more and more special cases and becomes less and less understandable.

Another possibility exists: Have the **Animal** class contain an object that has the appropriate movement behavior. I show this in Figure 8-3.

Handling variation in behavior with objects

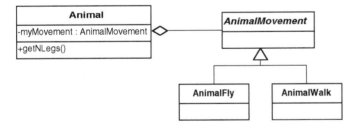

Figure 8-3 Animal containing AnimalMovement object.

This may seem like overkill at first. However, it's nothing more than an **Animal** containing a data member that is an object that contains the movement behavior of the **Animal**. This is very analogous to having a data member containing the number of legs—in which case an intrinsic type object is containing the number of legs (except the member, in this case, has a variation in behavior instead of a number). I suspect these appear more different in concept than they really are, because Figures 8-3 and 8-4 appear to be so different.

This is not overkill

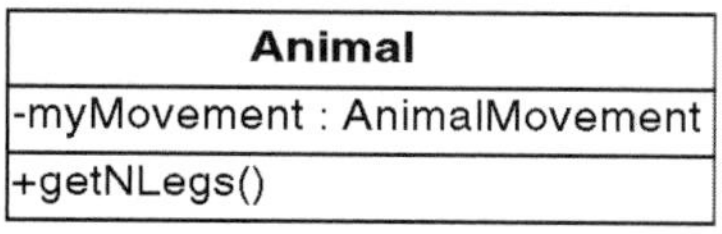

Animal
-myMovement : AnimalMovement
+getNLegs()

Figure 8-4 Showing containment as a member.

Comparing the two

Many developers tend to think that one object containing another object is inherently different from an object having a mere data member. But data members that appear not to be objects (integers and doubles, for example) really are. In true object-oriented languages, *everything* is an object, even intrinsic data types whose behavior is arithmetic. The special syntax of these objects (for instance, x+y is the same as x.addTo(y)) hides the fact that they are really objects with behavior.

Using objects to contain variation in attributes and using objects to contain variation in behavior are very similar; this can be most easily shown through an example. Suppose I am writing a point-of-sale system. In this system, there is a sales receipt. On this sales receipt, there is a total. I could start out by making this total be a type **double**. However, if I am dealing with an international application, I quickly realize I need to handle monetary conversions, and so forth. I might therefore make a **Money** class that contains an amount and a currency. Total can now be of type **Money**.

Using the **Money** class this way appears to be using an object just to contain more data. However, when I need to convert **Money** from one currency to the next, it is the **Money** object itself that should do the conversion, because objects should be responsible for themselves. At first it may appear that this conversion can be done by simply having another data member that specifies what the conversion factor is.

However, it may be more complicated than this. For example, perhaps I need to be able to convert currency based on past dates. I can make my currency attribute become a **Currency** class. Adding behaviors to the **Money** or **Currency** classes adds behaviors to the

SalesReceipt as well, based upon which **Money** objects (and therefore which **Currency** objects) it contains. However, doing it this way does not complicate the **SalesReceipt** class nor does it require any changes to the **SalesReceipt** class.

I demonstrate this strategy of using contained objects to perform required behavior in the next few design patterns.

Commonality and Variability Analysis and Abstract Classes

Coplien's work on commonality and variability analysis tells us how to find variations in the problem domain and identify what is common across the domain: Identify *where* things vary ("commonality analysis") and then identify *how* they vary ("variability analysis").

Commonality and variability analysis

According to Coplien, "Commonality analysis is the search for common elements that helps us understand how family members are the same."[4] By "family members," Coplien means elements related to each other by the situation in which they appear or the function they perform. The process of finding out how things are common defines the family in which these elements belong (and hence, where things vary). For example, if I show you a whiteboard marker, a pencil, and a ballpoint pen, you might say that what they all have in common is they are "writing instruments." The process you performed to identify them all in a common manner is commonality analysis. Given this commonality (writing instrument), you can now more easily discuss how they are different writing instruments (material to write on varies, shape varies, and so forth).

Commonality analysis

Variability analysis reveals how family members vary. Variability only makes sense within a given commonality:

Variability analysis

---

4. Coplien, J., *Multi-Paradigm Design for C++*, Boston: Addison-Wesley, 1998, p. 63.

> *Commonality analysis seeks structure that is unlikely to change over time, while variability analysis captures structure that is likely to change. Variability analysis makes sense only in terms of the context defined by the associated commonality analysis ... From an architectural perspective, commonality analysis gives the architecture its longevity; variability analysis drives its fitness for use.*[5]

In other words, if variations are the specific concrete cases in the domain, commonality defines the concepts in the domain that tie them together. The common concepts will be represented by abstract classes. The variations found by variability analysis will be implemented by the concrete classes (that is, classes derived from the abstract class with specific implementations).

A new paradigm for finding objects

Often the new object-oriented designer is told to begin by looking in the problem domain: "Identify the nouns present, and create objects representing them. Then, find the verbs relating to those nouns (that is, their actions) and implement them by adding methods to the objects." This process of focusing on nouns and verbs typically leads to larger class hierarchies than we might want. I suggest that using commonality and variability analysis as a primary tool in creating objects is a better approach than looking at just nouns and verbs. (This is consistent with, but not the full extent of Coplien's approach.)

Object-oriented design captures all three perspectives

Consider Figure 8-5. It shows the relationship among

- Commonality and variability analysis.

- The conceptual, specification, and implementation perspectives.

- An abstract class, its interface, and its derived classes.

As you can see in Figure 8-5, commonality analysis relates to the conceptual view of the problem domain, and variability analysis relates to the implementation (that is, to specific cases).

5. Ibid, pp. 60, 64.

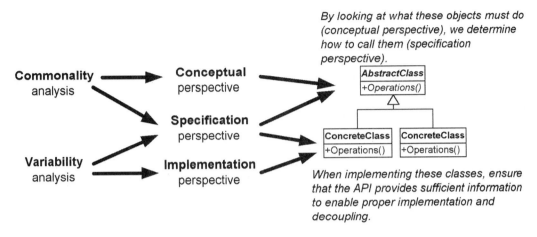

Figure 8-5 The relationship between commonality and variability analysis, perspectives, and abstract classes.

The specification perspective lies in the middle. Both commonality and variability are involved in this perspective. The specification describes how to communicate with a set of objects that are conceptually similar. Each of these objects represents a variation of the common concept. This specification becomes an abstract class or an interface at the implementation level.

Now, specification gives a better understanding of abstract classes

In my new way of looking at object-oriented design, I can now say with confidence the statements listed in Table 8-2.

Table 8-2 Benefits of Using Abstract Classes for Specialization

Mapping with Abstract Classes	Description
Abstract class vs. the central binding concept	An abstract class represents the core concept that binds together all the derivatives of the class. This core concept is what defines the commonality.
Commonality vs. which abstract classes to use	The commonalities define the abstract classes I need to use.
Variations vs. derivation of an abstract class	The variations identified within that commonality become derivations of the abstract classes.
Specification vs. interface for abstract class	The interface for these classes corresponds to the specification level.

This simplifies the design process of the classes into a two-step procedure, as listed in Table 8-3.

Table 8-3 A Two-Step Procedure for Design

When Defining	You Must Ask Yourself...
An abstract class (commonality)	What interface is needed to handle all the responsibilities of this class?
Derived classes	Given this particular implementation (this variation), how can I implement it with the given specification?

The relationship between the specification perspective and the conceptual perspective is this: *The specification identifies the interface I need to use to handle all the cases of this concept (that is, the commonality defined by the conceptual perspective).*

The relationship between the specification perspective and the implementation perspective is this: *Given this specification, how can I implement this particular case (this variation)?*

The Qualities of Agile Coding

Upfront design versus "design as you go"

The design pattern approach has often been described as "design up front." It advocates starting with the big concepts in the problem domain and working in, accounting for more details as you go.

There is an alternative approach, advocated in eXtreme programming (XP), which seems to contradict design patterns. XP focuses on doing things in small steps, validating them as you move forward. The big picture evolves from the small items.

Rather than being in opposition, I consider XP and design patterns to be quite complementary. They both can be used to achieve the same point:

effective, robust, flexible code. How is this possible? I believe it is because the principles upon which both approaches rely are related.

As a reasonably early adopter of agile coding practices, I found myself in a dilemma:

Lessons learned from agile coding

- I have had great success with upfront designs.
- Agile had me do significantly less of this (sometimes virtually none).
- I was even more successful.

My dilemma was that I was clear that design patterns had contributed to my success and I was not willing to abandon them. However, agile methods—the methods I hoped to follow—seemed not to prescribe that upfront design. Yet, intuitively, I felt there must be some common ground: Agile requires code that is changeable, and patterns result in code that is flexible. Maybe it was more a difference of approach rather than a difference of values.

Ultimately I resolved this dilemma when I realized that both approaches required the same qualities in the code; they just got there in different ways. The different code qualities are actually very much interrelated. For example, when a method is encapsulated, it is essentially decoupled as well. Agile practices focused on different qualities than the ones I've already mentioned. However, these qualities are highly correlated with mine. These additional qualities are (1) no redundancy, (2) readability, and (3) testability (not in order of importance).

A very important implementation strategy to follow is to have only one place where a rule is implemented. "One rule, one place" has been a mantra for object-oriented designers for a long time. It represents a best practice of designers. Most recently, Kent Beck called this the "Once and Only Once rule."[6]

No redundancy

---

6. Beck, K., *Extreme Programming Explained: Embrace Change*, Boston: Addison-Wesley, 2000, pp. 108–109.

He defines it as part of his constraints:

1. The system (code and tests together) must communicate everything you want to communicate.

2. The system must contain no duplicate code. (1 and 2 together constitute the Once and Only Once rule.)

In other words, if there is a rule on how to do things, only implement that once. This typically requires using several small methods. The extra cost is minimal, but it eliminates duplication and often saves many future problems. Duplication is bad not only because of the extra work in typing things in multiple times, but because of the likelihood of something changing in the future and then you perhaps forgetting to change it in all the required places.

I am not a purist, but if there is one place where I think it is important to always follow a rule, it is here. A powerful relationship exists between redundancy and coupling. If redundant code is present and it becomes necessary to change one of the sections of code, it is very likely the other section will need to be changed as well. Hence, these two sections of redundant code are also coupled to each other.

Interestingly enough, following the practices of designing to interfaces and pulling out what is varying and making things be strongly cohesive is pretty much what you need to do to eliminate redundant code. This is because instead of having the code in two places, you have it in one. To avoid coupling, the code needs to be encapsulated behind a well-defined interface.

Readability   Readability is another essential quality of good code that is advocated in agile methods. Readability is related to strong cohesion. However, Ron Jeffries (XP advocate) takes this to a new level with the mandate to "program by intention,"[7] Simply put, this mandate

---

7. Jeffries, R., Anderson, A., Hendrickson, C., *Extreme Programming Installed*, Boston: Addison-Wesley, 2001, pp. 73–74.

says that when you are writing code and you need to implement some piece of function, just pretend it already exists, give it an "intention-revealing name,"[8] write the method call to it, and move on (implementing this function later). In other words, coding becomes a series of calls to functions that are named in a way that clearly describes their use.

This results in very readable code because at the larger module level, the reader is seeing the intent of the code, not each little implementation. Martin Fowler further encourages this with this statement: "Whenever we feel the need to comment something, we write a method instead."[9] This results in shorter, more concise (and cohesive) methods.

Programming by intention is very similar to the design pattern mandate: Design to an interface. When you are creating the "intention-revealing name," you are creating the interface without worrying about the implementation. Again, it seems that agile coding techniques and design patterns have significant synergy in how to achieve code quality.

Testable code is an essential quality of good code. And testability lies at the core of agile methods. Before discussing this, I want to be clear about the difference between "testability" and the XP practice of writing unit tests before writing code.[10]   *Testability*

One of the more distinctive practices of XP is that you write your tests before you write your code. This serves several purposes:

- You end up with a suite of automated tests.

---

8. An "intention-revealing name" is a label or name that clearly and succinctly communicates what the function is responsible for doing.

9. Fowler, M., *Refactoring: Improving the Design of Existing Code*, Boston: Addison-Wesley Longman, 1999, p. 77.

10. Because this is a book on design patterns, I do not go into the excellent practices of upfront testing and test-driven design.

- You are forced to design to the method's interface and not its implementation, resulting in a more encapsulated, loosely coupled method.

- Focusing on tests has you focus on separating the functionality into testable pieces, which results in strong cohesion and loose coupling.

I call code that is easy to test *testable*. Testable code is code that can be tested in isolation and without having to worry about how it is coupled to other modules or entities. The XP practice of writing tests up front inherently results in highly testable code.

Testability is strongly correlated to the other practices:

- **Cohesive** code is easier to test because the code is only about one thing.

- **Loosely coupled** code is easier to test than tightly coupled code because there are minimal interactions to worry about.

- **Redundant code** is not harder to test in itself, but requires more tests to cover the redundancy. Therefore, the testability of the entire system degrades when you have more redundancy.

- **Readable** code is easier to test because method names and parameters describe precisely what each is supposed to do.

- **Encapsulated** code is easier to test because it will have little, if any, coupling to other code.

Let me give an example to illustrate this. I had a client once that I had discussed testing issues with before I was to do our Effective Object-Oriented Analysis and Design class. I was told, "Don't talk too much about unit testing—we've had bad experiences with that." I asked what happened. I was told that when they had tried to unit test their code on an earlier project, it was very difficult. To write tests, they had to build a framework because they couldn't instantiate the objects they were trying to test easily. These objects were intertwined with other objects.

I responded by asking them whether they had considered how they would test these functions prior to writing the code. My contact said they hadn't. I then asked him whether they would have designed their code any differently if they *had* considered how they would test it later. He paused and realized that if they had just considered how they would have tested their code later, it would have improved their designs.

Many developers take this notion even further and drive their development completely through testing. This approach is called *test-driven development* (TDD) and is beyond the scope of this book.[11] I have done a fair amount of TDD personally and believe it to be a great approach. Like other agile methods, TDD initially looks incompatible with a patterns approach. It is not. It is based on the same principles as patterns, but just approaches the task of writing code differently.

Summary

The traditional way of thinking about objects, encapsulation, and inheritance is very limiting. Encapsulation exists for so much more than simply hiding data. By expanding the definition to include any kind of hiding, I can use encapsulation to create layers between objects—enabling me to change things on one side of a layer without adversely affecting the other side.

In this chapter

Inheritance is better used as a method of consistently dealing with different concrete classes that are conceptually the same rather than as a means of specialization.

---

11. For more information on test-driven development, see this book's companion Web site at http://www.netobjectives.com/dpexplained.

The concept of using objects to hold variations in behavior is not unlike the practice of using data members to hold variations in data. Both allow for the encapsulation (and therefore extension) of the data/behavior being contained.

Commonality and variability analysis can be used to identify objects in our problem domain more effectively than looking for nouns and their corresponding actions.

The code qualities that result from the practices espoused by agile methods, particularly XP, are highly correlated with the long-recognized coding qualities of strong cohesion, loose coupling, and encapsulation.

Review Questions

Observations

1. What is the right way to think about encapsulation?

2. What are the three perspectives for looking at a problem? (You may need to review Chapter 1, "The Object-Oriented Paradigm.")

Interpretations

1. There are two different ways to understand objects: "data with methods" and "things with responsibilities."

   • In what ways is the second approach superior to the first?

   • What additional insights does it provide?

2. Can an object contain another object? Is this different from one object containing a data member?

3. What is meant by the phrase *find what varies and encapsulate it*? Give an example.

4. Explain the relationship between commonality/variability analysis and the three perspectives of looking at a problem.

5. An abstract class maps to the "central binding concept." What does this mean?

6. "Variability analysis reveals how family members vary. Variability only makes sense within a given commonality."

    • What does this mean?

    • What types of objects are used to represent the common concepts?

    • What types of objects are used to represent the variations?

Opinions and Applications

1. Why is it better to start out focusing on motivations rather than on implementation? Give an example where this has helped you.

2. Preconceived notions limit one's ability to understand concepts. This was shown to be the case with encapsulation. Can you think of a situation in which your preconceived notions got in the way of understanding requirements? What happened and how did you overcome it?

3. The term *inheritance* is used both when a class derives from an nonabstract class to make a specialized version of it and when an abstract class is used as a starting point for different implementations. Would it be better if we had two different terms for these concepts instead of using the same term?

4. How might you use commonality/variability analysis to help you think about ways to modify a system?

5. It is important to explore for variations early and often. Do you believe this? Why or why not? How does it help to avoid pitfalls?

6. Commonality/variability analysis is an important primary tool for identifying objects, better than "looking for the nouns." Do you agree? Why or why not?

7. This chapter tried to present a new perspective on objects. Did it succeed? Why or why not?

CHAPTER 9

The Strategy Pattern

Overview

This chapter introduces a new case study, which comes from the area of *e-commerce* (electronic commerce over the Internet). It also begins a solution using the Strategy pattern. I return to this case study in Chapter 16, "The Analysis Matrix."

In this chapter

This chapter

- Returns to the problem of new requirements and describes approaches to handling new variations of an existing theme.

- Explains which approach is consistent with the Gang of Four's philosophy and why.

- Introduces the new case study.

- Describes the Strategy pattern and shows how it handles a new requirement in the case study.

- Describes the key features of the Strategy pattern.

An Approach to Handling New Requirements

Many times in life and many times in software applications, you have to make choices about the general approach to performing a task or solving a problem. Most of us have learned that taking the easiest route in the short run can lead to serious complications in the long run. For example, none of us would ignore oil changes for our car beyond a certain point. True, I may not change the oil every

Disaster often comes in the long run from suboptimal decisions in the short run

3,000 miles, but I also do not wait until 30,000 miles before changing the oil. (If I did so, there would be no need to change the oil any more: The car would not work!) Or consider the "desktop filing system"—the technique of using the top of the desk as a filing cabinet. It works well in the short run, but in the long run, as the piles grow, it becomes tough to find *anything*. Disaster often comes in the long run from suboptimal decisions made in the short run.

This is true in software as well: We focus on immediate concerns and ignore the longer term

Unfortunately, when it comes to software development, many people have not learned these lessons yet. Many projects are only concerned with handling immediate, pressing needs, without concern for future maintenance. There are several reasons projects tend to ignore long-term issues such as ease of maintenance or ability to change. Common excuses include the following:

- We really can't figure out how the new requirements are going to change.

- If we try to see how things will change, we'll stay in analysis forever.

- If we try to write our software so we can add new functionality to it, we'll stay in design forever.

- We don't have the budget to do so.

- The customer is breathing down my neck to get this implemented right now. I don't have time to think.

- I'll get to it later.

There seem to be only two choices:

- Overanalyze or overdesign—I like to call this "paralysis by analysis," or

- Just jump in, write the code without concern for long-term issues, and then get on another project before this short-sightedness causes too many problems. I like to call this "abandon (by) ship (date)!"

Because management is under pressure to deliver and not to maintain, maybe these results are not surprising. But take a (*quick!*) moment to reflect. Could there be a third way? Could it be that my basic assumptions and belief systems keep me from being seeing alternatives? In this case, the belief is that it is more costly to design for change than to design without worrying about change.

But this belief is often false. In fact, the opposite is often true: Stepping back to consider how a system might change over time often results in a better design becoming apparent. And this often takes less time than the standard, "hurry-up-and-get-it-done-now" approach. Better quality code is easier to read, test, and modify. These factors compensate for any additional time it might take to do it right.

The following case study is a great illustration of the "design-with-change-in-mind" approach. Note that I am not trying to anticipate the exact nature of the change. Instead, I am assuming that change will happen and I am trying to anticipate *where* those changes will occur. This approach is based on the principles described in the Gang of Four book:

Designing for change

- "Program to an interface, not an implementation."[1]

- "Favor object [aggregation] over class inheritance."[2]

- "Consider what should be variable in your design. This approach is the opposite of focusing on the cause of redesign. Instead of considering what might *force* a change to a design, consider what you want to be *able* to change without redesign. The focus here is *on encapsulating the concept that varies*, a theme of many design patterns."[3]

---

1. Gamma, E., Helm, R., Johnson, R., Vlissides, J., *Design Patterns: Elements of Reusable Object-Oriented Software*, Boston.: Addison-Wesley, 1995, p. 18.

2. Ibid, p. 20. Note: "composition" (the word used by the Gang of Four) in OMT (the modeling language they used) is called "aggregation" in the UML (the common modeling language of today).

3. Ibid, p. 29.

Here is what I suggest: When faced with modifying code to handle a new requirement, you should at least consider following these strategies. If following these strategies will not cost significantly more to design and implement, then use them. You can expect a long-term benefit from doing so, with only a modest short-term cost (if any).

I am not proposing to follow these strategies blindly, however. I can test the value of an alternative design by examining how well it conforms to the good principles of object-oriented design. This is essentially the same approach I use in deriving the Bridge pattern in Chapter 10, "The Bridge Pattern." In that chapter, I measure the quality of alternative designs by seeing which one followed object-oriented principles the best.

The International E-Commerce System Case Study: Initial Requirements

e-commerce: A case study about requirements

In this new case study, I consider an order-processing system for an international e-commerce company in the United States. This system must be able to process sales orders in many different countries. In this chapter, I want to consider the challenges of changing requirements and ways to address them. In Chapter 16, I continue the case study, focusing on the problem of variations.

The general architecture of this system has a controller object that handles sales requests. It identifies when a sales order is being requested and hands the request off to a **SalesOrder** object to process the order.

The system looks something like Figure 9-1.

Some features of the system

The functions of **SalesOrder** include the following:

- Allow for filling out the order with a GUI

- Handle tax calculations

- Process the order, and print a sales receipt

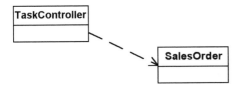

Figure 9-1 Sales order architecture for an e-commerce system.

Some of these functions are likely to be implemented with the help of other objects. For example, **SalesOrder** would not necessarily print itself; instead, it serves as a holder for information about sales orders. A particular **SalesOrder** object could call a **SalesTicket** object that prints the **SalesOrder**.

Handling New Requirements

After writing this application, suppose I receive a new requirement to change the way I have to handle taxes. For example, now I have to be able to handle taxes on orders from customers outside the United States. At a minimum, I will need to add new rules for computing these taxes.

New requirement for taxation rules

What approaches are available? How can I handle these new rules?

Before looking at this specific situation, allow me to take a slight detour. In general, what are ways for handling different implementations of tasks that are pretty much conceptually the same (such as handling different tax rules)? The following alternatives jump quickly to my mind:

- Copy and paste

- Switches or ifs on a variable specifying the case we have

- Use function pointers or delegates (a different one representing each case)

- Inheritance (make a derived class that does it the new way)

- Delegate the entire functionality to a new object

Copy and paste   The old standby. I have something that works and need something
close. So, just copy and paste and then make the changes. Of course,
this leads to maintenance headaches because now there are two versions of the same code that I — or somebody else — has to maintain.
I am ignoring the possibility of how to reuse objects. Certainly the
company as a whole ends up with higher maintenance costs.

Switches, etc.   A reasonable approach. But one with serious problems for applications that need to grow over time. Consider the how coupling and
testability are affected when one variable is used in several switches. For example, suppose I use the local variable **myNation** to identify the country that the customer is in. If the choices are just the
United States and Canada, then using a switch probably works well.
For example, I might have the following switches:

```
// Handle Tax switch (myNation) {          // Handle Currency switch (myNation) {
   case US:                                   case US:
   // US Tax rules here break;                // US Currency rules here break;
   case Canada:                               case Canada:
   // Canadian Tax rules here break;          // Canadian Currency rules here break;
}                                          }
```

```
// Handle Date Format switch (myNation){
   case US:
   // use mm/dd/yy format break;
   case Canada:
   // use dd/mm/yy format break;
}
```

But what happens when there are more variations? For example,
suppose I need to add Germany to the list of countries and also add
language as a result. Now the code looks like this:

```
// Handle Tax switch (myNation) {
    case US:
        // US Tax rules here break;
    case Canada:
        // Canadian Tax rules here break;
    case Germany:
        // Germany Tax rules here break;
}
```

```
// Handle Currency switch (myNation) {
    case US:
        // US Currency rules here break;
    case Canada:
        // Canadian Currency rules here break;
    case Germany:
        // Euro Currency rules here break;
}
```

```
// Handle Date Format switch (myNation) {
    case US:
        // use mm/dd/yy format break;
    case Canada:
    case Germany:
        // use dd/mm/yy format break;
}
```

```
// Handle Language switch (myNation) {
    case US:
    case Canada:
        // use English break;
    case Germany:
        // use German break;
}
```

This still is not too bad, but notice how the switches are not quite as nice as they used to be. There are now fall-throughs. But eventually I may need to start adding variations *within* a case. Suddenly, things get bad in a hurry. For example, to add French in Quebec, my code looks like this:

```
// Handle Language switch (myNation) {
    case Canada:
        if ( inQuebec) {
            // use French break;
        }
    case US:
        // use English break;
    case Germany:
        // use German break;
}
```

The flow of the switches themselves becomes confusing. Hard to read. Hard to decipher. When a new case comes in, the programmer must find every place it can be involved (often finding all but one of them). I like to call this "switch creep."

Function pointers and delegates

Function pointers in C++ and delegates in C# can be used to hide code in a nice, compact, cohesive function. However, function pointers/delegates cannot retain state on a per-object basis and therefore have limited use.

Inheritance

The new standby. More often than not, inheritance is used incorrectly and that gives it a bad reputation. There is nothing inherently wrong with inheritance (sorry for the pun). When used incorrectly, however, inheritance leads to brittle, rigid designs. The root cause of this misuse may lie with those who teach object-oriented principles.

When object-oriented design became mainstream, "reuse" was touted as being one of its primary advantages. To achieve "reuse," it was taught that you just take something you already have and make slight modifications of it in the form of a derived class.[4]

In our tax example, I could attempt to reuse the existing **SalesOrder** object. I could treat new tax rules like a new kind of sales order, only with a different set of taxation rules. For example, for Canadian sales, I could derive a new class called **CanadianSalesOrder** from **SalesOrder** that would override the tax rules. I show this solution in Figure 9-2.

...but this will cause problems

The difficulty with this approach is that it works once but not necessarily twice. For example, when we have to handle Germany or get other things that are varying (for example, date format, language, freight rules), the inheritance hierarchy we are building will not easily handle the variations we have. Repeated specialization such as this will cause either the code not to be understandable or result in

---

4. My belief is that reuse is not a reason to use object-oriented methods. Lowering maintenance costs and making code more flexible (easier to extend) are more important considerations. Reuse is possible using proper object-oriented techniques, but it is not achieved by directly using objects and reusing them just by deriving new variations. This results in hard-to-maintain code.

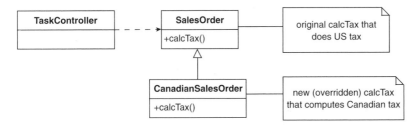

Figure 9-2 Sales order architecture for an e-commerce system.

redundancy. This is a consistent complaint with object-oriented designs: Tall inheritance hierarchies eventually result from specialization techniques. Unfortunately, these are hard to understand (have weak cohesion), have redundancy, are hard to test, and have concepts coupled together. No wonder many people say object-orientation is overrated—especially since it all comes from following the common object-orientation mandate of "reuse."

How could I approach this differently? Following the rules I stated earlier, attempt to "consider what should be variable in your design," "encapsulate the concept that varies," and (most importantly) "favor object-aggregation over class inheritance."[5]

Design patterns take a different approach

Following this approach, I should do the following:

1. Find what varies and encapsulate it in a class of its own.

2. Contain this class in another class.

In this example, I have already identified that the tax rules are varying. To encapsulate them would mean creating an abstract class that defines how to accomplish taxation conceptually, and then deriving

5. Gamma, E., Helm, R., Johnson, R., Vlissides, J., Design Patterns: Elements of Reusable Object-Oriented Software, Boston: Addison-Wesley, 1995, pp. 20 and 29.

*Step 1: Find what
varies and
encapsulate it*

concrete classes for each of the variations. In other words, I could create a **CalcTax** object that defines the interface to accomplish this task. I could then derive the specific versions needed. Figure 9-3 shows this.

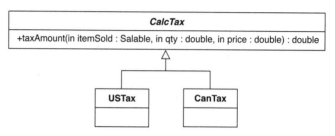

Figure 9-3 Encapsulating tax rules.

*Step 2: Favor
aggregation*

Continuing on, I now use aggregation instead of inheritance. This means, instead of making different versions of sales orders (using inheritance), I will contain the variation with aggregation. That is, I will have one **SalesOrder** class and have it contain the **CalcTax** class to handle the variations. Figure 9-4 shows this.

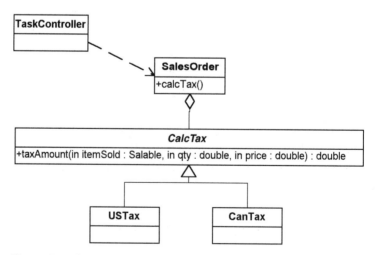

Figure 9-4 Favoring aggregation over inheritance.

Example 9-1 Java Code Fragments: Implementing the Strategy Pattern

---

```java
public class TaskController {
   public void process () {
       // this code is an emulation of a
       // processing task controller
       // . . .
       // figure out which country you are in
       CalcTax myTax;
       myTax= getTaxRulesForCountry();
       SalesOrder mySO= new SalesOrder();
       mySO.process( myTax);
   }
   private CalcTax getTaxRulesForCountry() {
       // In real life, get the tax rules based on
       // country you are in.  You may have the
       // logic here or you may have it in a
       // configuration file
       // Here, just return a USTax so this
       // will compile.
       return new USTax();
   }
}

public class SalesOrder {
   public void process (CalcTax taxToUse) {
       long itemNumber= 0;
       double price= 0;

       // given the tax object to use

       // . . .

       // calculate tax
       double tax=
          taxToUse.taxAmount( itemNumber, price);
   }
}

public abstract class CalcTax {
   abstract public double taxAmount(
      long itemSold, double price);
}

public class CanTax extends CalcTax {
   public double taxAmount(
      long itemSold, double price) {
```

```
            // in real life, figure out tax according to
            // the rules in Canada and return it
            // here, return 0 so this will compile
            return 0.0;
        }
    }
    public class USTax extends CalcTax {
        public double taxAmount(
            long itemSold, double price) {
            // in real life, figure out tax according to
            // the rules in the US and return it
            // here, return 0 so this will compile
            return 0.0;
        }
    }
```

UML Diagrams

In the UML, it is possible to define parameters in the methods. This is done by showing a parameter and its type in the parentheses following the method name.

Thus, in Figure 9-4, the *taxAmount* method has three parameters:

- *itemSold* of type **Saleable**

- *qty* of type **double**

- *price* of type **double**

All of these are inputs denoted by the "in." The *taxAmount* method also returns a **double**.

How this works

I have defined a fairly generic interface for the **CalcTax** object. Presumably, I would have a **Saleable** class that defines saleable items (and how they are taxed). The **SalesOrder** object would give that to the **CalcTax** object, along with the quantity and price. This would be all the information the **CalcTax** object would need.

Improves cohesion, aids flexibility

Another advantage of this approach is that cohesion has improved. Sales tax is handled in its own class. Another advantage is that as I get new tax requirements, I just need to derive a new class from **CalcTax** that implements them.

Finally, it becomes easier to shift responsibilities. For example, in the inheritance-based approach, I *had* to have the **TaskController** decide which type of **SalesOrder** to use. With the new structure, I can have either the **TaskController** do it or the **SalesOrder** do it. To have the **SalesOrder** do it, I would have some configuration object that would let it know which tax object to use (probably the same one the **TaskController** was using). Figure 9-5 shows this.

Easier to shift responsibilities

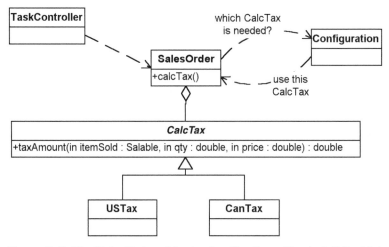

Figure 9-5 The SalesOrder object using Configuration to tell it which CalcTax to use.

Most people note that this approach also uses inheritance. This is true. However, it does it in a way different from just deriving a **CanadianSalesOrder** from **SalesOrder**. In the strict inheritance approach, I am using inheritance within **SalesOrder** to handle the variation. In the approach indicated by design patterns, I am using an object aggregation approach. (That is, **SalesOrder** *contains* a reference to the object that handles the function that is varying; that is, tax.) From the perspective of the **SalesOrder** (the class I am trying to extend), I am favoring aggregation over inheritance. How the contained class handles its variation is no concern of the **SalesOrder**.

Contrasting this approach with direct inheritance

One could ask, "Well, aren't you just pushing the problem down the chain?" There are three parts to answering this question. First, yes I am. But doing so simplifies the bigger, more complicated program. Second, the original design captured many independent variables (tax, date format, and so on) in one class hierarchy (**SalesOrder**), whereas the new approach captures each of these variables in its own class hierarchy. This allows them to be independently extended. Finally, in the new approach, other pieces of the system can use (or test) these smaller operations independently of the **SalesOrder**. The bottom line is, the approach espoused by patterns will scale, whereas the original use of inheritance will not.

Handling New Cases and Normalization

This process of moving some varying behavior outside of the class using it is very similar to the process of normalization in databases where you move columns into their own table and refer to them by a foreign key.

The Strategy pattern

This approach allows the business rule to vary independently from the **SalesOrder** object that uses it. Note how this works well for current variations I have as well as any future ones that might come along. Essentially, this use of encapsulating an algorithm in an abstract class (**CalcTax**) and using one of them at a time interchangeably is the Strategy pattern.

The Strategy Pattern

The intent, according to the Gang of Four

According to the Gang of Four, the Strategy pattern's intent is to

> *Define a family of algorithms, encapsulate each one, and make them interchangeable. Strategy lets the algorithm vary independently from clients that use it.*[6]

---

6. Ibid, p. 315.

The Strategy pattern is based on a few principles:

The motivations of the Strategy pattern

- Objects have responsibilities.

- Different, specific implementations of these responsibilities are manifested through the use of polymorphism.

- There is a need to manage several different implementations of what is, conceptually, the same algorithm.

It is a good design practice to separate behaviors that occur in the problem domain from each other—that is, to decouple them. This allows me to change the class responsible for one behavior without adversely affecting another.

The Strategy Pattern: Key Features	
Intent	Enables you to use different business rules or algorithms depending on the context in which they occur.
Problem	The selection of an algorithm that needs to be applied depends on the client making the request or the data being acted on. If you just have a rule in place that does not change, you do not need a Strategy pattern.
Solution	Separates the selection of algorithm from the implementation of the algorithm. Allows for the selection to be made based upon context.
Participants and collaborators	• **Strategy** specifies how the different algorithms are used. • **ConcreteStrategies** implement these different algorithms. • **Context** uses a specific **ConcreteStrategy** with a reference of type **Strategy**. **Strategy** and **Context** interact to implement the chosen algorithm. (Sometimes **Strategy** must query **Context**.) The **Context** forwards requests from its client to **Strategy**.
Consequences	• The Strategy pattern defines a family of algorithms. • Switches and/or conditionals can be eliminated. • You must invoke all algorithms in the same way. (They must all have the same interface.) The interaction between the **ConcreteStrategies** and the **Context** may require the addition of methods that get state to the **Context**.

Implementation	Have the class that uses the algorithm (**Context**) contain an abstract class (**Strategy**) that has an abstract method specifying how to call the algorithm. Each derived class implements the algorithm as needed. *Note:* This method wouldn't be abstract if you wanted to have some default behavior.
	Note: In the prototypical Strategy pattern, the responsibility for selecting the particular implementation to use is done by the **Client** object and is given to the **Context** object of the Strategy pattern.

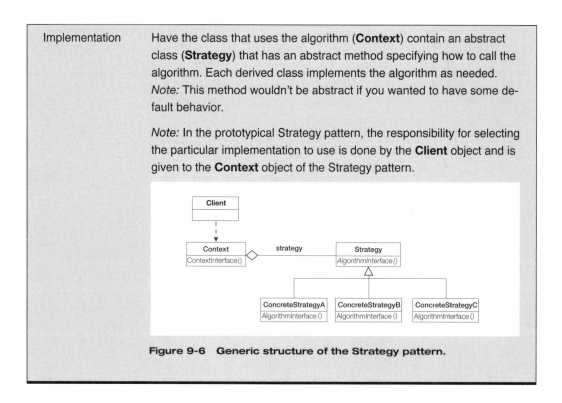

Figure 9-6   Generic structure of the Strategy pattern.

Field Notes: Using the Strategy Pattern

The limits prove the pattern

I had been using the e-commerce example in my pattern classes when someone asked, "Are you aware that in the U.K. people over a certain age don't get taxed on food?" I wasn't aware of this, and the interface for the **CalcTax** object did not handle this case. I could handle this in at least one of three ways:

1. Pass the age of the **Customer** to the **CalcTax** object and use it if needed.

2. Be more general by passing the **Customer** object itself and querying it if needed.

3. Be more general still by passing a reference to the **SalesOrder** object (that is, **this**) and letting the **CalcTax** object query it.

Although it is true I have to modify the **SalesOrder** and **CalcTax** classes to handle this case, it is clear how to do this. I am not likely to introduce a problem because of this.

Technically, the Strategy pattern is about encapsulating algorithms. In practice, however, I have found that it can be used for encapsulating virtually any kind of rule. In general, when I am doing analysis and I hear about applying different business rules at different times, I consider the possibility of a Strategy pattern handling this variation for me.

Encapsulating business rules

The Strategy pattern requires that the algorithms (business rules) being encapsulated now lie outside of the class that is using them (the **Context**). This means that the information needed by the strategies must either be passed to them or obtained in some other manner.

Coupling between context and strategies

The Strategy pattern simplifies unit testing because each algorithm is in its own class and can be tested through its interface alone. If the algorithms are not pulled out, as they are in the Strategy pattern, any coupling between the context and the strategies makes testing more difficult. For example, you may have preconditions before you can instantiate a context object. Or the context may supply some of what becomes the strategy through a protected data member. Testing is even further simplified if several different families of algorithms coexist. (That is, several Strategy patterns are present, which is typically the case.) This is because by using Strategy patterns the developer does not need to worry about interactions caused by coupling with the context. That is, we should be able to test each algorithm independently and not worry about all the combinations possible.

Lowers cost of unit tests

In the sales order example earlier, I had the **TaskController** pass the strategy object to the **SalesOrder** object each time it was needed. A little reflection would tell me that unless I were reusing the sales order object for different customers, I would always use the same strategy object for any one particular **SalesOrder** object. A variation of the Strategy pattern I often see is to assign the strategy object to the context in the

When I always use the same Strategy object

Strategy pattern (in this case, my **SalesOrder** object) in the context's constructor. Then any method that needs to reference it can, without requiring it be passed in. However, because the context still doesn't know what particular type of strategy object it has, the power of the pattern is still maintained. This can be done if which particular strategy object is needed is known at the time the context object is constructed.

Ways of eliminating class explosions with the Strategy pattern

I have sometimes had students complain that the Strategy pattern causes them to make a number of additional classes. Although I don't believe this is a real problem, I have done a few things to minimize this when I have control of all the strategies. In this situation, if I am using C++, I might have the abstract strategy header file contain all the header files for the concrete strategies. I also have the abstract strategy cpp file contain the code for the concrete strategies. If I am using Java, I use inner classes in the abstract strategy class to contain all the concrete strategies. I do not do this if I do not have control over all the strategies; that is, if other programmers need to implement their own algorithms.

Summary

In this chapter

The Strategy pattern is a way to define a family of algorithms. Conceptually, all of these algorithms do the same things. They just have different implementations.

I showed an example that used a family of tax calculation algorithms. In an international e-commerce system, there might be different tax algorithms for different countries. Strategy would enables me to encapsulate these rules in one abstract class and have a family of concrete derivations.

By deriving all the different ways of performing the algorithm from an abstract class, the main module (**SalesOrder** in the example above) does not need to worry about which of many possibilities is actually in use. This allows for new variations but also creates the need to manage these variations—a challenge I discuss in Chapter 16.

Review Questions

Observations

1. What are some alternatives for handling new requirements?

2. What are the three fundamental principles proposed by the Gang of Four that guide how to anticipate change?

3. What is the intent of the Strategy pattern?

4. What are the consequences of the Strategy pattern?

Interpretations

1. The Gang of Four suggests "considering what should be variable in your design." How is this different from focusing on the cause of redesign?

2. What is wrong with copy and paste?

3. What is meant by "switch creep"?

4. What are the advantages of the design patterns approach to handling variation?

5. Why is the object-aggregation approach to inheritance superior to direct class inheritance for handling variation?

Opinions and Applications

1. Have you ever been in a situation where you did not feel you could afford to anticipate change? What drove you that way? What was the result?

2. Should you ever use switch statements? Why or why not?

CHAPTER 10

The Bridge Pattern

Overview

This chapter continues the discussion of design patterns with the Bridge pattern. The Bridge pattern is quite a bit more complex than the other patterns you have learned. It is also much more useful.

In this chapter

This chapter

- Provides an example to help you derive the Bridge pattern. I go into great detail to help you learn this pattern.

- Presents the key features of the pattern.

- Presents some observations on the Bridge pattern from my own practice.

Introducing the Bridge Pattern

According to the Gang of Four, the intent of the Bridge pattern is to "decouple an abstraction from its implementation so that the two can vary independently."[1]

Intent: Decouple abstraction from implementation

I remember exactly what my first thoughts were when I read this: Huh?

This is hard to understand

1. Gamma, E., Helm, R., Johnson, R., Vlissides, J. *Design Patterns: Elements of Reusable Object-Oriented Software*, Boston: Addison-Wesley, 1995, p. 151.

And then: How come I understand every word in this sentence, but I have no idea what it means?

I knew that

- *Decouple* means to have things behave independently from each other or at least explicitly state what the relationship is.

- *Abstraction* is how different things are related to each other conceptually.

And I thought that *implementations* were the way to build the abstractions; but I was confused about how I was supposed to separate abstractions from the specific ways that implemented them.

It turns out that much of my confusion was due to misunderstanding what implementations meant. *Implementations* here means the objects that the abstract class and its derivations use to implement themselves (not the derivations of the abstract class, which are called concrete classes). To be honest, even if I had understood it properly, I am not sure how much it would have helped. The concept expressed in this sentence is just hard to understand at first.

If you are also confused about the Bridge pattern at this point, that is okay. If you understand the stated intent, you are that much ahead.

It *is* a challenging pattern to learn because it is so powerful.

The Bridge pattern is one of the toughest patterns to understand in part because it is so powerful and applies to so many situations. It also goes against a common tendency to handle special cases with inheritance. However, it is also an excellent example of following two of the mandates of the design pattern community: "Find what varies and encapsulate it" and "Favor aggregation over class inheritance" (as you will see).

Learning the Bridge Pattern: An Example

To help you understand the thinking behind the Bridge pattern and what it is trying to do, I will work through an example from scratch. Starting with requirements, I will derive the pattern and then see how to apply it.

Learn why it exists, then derive the pattern

Perhaps this example will seem basic. But look at the concepts discussed in this example and then try to think of situations that you have encountered that are similar, having

- Variations in abstractions of a concept.

- Variations in how these concepts are implemented.

You will see that this example has many similarities to the CAD/CAM problem discussed earlier. Rather than give you all the requirements up front, however, I am going to give them a little at a time, just as they were given to me. You can't always see the variations at the beginning of the problem.

Bottom line: During requirements definition, explore for variations early and often!

Start with a simple problem: Drawing shapes

Suppose I have been given the task of writing a program that will draw rectangles with either of two drawing programs. I have been told that when I instantiate a rectangle, I will know whether I should use drawing program 1 (**DP1**) or drawing program 2 (**DP2**).

The rectangles are defined as two pairs of points, as represented in Figure 10-1. The differences between the drawing programs are summarized in Table 10-1.

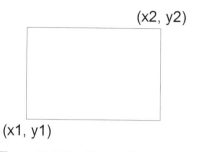

Figure 10-1 Positioning the rectangle.

Table 10-1 Different Drawing Programs

	DP1	DP2
Used to draw a line	`draw_a_line( x1, y1, x2, y2)`	`drawline( x1, x2, y1, y2)`
Used to draw a circle	`draw_a_circle( x, y, r)`	`drawcircle( x, y, r)`

Proper use of inheritance

Our analysis specifies that we don't want the code that draws the rectangles to worry about what type of drawing program it should use. It occurs to me that because the rectangles are told what drawing program to use when instantiated, I can have two different kinds of rectangle objects: one that uses **DP1** and one that uses **DP2**. Each would have a draw method but would implement it differently. Figure 10-2 shows this.

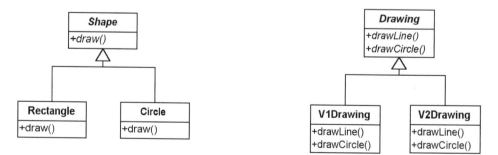

Figure 10-2 Design for rectangles and drawing programs (DP1 and DP2).

By having an abstract class **Rectangle**, I take advantage of the fact that the only difference between the different types of **Rectangle**s are how they implement the *drawLine* method. The **V1Rectangle** is implemented by having a reference to a **DP1** object and using that object's *draw_a_line* method. The **V2Rectangle** is implemented by having a reference to a **DP2** object and using that object's *drawline* method. However, by instantiating the right type of **Rectangle**, I no longer have to worry about this difference.

A note on the implementation

Example 10-1 Java Code Fragments

```
abstract public class Rectangle {
  private double _x1, _y1, _x2, _y2;
  public Rectangle
      (double x1, double y1, double x2, double y2) {
    _x1= x1; _y1= y1; _x2= x2; _y2= y2;
  }
  public void draw() {
    drawLine( _x1, _y1, _x2, _y1);
    drawLine( _x2, _y1, _x2, _y2);
    drawLine( _x2, _y2, _x1, _y2);
    drawLine( _x1, _y2, _x1, _y1);
  }
  abstract protected void drawLine
      (double x1, double y1, double x2, double y2);
}
```

Now suppose that after completing this code, one of the *inevitable three* (death, taxes, and changing requirements) comes my way. I am asked to support another kind of shape—this time, a circle. However, I am also given the mandate that the collection object does not want to know the difference between **Rectangle**s and **Circle**s.

But, although requirements always change

It occurs to me that I can just extend the approach I've already started by adding another level to my class hierarchy. I only need to add a new class, called **Shape**, from which I will derive the **Rectangle** and **Circle** classes. This way, the **Client** object can just refer to **Shape** objects without worrying about what kind of **Shape** it has been given.

…I can still have a simple implementation

Designing with
inheritance

As a beginning object-oriented analyst, it might seem natural to implement these requirements using only inheritance. For example, I could start out with something like Figure 10-2, and then, for each kind of **Shape**, implement the shape with each drawing program, deriving a version of **DP1** and a version of **DP2** for **Rectangle** and deriving a version of **DP1** and a version of **DP2** one for **Circle**. I would end up with Figure 10-3.

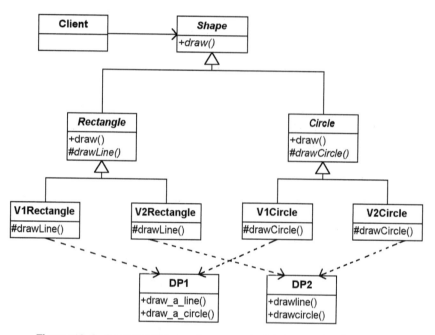

Figure 10-3 A straightforward approach: implementing two shapes and two drawing programs.

I implement the **Circle** class the same way that I implemented the **Rectangle** class. However, this time, I implement **draw** by using **drawCircle** instead of **drawLine**.

Example 10-2 Java Code Fragments

```
abstract class Shape {
 abstract public void draw();
}
```

```
// the only change to Rectangle is
abstract class Rectangle extends Shape {
//
// V1Rectangle and V2Rectangle don't change

abstract public class Circle extends Shape {
    protected double _x, _y, _r;
    public Circle (double x, double y, double r) {
        _x= x; _y= y; _r= r;
    }
    public void draw() {
        drawCircle();
    }
    abstract protected void drawCircle();
}
public class V1Circle extends Circle {
    public V1Circle
        (double x, double y, double r) {
        super(x,y,r);
    }
    protected void drawCircle () {
        DP1.draw_a_circle( _x, _y, _r);
    }
}
public class V2Circle extends Circle {
    public V2Circle(double x, double y, double r) {
        super( x, y, r);
    }
    protected void drawCircle () {
        DP2.drawCircle( _x, _y, _r);
    }
}
```

To understand this design, let's walk through an example. Consider what the **draw** method of a **V1Rectangle** does.

Understanding the design

- **Rectangle**'s **draw** method is the same as before (calling **drawLine** four times as needed).

- **drawLine** is implemented by calling **DP1**'s **draw_a_line**.

In action, this looks like Figure 10-4.

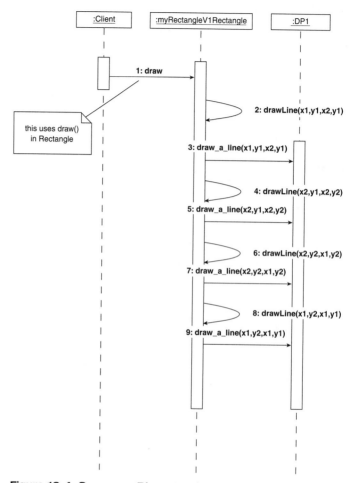

Figure 10-4 Sequence Diagram when have a V1Rectangle.

Even though the class diagram makes it look as if there are many objects, in reality I am only dealing with three objects (see Figure 10-5):

- The **Client** using the rectangle

- The **V1Rectangle** object

- The **DP1** drawing program

When the **Client** object sends a message to the **V1Rectangle** object (called **myRectangle**) to perform *draw*, it calls **Rectangle**'s
draw method resulting in Steps 2 through 9.

Reading a Sequence Diagram

As I discussed in Chapter 2, "The UML—The Unified Modeling Language," the diagram in Figure 10-4 is a special kind of interaction diagram called a *sequence diagram*. It is a common diagram in the UML. Its purpose is to show the interaction of objects in the system.

- Each box at the top represents an object. It may be named or not.

- If an object has a name, it is given to the left of the colon.

- The class to which the object belongs is shown to the right of the colon. Thus, the middle object is named **myRectangle** and is an instance of **V1Rectangle**.

You read the diagram from the top down. Each numbered statement is a message sent from one object to either itself or to another object.

- The sequence starts out with the unnamed **Client** object calling the *draw* method of **myRectangle**.

- This method calls its own *drawLine* method four times (shown in Steps 2, 4, 6, and 8). Note the arrow pointing back to the **myRectangle** in the lifeline.

- *drawLine* calls **DP1**'s *draw_a_line*. This is shown in Steps 3, 5, 7 and 9.

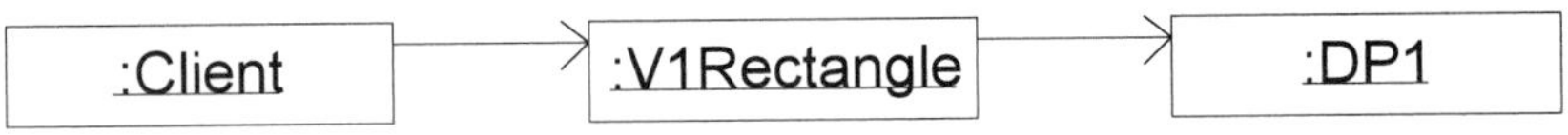

Figure 10-5 The objects present.

Unfortunately, this approach introduces new problems. Look back at Figure 10-3 and pay attention to the third row of classes. Consider the following:

This solution suffers from combinatorial explosion

- The classes in this row represent the four specific types of **Shape**s that I have.

- What happens if I get another drawing program—that is, another variation in implementation? I will have *six* different kinds of **Shape**s (two **Shape** concepts times three drawing programs).

- Imagine what happens if I then get another type of **Shape**, another variation in concept. I will have *nine* different types of **Shape**s (three **Shape** concepts times three drawing programs).

…because of tight coupling

The class explosion problem arises because in this solution the abstraction (the kinds of **Shape**s) and the implementation (the drawing programs) are tightly coupled. Each type of shape must know what type of drawing program it is using. I need a way to separate the variations in abstraction from the variations in implementation so that the number of classes only grows linearly (see Figure 10-6).

This is exactly the intent of the Bridge pattern: "[to] decouple an abstraction from its implementation so that the two can vary independently."[2]

Abstraction 1	Implementation A
Abstraction 2	Implementation B
Abstraction 3	Implementation C
. . .	. . .

Figure 10-6 The Bridge pattern separates variations in abstraction and implementation.

There are several other problems. Our poor approach to design gave us this mess!

Before showing a solution and deriving the Bridge pattern, I want to mention a few other problems (beyond the combinatorial explosion).

Looking at Figure 10-3, ask yourself what else is poor about this design.

---

2. Gamma, E., Helm, R., Johnson, R., Vlissides, J. *Design Patterns: Elements of Reusable Object-Oriented Software*, Boston: Addison-Wesley, 1995, p. 151.

- Does there appear to be redundancy?

- Would you say things have strong cohesion or weak cohesion?

- Are things tightly or loosely coupled?

Would you want to have to maintain this code?

The Overuse of Inheritance

As a beginning object-oriented analyst, I had a tendency to solve the kind of problem I have seen here by using special cases, taking advantage of inheritance. I loved the idea of inheritance because it seemed new and powerful. I used it whenever I could. This seems to be normal for many beginning analysts, but it is naive: Given this new "hammer," everything seems like a nail. Unfortunately, many approaches to teaching object-oriented design focus on the approach of handling variation through specialization, deriving new classes from existing classes. With an overfocus on the "*is*-ness" of objects, it has programmers create objects in monolithic hierarchies that work reasonably well at first but become more difficult to maintain as time goes on (as discussed in Chapter 9, "The Strategy Pattern").

As I became an experienced object-oriented designer, I was still stuck in this paradigm of designing based on inheritance—that is, looking at the characteristics of my classes based on their "*is*-ness" without regard for how complex the structures were becoming.

Thinking with design patterns eventually led me out of this mess. I learned to think about objects in terms of their responsibilities rather than in terms of their structure.

Experienced object-oriented analysts have learned to use inheritance selectively to realize its power. Using design patterns will help you move along this learning curve more quickly. It involves a transition from using a different specialization for each variation (inheritance) to moving these variations into used or owned objects (aggregation).

*An alternative
approach*

When I first looked at these problems, I thought that part of the difficulty might have been that I simply was using the wrong kind of inheritance hierarchy. Therefore, I tried the alternative hierarchy shown in Figure 10-7.

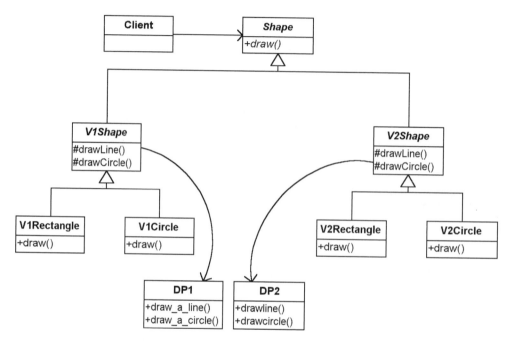

Figure 10-7   An alternative implementation.

*Not really a lot
better, just bad in a
different way*

I still have the same four classes representing all of my possible combinations. However, by first deriving versions for the different drawing programs, I eliminated the redundancy between the **DP1** and **DP2** classes.

Unfortunately, I am unable to eliminate the redundancy between the two types of **Rectangle**s and the two types of **Circle**s, each pair of which has the same *draw* method.

In any event, the class explosion that was present before is still present here.

The sequence diagram for this solution is shown in Figure 10-8.

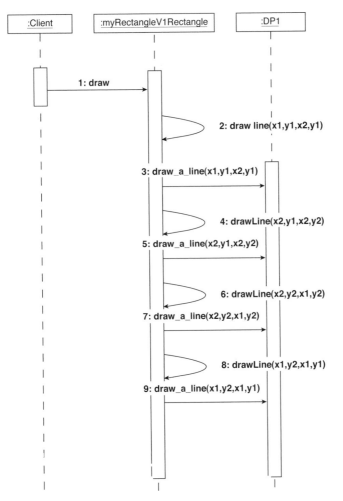

Figure 10-8 Sequence diagram for new approach.

Although this may be an improvement over the original solution, it still has a problem with scaling. It also still has some of the original cohesion and coupling problems.

It still has scaling problems

Bottom line: I do not want to have to maintain this version either! There must be a better way.

> ## Look For Alternatives in Initial Design
>
> Although my alternative design here was not significantly better than my original design, it is worth pointing out that finding alternatives to an original design is a good practice. Too many developers take what they first come up with and go with that. I am not endorsing an in-depth study of all possible alternatives (another way of suffering "paralysis by analysis"). However, stepping back and looking at how we can overcome the design deficiencies in our original design is a great practice. In fact, it was just this stepping back, a refusal to move forward with a known, poor design, that led me to understanding the powerful methods of using design patterns that this entire book is about.

An Observation About Using Design Patterns

A new way to look at design patterns

When people begin to look at design patterns, they often focus on the solutions the patterns offer. This seems reasonable because design patterns are advertised as providing good solutions to the problems at hand.

However, this is starting at the wrong end. Before trying to apply a solution to a problem, you should understand the problem. Taking an approach that looks for where you can apply patterns tells you *what to do* but not *when to use it* or *why to do it*.

I find it much more useful to focus on the context of the pattern—the problem it is trying to solve. This lets me know the *when* and the *why*. It is more consistent with the philosophy of Alexander's patterns: "Each pattern describes a problem which occurs over and over again in our environment, and then describes the core of the solution to that problem...."[3]

---

3. Alexander, C., Ishikawa, S., Silverstein, M. *A Pattern Language: Towns/Buildings/Construction*, New York: Oxford University Press, 1977, p. x.

What I have done so far in this chapter is a case in point. What is the problem being solved by the Bridge pattern?

The Bridge pattern is useful when you have an abstraction that has different implementations. It allows the abstraction and the implementation to vary independently of each other.

The characteristics of the problem fit this nicely. I can know that I ought to be using the Bridge pattern even though I do not know yet how to implement it. Allowing for the abstraction to vary independently from the implementation would mean I could add new abstractions without changing my implementations and vice versa.

The current solution does not allow for this independent variation. I can see that it would be better if I could create an implementation that would allow for this.

The bottom line: It is very important to realize that, without even knowing how to implement the Bridge pattern, you can determine that it would be useful in this situation. You will find that this is generally true of design patterns. That is, you can identify when to apply them to your problem domain before knowing exactly how to implement them.

Learning the Bridge Pattern: Deriving It

Now that you have been through the problem, we are in a position to derive the Bridge pattern together. Doing the work to derive the pattern will help you to understand more deeply what this complex and powerful pattern does.

Deriving a solution

Let's apply some of the basic strategies for good object-oriented design and see how they help to develop a solution that is very much like the Bridge pattern. To do this, I will be using the work of Jim Coplein[4] on commonality and variability analysis.

Design Patterns Are Solutions That Occur Again and Again

Design patterns are solutions that have recurred in several problems and have therefore proven themselves over time to be good solutions. The approach I am taking in this book is to *derive* the pattern to teach it so that you can understand its characteristics.

In this case, I know the pattern I want to derive—the Bridge pattern—because I was shown it by the Gang of Four and have seen how it works in my own problem domains. It is important to note that patterns are not really derived. By definition, they must be recurring—having been demonstrated in at least three independent cases—to be considered patterns. What I mean by "derive" is that we will go through a design process where you create the pattern as if you did not know it. This is to illustrate some key principles and useful strategies. It also demonstrates that it is at least equally important to know these principles as it is to know patterns because the principles always apply, whereas the patterns are found only in certain circumstances.

A new paradigm for finding objects

It is almost axiomatic with object-oriented design methods that the designer is supposed to look at the problem domain, identify the nouns present, and create objects representing them. Then the designer finds the verbs relating to those nouns (that is, their actions) and implements them by adding methods to the objects. This process of focusing on nouns and verbs typically leads to larger class hierarchies than we would like. I suggest that using commonality and variability analysis as a primary tool in creating objects is a better approach than looking at just nouns and verbs. (Actually, I believe this is a restatement of Jim Coplein's work.)

---

4. Coplein, J. *Multi-Paradigm Design for C++*, Boston: Addison-Wesley, 1998.

There are two basic strategies to follow in creating designs to deal with the variations:

Strategies to handle variations

- Find what varies and encapsulate it.
- Favor aggregation over inheritance.

In the past, developers often relied on extensive inheritance trees to coordinate these variations. However, the second strategy says to try aggregation when possible. The intent of this is to be able to contain the variations in independent classes, thereby allowing for future variations without affecting the code. One way to do this is to have each variation contained in its own abstract class and then see how the abstract classes relate to each other.

Reviewing Encapsulation

Most object-oriented developers learned that "encapsulation" is data hiding. Unfortunately, this is a very limiting definition. True, encapsulation does hide data, but it can be used in many other ways. If you look back at Figure 7-2, you will see encapsulation operates at many levels. Of course, it works at hiding data for each of the particular **Shape**s. However, notice that the **Client** object is not aware of the particular kinds of **Shape**s. That is, the **Client** object has no idea that the **Shape**s it is dealing with are **Rectangle**s and **Circle**s. Thus, the concrete classes that **Client** deals with are hidden (or encapsulated) from **Client**. This is the kind of encapsulation that the Gang of Four is talking about when they say "Find what varies and encapsulate it." They are finding what varies and encapsulating it "behind" an abstract class (see Chapter 6, "Expanding Our Horizons").

Follow this process for the rectangle-drawing problem.

Try it: Identify what is varying

First identify what it is that is varying. In this case, it is different types of shapes and different types of drawing programs. The common concepts are therefore shapes and drawing programs. I represent this in Figure 10-9. (Note that the class names are shown in italics because the classes are abstract.)

Figure 10-9 What is varying?

At this point, I intend **Shape** to encapsulate the concept of the types of shapes that I have. Shapes are responsible for knowing how to draw themselves. **Drawing** objects, on the other hand, are responsible for drawing lines and circles. I represent these responsibilities by defining methods in the classes.

Try it: Represent the variations The next step is to represent the specific variations that are present. For **Shape**, I have rectangles and circles. For drawing programs, I will have a program that is based on **DP1** (**V1Drawing**) and one based on **DP2** (**V2Drawing**), respectively. I show this in Figure 10-10.

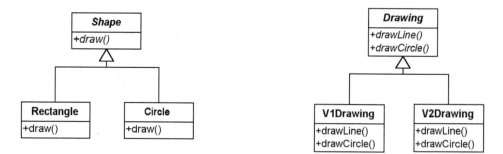

Figure 10-10 Represent the variations.

At this point, the diagram is simply notional. I know that **V1Drawing** will use **DP1** and **V2Drawing** will use **DP2**, but I have not said *how*. I have simply captured the concepts of the problem domain (shapes and drawing programs) and have shown the variations present.

Given these two sets of classes, I need to ask how they will relate to one another. I do not want to come up with a new set of classes based on an inheritance tree because I know what happens if I do that. (Look at Figures 10-3 and 10-7 to refresh your memory.) Instead, I want to see whether I can relate these classes by having one use the other (that is, follow the mandate to favor aggregation over inheritance). The question is, which class uses the other?

Tying the classes together: What uses what?

Consider these two possibilities: either **Shape** uses the **Drawing** programs or the **Drawing** programs use **Shape**.

Consider the latter case first. If drawing programs could draw shapes directly, they would have to know some things about shapes in general: what they are, what they look like. But this violates a fundamental principle of objects: An object should only be responsible for itself.

It also violates encapsulation. **Drawing** objects would have to know specific information about **Shape**s (that is, the kind of **Shape**) in order to draw them. The objects are not really responsible for their own behaviors.

Now consider the first case. What if I have **Shape**s use **Drawing** objects to draw themselves? **Shape**s wouldn't need to know what type of **Drawing** object they used because I could have **Shape**s refer to the **Drawing** class. **Shape**s also would be responsible for controlling the drawing.

This looks better to me. Figure 10-11 shows this solution.

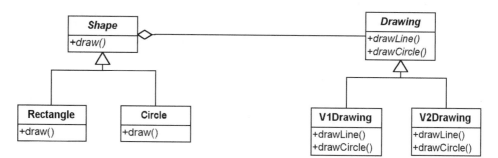

Figure 10-11 Tie the classes together.

Expanding the design

In this design, **Shape** uses **Drawing** to manifest its behavior. I left out the details of **V1Drawing** using the **DP1** program and **V2Drawing** using the **DP2** program. In Figure 10-12, I add this as well as the protected methods *drawLine* and *drawCircle* (in **Shape**), which calls **Drawing**'s *drawLine* and *drawCircle* respectively.

The pattern illustrated

Figure 10-13 illustrates the separation of the **Shape** abstraction from the **Drawing** implementation.

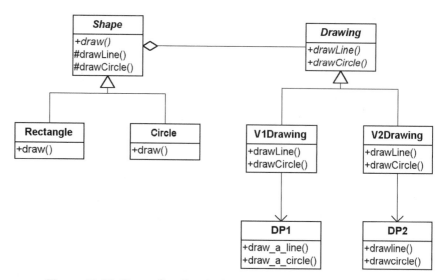

Figure 10-12 Expanding the design.

One Rule, One Place

A very important implementation strategy to follow is to have only one place where you implement a rule. In other words, if you have a rule how to do things, only implement that once. This typically results in code with a greater number of smaller methods. The extra cost is minimal, but it eliminates duplication and often prevents many future problems. Duplication is bad not only because of the extra work in typing things multiple times, but because of the likelihood of something changing in the future and then forgetting to change it in all of the required places.

Although the *draw* method or **Rectangle** could directly call the *drawLine* method of whatever **Drawing** object the **Shape** has, I can improve the code by continuing to follow the one rule, one place strategy and have a *drawLine* method in **Shape** that calls the *drawLine* method of its **Drawing** object.

I am not a purist (at least not in most things), but if there is one place where I think it is important to always follow a rule, it is here. In the following example, I have a *drawLine* method in **Shape** because that describes my rule of drawing a line with **Drawing**. I do the same with *drawCircle* for circles. By following this strategy, I prepare myself for other derived objects that might need to draw lines and circles.

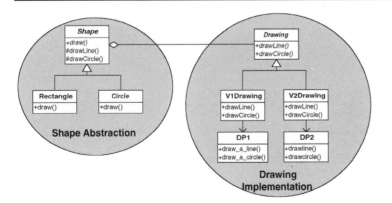

Figure 10-13 Class diagram illustrating separation of abstraction and implementation.

Relating this to the inheritance-based design

From a method point of view, this looks fairly similar to the inheritance-based implementation (such as shown in Figure 10-3). The biggest difference is that the methods are now located in different classes.

I said at the beginning of this chapter that my confusion over the Bridge pattern was due to my misunderstanding of the term *implementation*. I thought that implementation referred to how I implemented a particular abstraction.

The Bridge pattern let me see that viewing the implementation as something outside of my objects, something that is *used by* the objects, gives me much greater freedom by hiding the variations in implementation from my calling program. By designing my objects this way, I also noticed how I was containing variations in separate class hierarchies. The hierarchy on the left side of Figure 10-13 contains the variations in my abstractions. The hierarchy on the right side of Figure 10-13 contains the variations in how I will implement those abstractions. This is consistent with the new paradigm for creating objects (using commonality/variability analysis) that I mentioned earlier.

From an object perspective

It is easiest to visualize this when you remember that there are only three objects to deal with at any one time, even though there are several classes (see Figure 10-14).

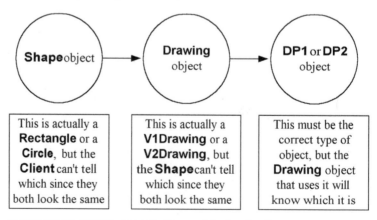

Figure 10-14 There are only three objects at a time.

Example 10-3 shows a reasonably complete Java code example.   *Code examples*

Example 10-3 Java Code Fragments

```java
public class Client {
   static public void main () {
      Shape myShapes[];
      Factory myFactory= new Factory();

      // get rectangles from some other source
      myShapes= myFactory.getShapes();
      for (int i= 0; i < myShapes.length; i++) {
         myShapes[i].draw();
      }
   }
}

abstract public class Shape {
   protected Drawing myDrawing;
   abstract public void draw();

   Shape (Drawing drawing) {
      myDrawing= drawing;
   }
   protected void drawLine (
      double x1,double y1, double x2,double y2) {
      myDrawing.drawLine(x1,y1,x2,y2);
   }

   protected void drawCircle (
      double x,double y,double r) {
      myDrawing.drawCircle(x,y,r);
   }
}

public class Rectangle extends Shape {
   private double _x1, _y1, _x2, _y2;
   public Rectangle (Drawing dp, double x1,
      double y1, double x2, double y2) {
      super( dp);
      x1= x1; _y1= y1; _x2= x2; _y2= y2;
   }
   public void draw() {
      drawLine( _x1, _y1, _x2, _y1);
      drawLine( _x2, _y1, _x2, _y2);
      drawLine( _x2, _y2, _x1, _y2);
```

```
            drawLine( _x1, _y2, _x1, _y1);
         }
         protected void drawLine(double x1, double y1,
            double x2, double y2) {
            myDrawing.drawLine( x1, y1, x2, y2);
         }
}

public class Circle extends Shape {
    private double _x, _y, _r;
    public Circle (Drawing dp,
        double x, double y, double r) {
        super(dp);
        x= x; _y= y; _r= r;
    }
    public void draw() {
        myDrawing.drawCircle( _x, _y, _r);
    }
}

abstract public class Drawing {
    abstract public void drawLine(double x1,
        double y1, double x2, double y2);
        abstract public void drawCircle(
        double x, double y, double r);
}

public class V1Drawing extends Drawing {
    public void drawLine (
        double x1,double y1,
        double x2,double y2) {
        DP1.draw_a_line(x1,y1,x2,y2);
    }
    public void drawCircle (
        double x,double y,double r) {
        DP1.draw_a_circle(x,y,r);
    }
}

public class V2Drawing extends Drawing {
    public void drawLine (
        double x1,double y1,
        double x2,double y2) {
        // arguments are different in DP2
        // and must be rearranged
        DP2.drawLine(x1,x2,y1,y2);
    }
    public void drawCircle (
        double x, double y,double r) {
```

```
        DP2.drawCircle(x,y,r);
    }
}
```

The Bridge Pattern in Retrospect

Now that you've seen how the Bridge pattern works, it is worth looking at it from a more conceptual point of view. As shown in Figure 10-13, the pattern has an abstraction part (with its derivations) and an implementation part. When designing with the Bridge pattern, it is useful to keep these two parts in mind. The implementation's interface should be designed considering the different derivations of the abstract class that it will have to support. Note that a designer shouldn't necessarily define an interface that will account for all conceivable derivations of the abstract class (yet another possible route to paralysis by analysis). Only those derivations that actually are being built need be supported. Time and time again, the authors have seen that the mere consideration of flexibility at this point often greatly improves a design.

The essence of the pattern

Note: In C++, the Bridge pattern's implementation must be implemented with an abstract class defining the public interface. In C# and Java, either an abstract class or an interface can be used. The choice depends on whether implementations share common traits that abstract classes can take advantage of.[5]

Field Notes: Using the Bridge Pattern

Print drivers are perhaps the class example of the Bridge. They are also the easiest to see when to apply the Bridge. The real power of the Bridge pattern, in my mind, however, is that it helps me see

Classic Bridge pattern example

---

5. For more on this, see Coad, Peter, *Java Design*, Upper Saddle River, N.J.: Prentice Hall, 2000.

when to abstract out the implementations that are present in my problem domain. In other words, sometimes I'll have an entity X that uses a system S and an entity Y that uses a system T. I may think that X always and only comes with S and Y always and only comes with T and link them (couple) them together. The Bridge reminds me that I may be better off abstracting out the differences between S and T (the implementations of X and Y) and allowing X and Y to use either S and T. In other words, the Bridge is most useful when I might not have decoupled my abstraction from my implementation unless I considered whether the Bridge pattern applied.

The Bridge pattern often incorporates the Adapter pattern

Note that the solution presented in Figures 10-12 and 10-13 integrates the Adapter pattern with the Bridge pattern. I do this because I was given the drawing programs that I must use. These drawing programs have preexisting interfaces with which I must work. I must use the Adapter to adapt them so that they can be handled in the same way.

Although it is very common to see the Adapter pattern used with the Bridge pattern, the Adapter pattern is not part of the Bridge pattern.

Compound design patterns

When two or more patterns are tightly integrated (like my Bridge and Adapter), the result is called a compound design pattern.[6,7] It is now possible to talk about patterns of patterns!

Instantiating the objects of the Bridge pattern

Another thing to notice is that the objects representing the abstraction (the **Shape**s) were given their implementation while being instantiated. This is not an inherent part of the pattern, but it is very common.

---

6. Compound design patterns used to be called composite design patterns, but are now called compound design patterns to avoid confusion with the Composite pattern.

7. For more information, refer to Riehle, D., "Composite Design Patterns," in, *Proceedings of the 1997 Conference on Object-Oriented Programming Systems, Languages and Applications* (OOPSLA '97), New York: ACM Press, 1997, pp. 218–228. Also refer to "Composite Design Patterns (They Aren't What You Think)," *C++ Report,* June 1998.

The Bridge Pattern: Key Features

Intent	Decouple a set of implementations from the set of objects using them.
Problem	The derivations of an abstract class must use multiple implementations without causing an explosion in the number of classes.
Solution	Define an interface for all implementations to use and have the derivations of the abstract class use that.
Participants and collaborators	**Abstraction** defines the interface for the objects being implemented. **Implementor** defines the interface for the specific implementation classes. Classes derived from **Abstraction** use classes derived from **Implementor** without knowing which particular **ConcreteImplementor** is in use.
Consequences	The decoupling of the implementations from the objects that use them increases extensibility. Client objects are not aware of implementation issues.
Implementation	• Encapsulate the implementations in an abstract class.
	• Contain a handle to it in the base class of the abstraction being implemented. **Note:** In Java, you can use interfaces instead of an abstract class for the implementation.

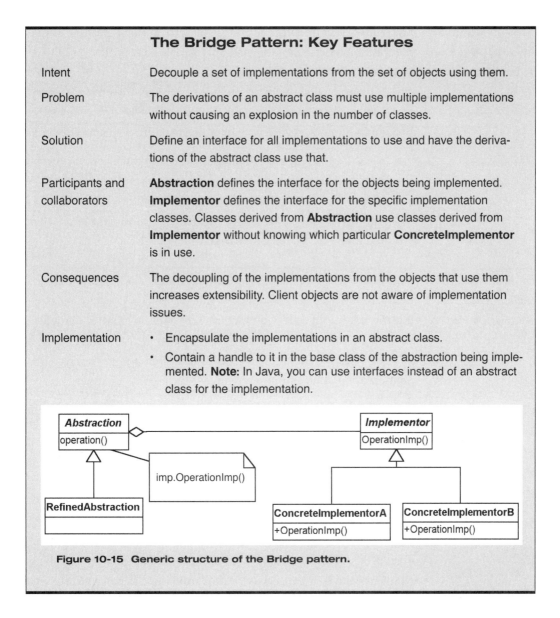

Figure 10-15 Generic structure of the Bridge pattern.

Now that you understand the Bridge pattern, it is worth reviewing the Gang of Four's implementation section in their description of the pattern. They discuss different issues relating to how the abstraction creates and/or uses the implementation.

An advantage of C#
and Java over C++
in the Bridge pattern

Sometimes when using the Bridge pattern, I will share the implementation objects across several abstraction objects.

- In C# and Java, this is no problem; when all the abstraction objects go away, the garbage collector will realize that the implementation objects are no longer needed and will clean them up.

- In C++, I must somehow manage the implementation objects. There are many ways to do this; keeping a reference counter or even using the Singleton pattern are possibilities. It is nice, however, not to have to consider this effort. This illustrates another advantage of automatic garbage collection.

The Bridge pattern
solution is good, but
not always perfect

Although the solution I developed with the Bridge pattern is far superior to the original solution, it is not perfect. One way of measuring the quality of a design is to see how well it handles variation. Handling a new implementation is very easy with a Bridge pattern in place. The programmer just needs to define a new concrete implementation class and implement it. Nothing else changes.

However, things may not go so smoothly if I get a new concrete example of the abstraction. I may get a new kind of **Shape** that can be implemented with the implementations already in the design. However, I may also get a new kind of **Shape** that requires a new drawing function. For example, I may have to implement an ellipse. The current **Drawing** class does not have the proper method to do ellipses. In this case, I have to modify the implementations. However, even if this occurs, at least I have a well-defined process for making changes: Modify the interface of the **Drawing** class or interface and then modify each **Drawing** derivative accordingly. This process localizes the impact of the change and lowers the risk of an unwanted side effect.

I am left with a fine solution, even if it is not "perfect." And the Bridge pattern has given me a handle on the problem if I need to consider a more general implementation. Design patterns help me think more abstractly and more generally about my solutions. Whether I want to implement this more general solution is up to me; the pattern doesn't mandate that.

Bottom line: Patterns do not always give perfect solutions. Because patterns represent the collective experience of many designers over the years, however, they are often better than the solutions you or I might come up with on our own in the often limited time we have.

Follow one rule, one place to help with refactoring

In the real world, I do not always start out with multiple implementations. Sometimes, I know that new ones are *possible*, but they show up unexpectedly. One approach is to prepare for multiple implementations by always using abstractions. You get a very generic application.

But I do not recommend this approach. It leads to an unnecessary increase in the number of classes you have. It is important to write code in such a way that when multiple implementations do occur (which they often will), it is not difficult to modify the code to incorporate the Bridge pattern. Modifying code to improve its structure without adding function is called *refactoring*. As defined by Martin Fowler, "Refactoring is the process of changing a software system in such a way that it does not alter the external behavior of the code yet improves its internal structure."[8]

When designing code, I was always attending to the possibility of refactoring by following the one rule, one place mandate. The **drawLine** method was a good example of this. Although the place the code was actually implemented varied, moving it around was fairly easy.

---

8. Fowler, M. *Refactoring: Improving the Design of Existing Code,* Boston: Addison-Wesley, 1999, p. xvi.

> ## Refactoring
>
> Refactoring is commonly used in object-oriented design. However, it is not strictly an object-oriented thing ...It is modifying code to improve its structure without adding function.

A useful way to look at the Bridge pattern

While deriving the pattern, I took the two variations present (shapes and drawing programs) and encapsulated each in its own abstract class. That is, the variations of shapes are encapsulated in the **Shape** class, the variations of drawing programs are encapsulated in the **Drawing** class.

Stepping back and looking at these two polymorphic structures, I should ask myself, "What do these abstract classes represent?" For the shapes, it is pretty evident that the class represents different kinds of shapes. The **Drawing** abstract class represents how I will implement the **Shape**s. The pattern is about the relationship between these different abstractions. Thus, in the case where I described how new requirements for the **Drawing** class may arise (say, if I need to implement ellipses) there is a clear relationship between the classes that tells me how to implement it.

Summary

In this chapter

While reviewing the Bridge pattern, I looked at a problem where there were two variations in the problem domain—shapes and drawing programs. In the problem domain, each of these varied. The challenge came when trying to implement a solution based on all the special cases that existed. The initial solution, which naively used inheritance too much, resulted in a redundant design that had tight coupling and weak cohesion, and was thus difficult to maintain.

You learned the Bridge pattern by following the basic strategies for dealing with variation:

- Find what varies and encapsulate it.

- Favor aggregation over inheritance.

Finding what varies is always a good step in learning about the problem domain. In the drawing program example, I had one set of variations using another set of variations. This indicates that the Bridge pattern will probably be useful.

In general, you should identify which patterns to consider by matching them with the characteristics and behaviors in the problem domain. By understanding the *whys* and *whats* of the patterns in your repertoire, you can be more effective in picking the ones that will help you. You can select patterns to consider before deciding how the pattern's implementation will be done.

Consideration vs. Use

I used the word *consider* rather than *use* in the prior paragraph deliberately. Actually, you should "use" patterns by "considering" the issues they imply and the body of knowledge about them. Unfortunately, when people hear the word *use* regarding a pattern, they tend to think about "using the implementation" of the pattern. The word *consider* helps people realize that they need to use the pattern as a guideline, a list of considerations.

If you use[9] the Bridge pattern, the design and implementation are more robust and better able to handle changes in the future.

Although I focused on the Bridge pattern during the chapter, it is worth pointing out several object-oriented principles that are used in the Bridge pattern.

Summary of object-oriented principles used in the Bridge pattern

---

9. Of course, now I mean use as in "using the pattern to consider the issues, forces, etc., present."

Concept	Discussion
Objects are responsible for themselves	I had different kinds of **Shapes**, but all drew themselves (via the *draw* method). The **Drawing** classes were responsible for drawing elements of objects.
Abstract class	I used abstract classes to represent the concepts. I actually had rectangles and circles in the problem domain. The concept "shape" is something that lives strictly in our head, a device to bind the two concepts together; therefore, I represent it in the **Shape** class as an *abstract* class. **Shape** will never get instantiated because it never exists in the problem domain (only **Rectangle**s and **Circle**s do). The same thing is true with drawing programs.
Encapsulation via an abstract class	I have two examples of encapsulation through the use of an abstract class in this problem:
	• A client dealing with the Bridge pattern will have only a derivation of **Shape** visible to it. However, the client will not know what type of **Shape** it has. (It will be just a **Shape** to the client.) Thus, I have encapsulated this information. The advantage of this is if a new type of **Shape** is needed in the future, it does not affect the client object.
	• The **Drawing** class hides the different drawing derivations from the **Shape**s. In practice, the abstraction may know which implementation it uses because it might instantiate it. See page 155 of the Gang of Four book for an explanation as to why this might be a good thing to do. However, even when that occurs, this knowledge of implementations is limited to the abstraction's constructor and is easily changed.
One rule, one place	The abstract class often has the methods that actually use the implementation objects. The subclasses of the abstract class call these methods. This allows for easier modification if needed, and allows for a good starting point even before implementing the entire pattern.
Testability	Imagine writing tests for the shapes and drawing programs with both our original solution and our later solution. For example, suppose you have N shapes and M implementations. The first solution would require N*M tests. The second solution only requires M+N tests: First test the M implementations, and then test the N shapes with arbitrarily chosen implementations (because all of the shapes work with all of the implementors in exactly the same way).

Review Questions

Observations

1. Define *decouple* and *abstraction*.

2. How is *implementation* defined in the context of the Bridge pattern?

3. What are the basic elements of a sequence diagram?

4. What is Alexander's view of how to use patterns? Does he advocate starting with the solution first or the problem to be solved first?

5. What does commonality analysis seek to identify? What does variability analysis seek to identify?

6. What is the basic problem being solved by the Bridge pattern?

7. Define the "one rule, one place" strategy.

8. What are the consequences of the Bridge pattern?

Interpretations

1. The Gang of Four says that the intent of the Bridge pattern is to "decouple an abstraction from its implementation so that the two can vary independently."

   • What does this mean?

   • Give an example.

2. Why can tight coupling lead to an explosion in the number of classes?

Opinions and Applications

1. "Look at objects in terms of their responsibilities rather than their behaviors." How does this affect your view of the use of inheritance in an object-oriented system?

2. Why do you think the Gang of Four call this pattern "Bridge"? Is it an appropriate name for what it is doing? Why or why not?

CHAPTER 11

The Abstract Factory Pattern

Overview

This chapter continues our study of patterns with the Abstract Factory pattern, which is used to create families of objects.

In this chapter

This chapter

- Provides an example to help you derive the Abstract Factory pattern.
- Presents the key features of the Abstract Factory pattern.
- Relates the Abstract Factory pattern to the CAD/CAM problem.

Introducing the Abstract Factory Pattern

According to the Gang of Four, the intent of the Abstract Factory pattern is to "provide an interface for creating families of related or dependent objects without specifying their concrete classes."[1]

Intent: Coordinate the instantiation of objects

Sometimes several objects need to be instantiated in a coordinated fashion. For example, when dealing with user interfaces, the system might need to use one set of objects to work on one operating system and another set of objects to work on a different operating system. The Abstract Factory pattern ensures that the system always gets the correct objects for the situation.

---

1. Gamma, E., Helm, R., Johnson, R., Vlissides, J. *Design Patterns: Elements of Reusable Object-Oriented Software*, Boston: Addison-Wesley, 1995, p.87.

Learning the Abstract Factory Pattern: An Example

A motivating example: Select device drivers according to the machine capacity

Suppose I have been given the task of designing a computer system to display and print shapes from a database. The type of resolution to use to display and print the shapes depends on the computer that the system is currently running on: the speed of its CPU and the amount of memory that it has available. My system must be careful about how much demand it is placing on the computer.

The challenge is that my system must control the drivers that it is using: low-resolution drivers in a less-capable machine and high-resolution drivers in a high-capacity machine, as shown in Table 11-1.

Table 11-1 Different Drivers for Different Machines

For Driver	In a Low-Capacity Machine, Use	In a High-Capacity Machine, Use
Display	LRDD Low-resolution display driver	HRDD High-resolution display driver
Print	LRPD Low-resolution print driver	HRPD High-resolution print driver

Define families based on a unifying concept

In this example, the families of drivers are mutually exclusive, but this is not usually the case. Sometimes different families contain objects from the same classes. For example, a midrange machine might use a *low-resolution display driver* (LRDD) and a *high-resolution print driver* (HRPD).

The families to use are based on the problem domain: which sets of objects are required for a given case? In this case, the unifying concept focuses on the demands that the objects put on the system:

- **A low-resolution family**—LRDD and LRPD, those drivers that put low demands on the system

- **A high-resolution family**—HRDD and HRPD, those drivers that put high demands on the system

My first attempt might be to use a switch to control the selection of driver, as shown in Example 11-1.

Alternative 1: Use a switch to select the driver

Example 11-1 Java Code Fragments: A Switch to Control Which Driver to Use

```java
// JAVA CODE FRAGMENT

class ApControl {
    .  .  .
    public void doDraw() {
        .  .  .
        switch (RESOLUTION) {
            case LOW:
                // use lrdd
            case HIGH:
                // use hrdd
        }
    }
    public void doPrint() {
        .  .  .
        switch (RESOLUTION) {
            case LOW:
                // use lrpd
            case HIGH:
                // use hrpd
        }
    }
}
```

Although this does work, it presents problems. The rules for determining which driver to use are intermixed with the actual use of the driver. There are problems both with coupling and with cohesion:

...but there are problems with coupling and cohesion

- **Tight coupling**—If I change the rule on the resolution (say, I need to add a MIDDLE value), I must change the code in two places that are otherwise not related.

- **Weak cohesion**—I am giving *doDraw* and *doPrint* two unrelated assignments: They must both create a shape and must also worry about which driver to use.

Tight coupling and weak cohesion may not be a problem right now. However, they usually increase maintenance costs. Also, in the real world, I would likely have many more places affected than just the two shown here.

Switches May Indicate a Need for Abstraction

Often a switch indicates (1) the need for polymorphic behavior or (2) the presence of misplaced responsibilities. Consider instead a more general solution such as abstraction or giving the responsibility to other objects.

Alternative 2: Use inheritance

Another alternative is to use inheritance. I could have two different **ApControl**s: one that uses low-resolution drivers and one that uses high-resolution drivers. Both would be derived from the same abstract class, so common code could be maintained. I show this in Figure 11-1.

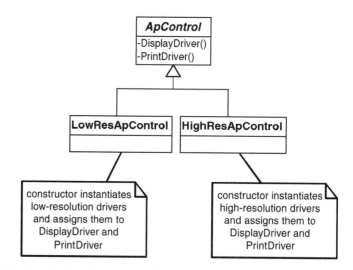

Figure 11-1 Alternative 2—handling variation with inheritance.

Although inheritance could work in this simple case, it has so many disadvantages that I would rather stay with the switches. For example:

...but this also has problems

- **Combinatorial explosion**—For each different family and each new family I get in the future, I must create a new concrete class (that is, a new version of **ApControl**). For example, if I had a requirement for a medium-capacity application (one with an **LRPD** and an **HRDD**), I would need to make a new class that handled that case. If I needed one to handle an **HRPD** and an **LRDD**, I would need yet another class. The diagram above would have many derivations under **ApControl**.

- **Unclear meaning**—The resultant classes do not help clarify what is going on. I have specialized each class to a particular special case. If I want my code to be easy to maintain in the future, I need to strive to make it as clear as possible what is going on. Then I do not have to spend a lot of time trying to relearn what that section of code is trying to do.

- **Need to favor aggregation**—Finally, it violates the basic rule to "favor aggregation over inheritance." Not following this rule means when other variations happen my classes will degrade even further.

In my experience, I have found that switches often indicate an opportunity for abstraction. In this example, **LRDD** and **HRDD** are both display drivers, and **LRPD** and **HRPD** are both print drivers. The abstractions would therefore be *display drivers* and *print drivers*. Figure 11-2 shows this conceptually. I say "conceptually" because **LRDD** and **HRDD** may not actually derive from the same abstract class. At this point, I do not have to be concerned that they may derive from different classes because I know I can use the Adapter pattern to wrap the drivers, making it appear they belong to the appropriate abstract class.

Alternative 3: Replace switches with abstraction

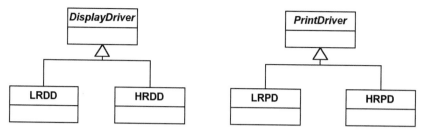

Figure 11-2 Drivers and their abstractions.

The code is simpler to understand

Defining the objects this way would allow for **ApControl** to use **DisplayDriver** and **PrintDriver** without using switches. **ApControl** is much simpler to understand because it is not concerned about the type of drivers it uses. In other words, **ApControl** would use a **DisplayDriver** object or a **PrintDriver** object without concerning itself about the driver's resolution. This use of **ApControl** with the drivers is likely a manifestation of the Bridge pattern. We are using the Abstract factory pattern (which we haven't yet defined) to set this up.

See Figure 11-3 and the code in Example 11-2.

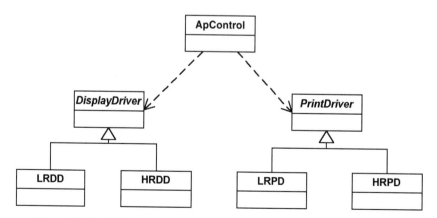

Figure 11-3 ApControl using drivers in the ideal situation.

Example 11-2 Java Code Fragments: Using Polymorphism to Solve the Problem

```
// JAVA CODE FRAGMENT

class ApControl {
   .   .   .
   public void doDraw() {
      .   .   .
      myDisplayDriver.draw();
   }
   public void doPrint() {
      .   .   .
      myPrintDriver.print();
   }
}
```

One question remains: How do I create the appropriate objects?   *Factory objects*

I could have **ApControl** do it, but this can cause maintenance problems in the future. If I have to work with a new set of objects, I will have to change **ApControl**. Instead, if I use a "factory" object to instantiate the objects I need, I will have prepared myself for new families of objects.

In this example, I will use a factory object (of type **ResFactory**, also known as Resolution Factory) to control the creation of the appropriate family of drivers. The **ApControl** object will use another object—the factory object—to get the appropriate type of display driver and the appropriate type of print driver for the current computer being used. The interaction would look something like the one shown in Figure 11-4.

The factory is responsible ...*and* cohesive

From **ApControl**'s point of view, things are now pretty simple. It lets **ResFactory** worry about keeping track of which drivers to use. Although I am still faced with writing code to do this tracking, I have decomposed the problem according to responsibility. **ApControl** has the responsibility for knowing how to work with the appropriate objects. **ResFactory** has the responsibility for deciding which objects are appropriate. I can use different factory objects or even just one object (that might use switches). In any case, it is better than what I had before.

This strengthens cohesion: All that **ResFactory** does is create the appropriate drivers; all **ApControl** does is use them.

…and it encapsulates variation in a class

There are ways to avoid the use of switches in **ResFactory** itself. This would enable me to make future changes without affecting any existing factory objects. I can encapsulate a variation in a class by defining an abstract class that represents the factory concept. In the case of **ResFactory**, I have two different behaviors (methods):

- Give me the display driver I should use.

- Give me the print driver I should use.

ResFactory can be instantiated from one of two concrete classes and derived from an abstract class that has these public methods, as shown in Figure 11-5.

Approach to Bridging Analysis and Design

Following are three key conceptual steps in the Abstract Factory.

Strategy	Shown in the Design
Find what varies and encapsulate it.	The choice of which driver object to use was varying, so I encapsulated it in **ResFactory**.
Favor aggregation over inheritance.	Put this variation in a separate object—**ResFactory**—and have **ApControl** use it as opposed to having two different **ApControl** objects.
Design to interfaces, not to implementations.	**ApControl** knows how to ask **ResFactory** to instantiate drivers—it does not know (or care) how **ResFactory** is actually doing it.

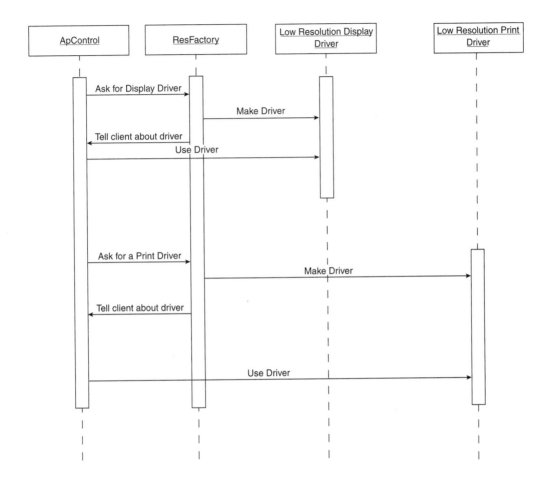

Figure 11-4 ApControl gets its drivers from a factory object.

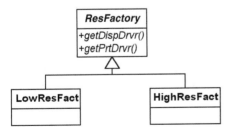

Figure 11-5 The ResFactory encapsulates the variations.

Learning the Abstract Factory Pattern: Implementing It

Implementation of the design

Example 11-3 shows how to implement the Abstract Factory objects for this design.

Example 11-3 Java Code Fragments: Implementation of ResFactory

```java
abstract class ResFactory {
   abstract public DisplayDriver getDispDrvr();
   abstract public PrintDriver getPrtDrvr();
}

class LowResFact extends ResFactory {
   public DisplayDriver getDispDrvr() {
      return new LRDD();
   }
   public PrintDriver getPrtDrvr() {
      return new LRPD();
   }
}

class HighResFact extends ResFactory {
   public DisplayDriver getDispDrvr() {
      return new HRDD();
   }
   public PrintDriver getPrtDrvr() {
      return new HRPD();
   }
}
```

Putting it together: the Abstract Factory

To finish the solution, I have **ApControl** talk with the appropriate factory object (either **LowResFact** or **HighResFact**); this is shown in Figure 11-6. Note that **ResFactory** is abstract, and that this hiding of **ResFactory**'s implementation is what makes the pattern work. Hence, the name Abstract Factory for the pattern.

How this works

ApControl is given either a **LowResFact** object or a **HighResFact** object. It asks this object for the appropriate drivers when it needs them. The factory object instantiates the particular driver (low or

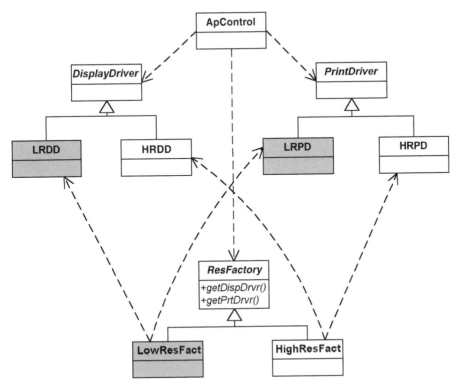

Figure 11-6 Intermediate solution using the Abstract Factory.

high resolution) that it knows about. **ApControl** does not need to worry about whether a low-resolution or a high-resolution driver is returned because it uses both in the same manner.

I have ignored one issue: **LRDD** and **HRDD** may not have been derived from the same abstract class (as may be true of **LRPD** and **HRPD**). Knowing the Adapter pattern, this does not present much of a problem. I can simply use the structure I have in Figure 11-6, but adapt the drivers as shown in Figure 11-7.

The LRDD/HRDD and LRPD/HRPD pairs do not necessarily derive from the same classes

The implementation of this design is essentially the same as the one before it. The only difference is that now the factory objects instantiate objects from classes I have created that adapt the objects I started with. This is an important modeling method. By combining the Adapter

How this works

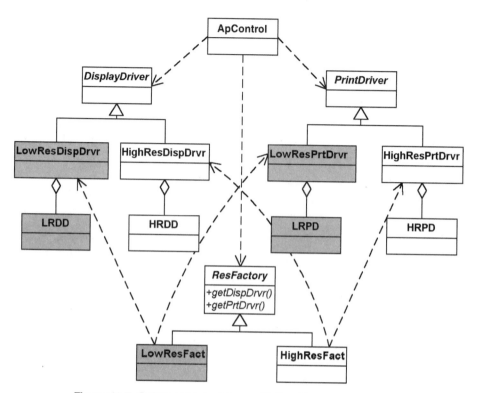

Figure 11-7 Solving the problem with the Abstract Factory and Adapter.

pattern with the Abstract Factory pattern in this way, I can treat these conceptually similar objects as if they were siblings even if they are not. This enables the Abstract Factory to be used in more situations.

The roles of the objects in the Abstract Factory

In this pattern

- The client object just knows who to ask for the objects it needs and how to use them.

- The Abstract Factory class specifies which objects can be instantiated by defining a method for each of these different types of objects. Typically, an Abstract Factory object will have a method for each type of object that must be instantiated.

- The concrete factories specify which objects are to be instantiated.

The example I just showed implemented the Abstract Factory by having one concrete class per potential situation. In this case, I had two situations: low resolution and high resolution. In practice, the number of cases can be very large and can grow combinatorially with each new variable (that is, new family member).

The Abstract Factory in the real world

For example, it might be that the "family" of objects relates to each customer in an e-commerce system. That is, each family of objects represents the choices a particular customer has made. In this case, having a concrete class for each "family" would not work at all. A better solution would simply be to have one class to create all of the families. There would still be a method relating to each family member but the decision on which particular object to create would be handled with a switch. The question becomes, "How do you know which option each customer wants?" That is, what should be the value of the switch variable?

Of course, the question was there all along. The Abstract Factory did not eliminate the need. Instead, it tells us what to do. It says to put the option in an object that is responsible for creating the used objects and to keep this separate from the objects that are using these objects. It says to separate the use of objects from the construction of objects. I talk more about this in Chapter 18, "Design Implications of Patterns."

Therefore, the issues in the pattern are as follows:

- Which case do I have?
- How do I manage this information?
- Where do I put the construction logic?

As I mentioned, these issues were here all along. We were just hidden by the other issues. Let's consider the different ways these questions were answered in our original solution and the solution with the Abstract Factory pattern as given.

Which case do I have?

- Original solution: **ApControl** knew this.

- Abstract Factory solution: A configuration file saying which concrete factory object to create.

How do I manage this information?

- Original solution: **ApControl** managed this.

- Abstract Factory solution: Each concrete object knew which objects it was to create.

Where do I put the construction logic?

- Original solution: **ApControl** managed this.

- Abstract Factory solution. In the factory objects.

In the e-commerce solution, managing the information—that is, which customer do I have (or, rather, which family I have) —is a little more complicated. We can handle this by passing in the customer ID to the factory and letting it resolve the issue. There are many possible solutions to resolving this:

- The factory could look in a configuration file or database for the information

- In a Web application, the information could be stored in a cookie

The Abstract Factory does not tell how to solve these issues other than to remove them from the objects using the family of objects. This both decouples the instantiation logic from the using logic and strengthens the cohesion. Strengthening cohesion makes the main code more readable, encapsulates the rules for choosing objects, and encourages the use of concrete objects in a more abstract fashion.

Aren't we back to switches?

I am often asked the question, "Haven't you just gone back to using switches?" The answer is yes. But switches aren't bad. They are only bad when switches get coupled together, as when one variable becomes the switch variable for many switches: That point of connection becomes a dependency that leads to complexity and bugs.

In any event, the factory code is well isolated now. No matter what method I use to implement it, I will not have impact the code that I am trying to simplify. It also means that my coding methods do not have to be quite as pristine because the code is so much smaller and decoupled from other logic.

Why does the Gang of Four call this pattern the "Abstract Factory"? At first glance, you might be tempted to conclude it is because the factory is implemented as an abstract class with a derivation for each case. But that is not the case. This pattern is called the "Abstract Factory" because the things it is intended to build are *themselves* defined by abstractions (**DisplayDriver** and **PrintDriver** in the example above). How you choose to implement the factory variations is not specific to the pattern.

Why call it "abstract" factory?

Field Notes: The Abstract Factory Pattern

Deciding which factory object is needed is really the same as determining which family of objects to use. For example, in the preceding driver problem, I had one family for low-resolution drivers and another family for high-resolution drivers. How do I know which set I want? In a case like this, it is most likely that a configuration file will tell me. I can then write a few lines of code that instantiate the proper factory object based on this configuration information.

How to get the right factory object

I can also use an Abstract Factory so that I can use a subsystem for different applications. In this case, the factory object will be passed to the subsystem, telling the subsystem which objects it is to use. In this case, it is usually known by the main system which family of objects the subsystem will need. Before the subsystem is called, the correct factory object is instantiated.

The Abstract Factory Pattern: Key Features

Intent	You want to have families or sets of objects for particular clients (or cases).
Problem	Families of related objects need to be instantiated.
Solution	Coordinates the creation of families of objects. Gives a way to take the rules of how to perform the instantiation out of the client object that is using these created objects.
Participants and collaborators	The **AbstractFactory** defines the interface for how to create each member of the family of objects required. Typically, each family is created by having its own unique **ConcreteFactory**.
Consequences	The pattern isolates the rules of which objects to use from the logic of how to use these objects.
Implementation	Define an abstract class that specifies which objects are to be made. Then implement one concrete class for each family. Tables or files can also be used to accomplish the same thing.

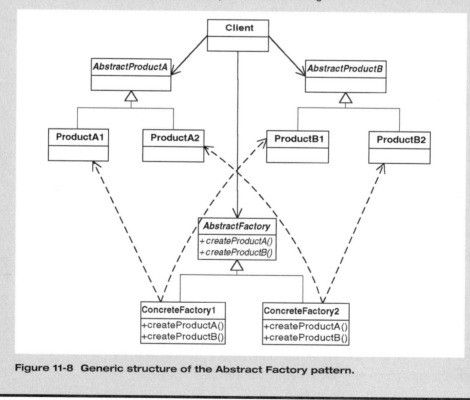

Figure 11-8 Generic structure of the Abstract Factory pattern.

Figure 11-8 shows a **Client** using objects derived from two different server classes (**AbstractProductA** and **AbstractProductB**). It is a design that simplifies, hides implementations, and makes a system more maintainable.

How Abstract Factory works and what its benefits are

- The **Client** object does not know which particular concrete implementations of the server objects it has because the factory object has the responsibility to create them.

- The client object does not even know which particular factory it uses because it only knows that it has an **AbstractFactory** object. It has a **ConcreteFactory1** or a **ConcreteFactory2** object, but it doesn't know which one.

I have hidden (encapsulated) from **Client** the choice about which server objects are being used. This will make it easier in the future to make changes in the algorithm for making this choice because **Client** is unaffected.

The Abstract Factory pattern affords us a new kind of decomposition—decomposition by responsibility. Using it decomposes our problem into

- Who is using our particular objects (**ApControl**).

- Who is deciding upon which particular objects to use (**AbstractFactory**).

Using the Abstract Factory is indicated when the problem domain has different families of objects present and each family is used under different circumstances.

Abstract Factory applies when there are families of objects

You may define families according to any number of reasons. Examples include the following:

- Different operating systems (when writing cross-platform applications)

- Different performance guidelines

- Different versions of applications

- Different traits for users of the application

- Different sets of locale-dependent resources (e.g., dialogs, date formats)

After you have identified the families and the members for each family, you must decide how you are going to implement each case (that is, each family). In my example, I did this by defining an abstract class that specified which family member types could be instantiated. For each family, I then derived a class from this abstract class that would instantiate these family members.

A variation of the Abstract Factory pattern: Configuration files

Sometimes you will have families of objects but do not want to control their instantiation with a different derived class for each family. Perhaps you want something more dynamic.

Examples might be

- You want to have a configuration file that specifies which objects to use. You can use a switch based on the information in the configuration file that instantiates the correct object.

- Each family can have a record in a database that contains information about which objects it is to use. Each column (field) indicates which specific class type to use for each make method in the Abstract Factory.

A further variation: Using the Class class in Java

If you are working in Java or C#, you can take the configuration file concept one step further. Have fields represent the class name to use. Using Java's Class class you can instantiate the correct object based on these names.[2] For example, a field could contain the value LRDD

---

2. C# has an equivalent mechanism. For a good description of Java's Class class, see Eckel, B., *Thinking in Java,* Upper Saddle River, N.J.: Prentice Hall, 2000.

to indicate an object of class **LRDD** is needed. Realize that you do not need to store the full class name as long as you have a well-defined convention. For example, you could have a set prefix or suffix to add to the name in the file.

In real-world projects, members in different families do not always have a common parent. For example, in the earlier driver example, it is likely that the **LRDD** and **HRDD** driver classes are not derived from the same class. In cases like this, it is necessary to adapt them so an Abstract Factory pattern can work.

Adapters and the Abstract Factory

Relating the Abstract Factory Pattern to the CAD/CAM Problem

In the CAD/CAM problem, the system will have to deal with many sets of features, depending on which CAD/CAM version it is working with. In the V1 system, all the features will be implemented for V1. Similarly, in the V2 system, all the features will be implemented for V2.

The families that I will use for the Abstract Factory pattern will be V1 features and V2 features.

Summary

The Abstract Factory is used when you must coordinate the creation of families of objects. It gives a way to take the rules regarding how to perform the instantiation out of the client object that is using these created objects:

In this chapter

- First identify the rules for instantiation and define an abstract class with an interface that has a method for each object that needs to be instantiated.

- Then implement concrete classes from this class for each family.

- The client object uses this factory object to create the server objects that it needs.

Review Questions

Observations

1. Although using "switches" can be a reasonable solution to a problem that requires choosing among alternatives, it caused problems for the driver problem discussed in this chapter.

   - What were these problems?

   - What might a switch indicate the need for?

2. Why is this pattern named "Abstract Factory"?

3. What are the three key strategies in the Abstract Factory?

4. In this pattern, there are two kinds of factories.

   - What does the "Abstract Factory" class do?

   - What do the "concrete factory" classes do?

5. What are the consequences of the Abstract Factory pattern?

Interpretations

1. The Gang of Four says that the intent of the Abstract Factory pattern is to "provide an interface for creating families of related or dependent objects without specifying their concrete classes."

   - What does this mean?

   - Give an example.

Opinions and Applications

1. Why do you think the Gang of Four call this pattern "Abstract Factory"? Is it an appropriate name for what it is doing? Why or why not?

2. How do you know when to use the Abstract Factory pattern?

PART IV

Putting It All Together: Thinking in Patterns

Part Overview

In this part, I propose an approach to designing object-oriented systems based on patterns. I have proven this approach in my own design practice. I apply this approach to the CAD/CAM problem that we have been examining since Chapter 3, "A Problem That Cries Out for Flexible Code."

In this part

This approach first tries to understand the context in which objects show up. Although this approach is limited in application, it sets the stage for the more general approach that I propose in the next part of the book.

Chapter	Discuss These Topics
12	**How Do Experts Design?**
	Christopher Alexander's ideas and how experts use these ideas to design.
13	**Solving the CAD/CAM Problem**
	Application of this approach to solve the CAD/CAM problem first presented in Chapter 3.
	Compares this solution with the solution I developed in Chapter 4, "A Standard Object-Oriented Solution."

CHAPTER 12

How Do Experts Design?

Overview

When trying to design, how do you start? Do you first get the details and see how they are put together? Or do you start with the big picture and break it down? Or is there another way?

In this chapter

Christopher Alexander's approach is to focus on the high-level relationships—in a sense, working from the top down. Before making any design decision, he feels it is essential to understand the context of the problem we are solving. He uses patterns to define these relationships. However, more than just presenting a collection of patterns, he offers us an entire approach to design. The area about which he is writing is architecture, designing places where people live and work, but his principles apply to software design as well.

This chapter

- Discusses Alexander's approach to design.

- Describes how to apply this in the software arena.

Building by Adding Distinctions

Now that you have a handle on some of the design patterns, it is time to see how they can work together. For Alexander, it is not enough just to describe individual patterns. He uses them to develop a new paradigm for design.

The Timeless Way of Building: *A book about architecture…*

...that came to shape me as a designer

His book, *The Timeless Way of Building*, is both about patterns and how they work together. This is a beautiful book. It is one of my favorite books both on a personal level and on a professional level. It has helped me appreciate things in my life, to understand the environment in which I live, and to achieve better software design.

How can this be? How can a book about designing buildings and towns have such a profound influence on designing software? I believe it is because it describes a paradigm that Alexander says a designer should work from. *Any* designer. It is this paradigm of design that I find most interesting.

I wish that I could say I had immediately adopted Alexander's insights the first time I read his book; however, that was not the case. My initial reaction to this book was, "This is very interesting. It makes sense." And then I went back to the traditional design methods that I had been using for so long.

But sometimes the old sayings turn out to be true. As in, "Luck is when opportunity meets with preparedness." Or, "Chance favors the prepared mind." I got "lucky" and that has made all the difference.

Within a few weeks of reading *The Timeless Way of Building*, I was faced with an opportunity. I was on a design project and my standard approaches weren't working. I had designs, but they weren't good enough. All of my tried-and-true design methods were failing me. I was very frustrated. Fortunately, I was wise enough to try a new way—Alexander's way—and was delighted with the results.

Building by fitting things together

In the next chapter, I describe what I did. But first, let's look at what Alexander offers us.

> Design is often thought of as a process of synthesis, a
> process of putting together things, a process of

combination. *According to this view, a whole is created by putting together parts. The parts come first: and the form of the whole comes second.*[1]

It is natural to design from parts to the whole, starting with the concrete things that I know.

When I first read this, I thought, "Yes. That is pretty much how I look at things. I figure out what I need and then put it together." That is, I identify my classes and then see how they work together. After assembling the pieces, I may step back to see that they fit in the big picture. But even when I switch my focus from local to global, I am still thinking about the pieces throughout the process.

As an object-oriented developer, these *pieces* are objects and classes. I identified them. I defined behavior and interfaces. But I started with pieces and typically stayed focused on them.

Think about the original CAD/CAM solution in Chapter 4, "A Standard Object-Oriented Solution." I started out thinking about the different classes I needed: slots, holes, cutouts, and so on. Knowing that I needed to relate these to a V1 system and a V2 system, I thought I needed a set of these classes that worked with V1 and another set of these classes that worked with V2. Finally, after coming up with these classes, I saw how they tied together.

But, this may not be a good way to think about it

But it is impossible to form anything which has the character of nature by adding preformed parts.[2] Alexander's thesis is that building from the pieces is not a good way to design.

Even though Alexander is talking about architecture, many software design practitioners whom I respect said that his insights were valid

---

1. Alexander, C. *The Timeless Way of Building*, New York: Oxford University Press, 1979, p. 368. Italics Alexander's

2. Ibid, p. 368.

for us as well. I had to open my mind to this new way of thinking. And when I did so, I heard Alexander say that "good software design cannot be achieved simply by adding together preformed parts." In the software world, this would mean looking first to create a library of useful routines and then tying them together to build the system.

Building by pieces will not get us elegance

> *When parts are modular and made before the whole, by definition then, they are identical, and it is impossible for every part to be unique, according to its position in the whole. Even more important, it simply is not possible for any combination of modular parts to contain the number of patterns which must be present simultaneously in a place which is alive.[3]*

Alexander's talk about modularity was confusing to me at first. It seemed that for reuse to work, one had to come up with generic routines and he was saying *not* to do this. Then I realized that by "modular," Alexander was talking about those identical, interchangeable parts used in the construction industry. He was not using the term *module* as we use it in software. What he means is that if one starts out building modules before having the big picture, it is unlikely that the modules will be able to handle special needs.

If it appears to you that there is a dilemma between Alexander's approach and the goal of reuse, you would not be alone. It was not apparent to me, either. I will resolve this dilemma by the end of the book. I hope that understanding what Alexander meant will be as useful to you as it has been for me. I find that now I create better, more reusable classes when I follow Alexander's approach than when I start with generic pieces.

Good design requires keeping the big picture in mind

> *It is only possible to make a place which is alive by a process in which each part is modified by its position in the whole.[4]*

When you read *alive*, think *robust and flexible systems*.

---

3. Ibid, pp. 368–369.

4. Ibid, p. 369.

Earlier, Alexander said that parts need to be unique so that they can take advantage of their particular situation. Now he takes this deeper. It is in coping with and fitting into the surroundings that a place gets its character. Think of examples in architecture:

- **A Swiss village**—Your mind's eye brings up a village of closely nestled cottages, each looking quite similar to the one next to it, but each one different in its own way. The differences are not arbitrary, but reflect the financial means of the builder and owner as well as the need of the building to blend in with its immediate surroundings. The effect is a very nice, comfortable image.

- **An American suburb**—All the houses are pretty much cookie-cutter designs. Attention is rarely paid to the natural surroundings of the house. Covenants and standards attempt to enforce this homogeneity. The effect is a depersonalization of the houses and is not at all pleasing.

Applying this to software design might seem a bit too "conceptual" at this point. For now, it is enough to understand that the goal is to design pieces—classes, objects—within the context in which they must live in order to create robust and flexible systems. Of course, the question is, "How do we do this?"

In short, each part is given its specific form by its existence in the context of the larger whole.

The design process involves complexification

This is a differentiating process. It views design as a sequence of acts of complexification; *structure is injected into the whole by operating on the whole and crinkling it, not by adding little parts to one another. In the process of differentiation, the whole gives birth to its parts: The form of the whole, and its parts, come into being simultaneously. The image of the differentiating process is the growth of an embryo.*[5]

5. Ibid, p. 370.

"Complexification." What in the world does that mean? Isn't the goal to make things simpler, not more complex?

What Alexander is describing is a way to think about design that starts by looking at the problem in its simplest terms (the conceptual level) and then adding additional features (distinctions), making the design more complex as we go because we are adding more information.[6]

This is a very natural process. We do it all the time. For example, suppose you need to arrange a room for a lecture with an audience of 40 people. As you describe your requirements to someone, you might say something like, "I'll need a room 30 feet by 30 feet" (starting simple). Then, "I'd like the chairs arranged theater style: 4 rows of 8" (adding information, you have made the description of the room more complex). And then, "I need a lectern at the front of the room" (even more complex).

How do we do this? What is the process of design?

The unfolding of a design in the mind of its creator, under the influence of language, is just the same.

Each pattern is an operator that differentiates space: that is, it creates distinctions where no distinction was before.

And in the language the operations are arranged in sequence: so that, as they are done, one after another, gradually a complete thing is born, general in the sense that it shared its patterns with other comparable things; specific in the sense that it is unique, according to its circumstances.

The language is a sequence of these operators, in which each one further differentiates the image, which is the product of the previous differentiations.[7]

---

6. This is also called the "dependency inversion principle" and is a central tenet of design patterns. See the discussion in Chapter 14 for more information.

7. Ibid, pp. 372–373.

Alexander asserts that design should start with a simple statement of the problem, then make it more detailed (complex) by injecting information into the statement. This information takes the form of a pattern. To Alexander, a pattern defines relationships between the entities in his problem domain.

For example, consider the Courtyard pattern discussed in Chapter 5, "An Introduction to Design Patterns." The pattern must describe the entities that are involved in a courtyard and how they relate, entities such as the following:

- The open spaces of the courtyard
- The crossing paths
- The views outward
- Even the people who are going to use the courtyard

Thinking in terms of how these entities need to relate to each other gives us a considerable amount of information with which to design the courtyard. We refine the design of the courtyard by thinking about the other patterns that would exist in the context of the courtyard pattern, such as porches or verandas facing the courtyard.

What makes this analytical method so powerful is that it does not have to rely on my experience or my intuition or my creativity. Alexander's thesis is that these patterns exist independent of any person. A space is alive because it follows a natural process, not just because the designer was a genius. Because the quality of a design depends following this natural process, it should not be surprising that quality solutions for similar problems appear very much alike.

Based on this, he gives us the rules a good designer would follow.

- **One at a time**—Patterns should be applied one at a time in sequence.

  • **Context first**—Apply those patterns first that create the context for the other patterns.

Patterns Define Relationships

The patterns that Alexander describes define relationships between the entities in the problem domain. These patterns are not as important as the relationships, but give us a way to talk about them.

The steps to follow

Alexander's approach also applies to software design. Perhaps not literally, but certainly philosophically. What would Alexander say to software designers?

Alexander's Steps	Discussion
Identify patterns	Identify the patterns that are present in your problem. Think about your problem in terms of the patterns that are present. Remember, the purpose of the pattern is to define relationships among entities.
Start with context patterns	Identify the patterns that create the context for the other patterns. These should be your starting point.
Then, work inward from the context	Look at the remaining patterns and at any other patterns that you might have uncovered. From this set, pick the patterns that define the context for the patterns that would remain. Repeat.
Refine the design	As you refine, always consider the context implied by the patterns.
Implement	The implementation incorporates the details dictated by the patterns.

In a word—sometimes. The problem with this approach is that it as- *Does this really* sumes you can find known patterns in your problem. This does hap- *work?* pen, sometimes. But not very often. However, a more generic approach that doesn't require foreknowledge of *any* patterns is possible. Before describing that approach, however, I will describe an example of where Alexander's approach as described does, in fact, work: The CAD/CAM problem.

Using Alexander in Software Design: A Personal Observation

The first time I used Alexander's approach, I took his words too literally. His concepts—rooted in architecture—do not usually translate directly to software design (or other kinds of design). In some ways, I was lucky in my early experiences in using design patterns in that the problems I solved had the patterns follow pretty well-defined orders of context. However, this also worked against me in that I naively assumed that this method would work in general. (It does not.) This was compounded by the fact that at this time, many key designers in the software community were espousing the development of "pattern languages"—looking for formal ways to apply Alexander to software. I interpreted this to mean that we were close to being able to apply Alexander's approach directly in software design. (I no longer believe this to be true.) Because Alexander said patterns in architecture had predetermined orders of context, I assumed patterns in software also had this predetermined order. That is, one type of pattern would always create the context for another type. I began to evangelize about Alexander's approach—as I understood it—while teaching others. A few months and a few projects later, I began to see the problems. There were cases where a preset order of contexts did not work. That is, sometimes a Bridge pattern could create the context for a Composite pattern, but sometimes it could be exactly the opposite.

Having been trained as a mathematician, I only needed one counterexample to disprove my theory. This started me questioning everything about my approach—something I usually did, but had forgotten in my excitement.

Since that early stage, I now look at the *principles* upon which Alexander's work is based. Although they manifest themselves differently in architecture and in software development, these principles do apply to software design. I see it in improved designs. I see it in more rapid and robust analysis. I experience it every time I have to maintain my software.

Summary

In this chapter   Design is normally thought of as a process of synthesis, a process of putting things together. In software, a common approach is to look immediately for objects and classes and components and then think about how they should fit together.

In *The Timeless Way of Building*, Christopher Alexander described a better approach, one that is based on patterns:

1. Start out with a conceptual understanding of the whole in order to understand what needs to be accomplished.

2. Identify the patterns that are present in the whole.

3. Start with those patterns that create the context for the others.

4. Work inward from the context: Apply the pattern, identify new patterns, and repeat

5. Finally, refine the design and implement within the context created by applying these patterns one at a time.

As a software developer, you may not be able to apply Alexander's pattern language approach directly. However, designing by adding concepts within the context of previously presented concepts is surely something that all of us can do. Keep this in mind as you learn new patterns later in this book. Many patterns create robust software because they define contexts within which the classes that implement them can work.

Review Questions

Observations

1. Alexander uses the term *alive* to characterize good designs. What terms did I suggest using when it comes to software?

2. Good design requires keeping what in mind?

3. Alexander suggests that the best approach to design involves "complexification." What does this mean?

4. To Alexander, what relationships does a pattern define?

5. What are Alexander's five steps to design?

Interpretations

1. Alexander says, "But it is impossible to form anything which has the character of nature by adding preformed parts." What does he mean by this?

Opinions and Applications

1. Sometimes, the case that is made for object-oriented programming is that it gives you small, reusable components that you can assemble to create a program. Does this align with Alexander or contradict him? Or is Alexander speaking at a different level? Why?

2. Have you ever seen a courtyard or entryway in a house or building that has felt particularly "dead" or uninviting? As you look at Alexander's description of the Courtyard pattern, what entities did your courtyard fail to resolve or involve?

3. Think of one software project in which you think Alexander's approach would apply and a project in which it would not apply. What are the issues? Keep this case in mind as you read the rest of the book.

CHAPTER 13

Solving the CAD/CAM Problem
with Patterns

Overview

In this chapter, I apply Alexander's suggested approach[1] with design patterns to solve the CAD/CAM problem presented in Chapter 3, "A Problem That Cries Out for Flexible Code."

In this chapter

This chapter

- Walks you through the methods needed to solve the earlier CAD/CAM problem.

- Takes you through the initial design phase. The details of implementation are left to you.

- Compares the new solution with the previous solution.

Review of the CAD/CAM Problem

Chapter 3 described the requirements for the CAD/CAM problem, a real-world problem that first got me on the road to using design patterns.

The requirements

The problem domain is in computer systems to support a large engineering organization (specifically, to support their CAD/CAM system).

The basic requirement is to create a computer program that can read a CAD/CAM dataset and extract the features that an existing expert system needs to be able to do intelligent design. This system is supposed to shield the expert system from the CAD/CAM system. The complication

---

1. More precisely, what I imagine he would suggest as I have actually never asked him.

is that the CAD/CAM system was in the midst of changes. Potentially, there could be multiple versions of the CAD/CAM system that the expert system would have to interface with.

After initial interviews, I developed the high-level system architecture shown in Figure 13-1 and the following set of requirements for the system:

Requirement	Description
Read a CAD/CAM model and extract features	My system must be able to analyze and extract CAD/CAM descriptions of pieces of sheet metal.
	The expert system then determines how the sheet metal should be made and generates the required instructions so that a robot can make it.
Be able to deal with many kinds of parts	Initially, I am concerned with sheet-metal parts.
	Each sheet-metal part can have multiple kinds of features, including slots, holes, cutouts, specials, and irregulars. It is unlikely that there will be other features in the future.
Handle multiple versions of the CAD/CAM system	From Figure 13-1, you can infer that I need the ability to plug and play different CAD/CAM systems without having to change the expert system.

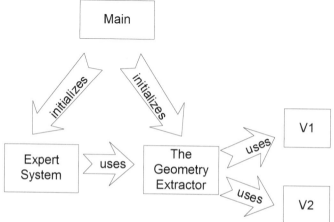

Figure 13-1 High-level view of the solution.

Thinking in Patterns

When I approach a design problem, I do not always try to "think in patterns." However, it has certainly helped me in the past to get breakthrough insights. It shapes my thoughts. And it has guided me in the development of my own useful, generalizable approach to design that I describe later in this book.

The steps to thinking in patterns

I came to understand Alexander's approach after spending many unfruitful hours trying to develop a solution to the CAD/CAM problem that was better than what I showed in Chapter 4, "A Standard Object-Oriented Solution." Instinctively, I knew a better solution had to exist, but I could not come up with it.

I decided to take a break. I went for a walk, just to clear my head and to stop thinking about the problem for a while. You won't be surprised to hear that I only got about 30 feet before I started up again! But I took a new tack. I imagined myself having a conversation with Alexander. I asked him, "So, what would *you* do?" And I could hear him answer, "Think in terms of the patterns!" And did I hear him smilingly add, "You idiot!"

Thinking back to the concepts in the earlier chapter, I knew immediately what he meant: Think in terms of the patterns that I had identified in the problem domain. Look at the essential concepts and do not worry about the details yet.

I have since formalized into the process of thinking in patterns (see box on page 232).

Admittedly, this works only when you can understand the entire problem domain in terms of patterns. And it does not work all the time, but it gives you a place to start. Design patterns are perhaps most useful in giving you a way to get started. You still have to fill in the rest by identifying relationships amongst the concepts in the problem domain. The method for doing this uses *commonality and*

The Process of Thinking in Patterns

1. **Identify the patterns.** Find the patterns in the problem domain.

2. **Analyze and apply the patterns.** For the set of patterns to be analyzed, perform steps 2a through 2d:

   2a. **Order the patterns by context creation.** Order the patterns according to how they create context for each other pattern. The idea is that one pattern will create a context for another, not two patterns co-creating contexts for each other.

   2b. **Select pattern and expand design.** Using your ordering, select the next pattern in this list and use it to create a high-level conceptual design

   2c. **Identify additional patterns.** Identify any additional patterns that might have come up during your analysis. Add them to the set of patterns to be analyzed.

   2d. **Repeat.** Repeat for the sets of patterns that have not yet been integrated into our conceptual design.

3. **Add detail.** Add detail as needed to the design. Expand method and class definitions.

variability analysis (CVA), as discussed in Chapter 15, "Commonality and Variability Analysis." CVA is generally usable, whereas "thinking in patterns" typically is not. I start with "thinking in patterns" because it is an easier process to learn and gives insight into the more useful CVA.

Let me walk you through the steps to thinking in patterns that I used in the CAD/CAM problem.

Thinking in Patterns: Step 1

In the previous chapters, I identified four patterns in the CAD/CAM problem, as follows:

1. Identify the patterns

- Abstract Factory
- Adapter
- Bridge
- Facade

No other patterns stand out at this point, but I am open to some additional ones showing up.

Note: If I were coming fresh to this problem, I would be going through the thought processes outlined earlier: What are the forces, what are the issues in the problem domain and how do they line up with the patterns I know, etc.?

Thinking in Patterns: Step 2a

I will work through the patterns that I have identified as being in the problem domain. I then select them based on how each pattern creates the context for the other patterns.

Work through the patterns by context

When determining which patterns create the context for others in my problem domain, I apply an easy technique: I look through all possible pairings of the patterns, taken two at a time. In this case, there are six possible pairings, as shown in Figure 13-2.

2a. See which one creates the context for the others

If you have several other patterns, it may look as if this process could get very involved. That turns out not to be the case. With a little experience, many of the patterns can easily be eliminated up front from contention for the primary pattern. In any event, you usually have to deal with only a handful or so.

This doesn't take very long

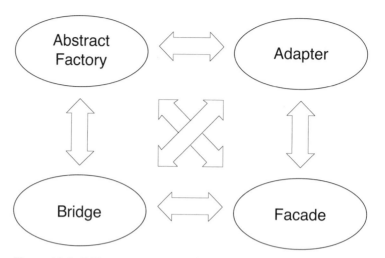

Figure 13-2 Different possible relationships between the patterns.

In this case, there are few enough combinations that we can look at all the possibilities.

We look for what creates context

What exactly do we mean when we say one pattern creates the context for another? One definition of *context* is the interrelated conditions in which something exists or occurs—an environment, a setting.

In the courtyard example in Chapter 5, "An Introduction to Design Patterns," Alexander said that a porch exists in the context of the courtyard. The courtyard defines the environment or the settings in which the porch exists.

A pattern in a system often relates to other patterns in the system by providing a context for these other patterns. In your analysis, it is always valuable to look for whether and how a pattern relates to the other patterns, to look for the contexts that the pattern creates or provides for the other patterns as well as those contexts in which the pattern itself exists. You may not be able to find these every time. But, by looking, you will create higher-quality solutions.

Looking for context is an essential tool to add to your bag of analysis and design tools. Deciding on which pattern creates the context for which is often assisted by looking at the pattern conceptually. For example:

- The **Abstract Factory pattern** creates sets of related objects (families).

- The **Adapter pattern** adapts an existing class A to the interface needed by a using class B.

- The **Bridge pattern** allows for different implementations to be used by a set of related using objects (concrete classes of the abstraction in the pattern).

- The **Facade pattern** simplifies an existing system A for a using class B.

When considering two patterns, I can use these "meta" descriptions of the pattern to see which one creates the context for the other. Although I can reject the Abstract Factory as the topmost pattern in my list out of hand (if I read the sidebar), I can also use its meta description to realize its context is defined by the organization (the families) of the objects it is creating. Therefore, other patterns must be creating its context and it will not be first on the list.

Using these concepts

In fact, the Abstract Factory will be the last pattern I do (unless another creational pattern shows up during my initial design, in which case, both creational patterns will vie for being last).

There are three pairs of patterns left to consider:

Three pairs left

- Adapter–Bridge

- Bridge–Facade

- Facade–Adapter

A Rule to Use
When Considering Context

During one of my projects, I was reflecting on my design approaches. I noticed something that I did consistently, almost unconsciously: I never worried about how I was going to instantiate my objects until I knew what I wanted my objects to be. My chief concern was with relationships between objects as if they already existed. I assumed that I would be able to construct the objects that fit in these relationships when the time came to do so.

The reason I do this is that I need to minimize the number of things that I have to keep in my head during a design. Usually I can do so with a minimal amount of risk when I delay thinking about how to instantiate objects that meet my requirements. Worrying too early is counterproductive; it is better not to worry about instantiating objects until I know what it is that I need to instantiate. I will let tomorrow take care of itself—at least when it comes to instantiation!

Perhaps this seems sensible to you. I had never heard it stated as a rule, and I wanted to check it out before adopting it as universal. I trust my intuition as a designer, but I am certainly not perfect. So I have conferred with several other experienced developers on this subject; without exception, they also follow this rule. That gives me confidence to offer it to you:

Rule: Consider what you need to have in your system before you concern yourself with how to create it.

When considering context à la Alexander, it means that patterns that are motivated by using objects create the context for patterns that are about instantiating objects (often classified as creation patterns). That is, we define our factories after we decide what our objects are.[*]

---

[*] More on this can be found in Joshua Bloch's brilliant book, *Effective Java Programming.* In particular, check out the section "Creating and Destroying Objects."

Seniormost Patterns Constrain the Other Patterns

Seniormost is my term for the one or two patterns that establish a context for the other patterns in my system. This is the pattern that constrains what the other patterns can do. Other terms you could use are outermost patterns or context-setting patterns.

As someone new to patterns, I may not see any pattern that is obviously dependent on another pattern, or any pattern that sets the context for all others.

When there is not an obvious choice, I have to work through the combination of patterns systematically looking for the following:

- Does one pattern define how the other pattern behaves?

- Do two patterns mutually influence each other?

The Adapter pattern is about modifying the interface of a class into another interface that the client is expecting. In this case, the interface that needs adapting is **OOGFeature**. The Bridge pattern is about separating multiple concrete examples of an abstraction from their implementation. In this case, the abstraction is **Feature** and the implementations are the V1 and V2 systems. It sounds like the Bridge will need the Adapter to modify **OOGFeature**'s interface; that is, the Bridge will use the Adapter.

Is there a relationship between the patterns?

Clearly there is some relationship between Bridge and Adapter.

Can I define one of the patterns without another, or is one of the patterns needed by another?

Are the patterns interrelated?

Looking at the patterns tells us what to do:

- I can talk about the Bridge pattern as separating the **Features** from the V1 and V2 systems without actually knowing how I will use the V1 and V2 systems. In fact, a standard way of using the Bridge is to define the abstract Implementation that the Abstraction uses without concerning oneself with differences in the actual concrete implementations. Then, after this is defined, the concrete implementations are adapted to be able to derive from this abstract implementation class.

- However, I cannot talk about using an Adapter pattern to modify the V2 system's interface without knowing what it will be modified into. Without the Bridge pattern, this interface doesn't exist. The Adapter pattern exists to modify the V2 system's interface to the implementation interface the Bridge pattern defines.

Thus, the Bridge pattern creates the context for the Adapter pattern. I can eliminate the Adapter pattern as a candidate for seniormost pattern.

The Relationship Between Context and Used By

Often it seems that when one pattern uses another pattern, the pattern that is used is within the context of the pattern doing the using. There are likely exceptions to this rule, but it seems to hold most of the time.

One down, two to go   Now I only have to compare Bridge–Facade and Facade–Adapter.

I will look at the Bridge and Facade relationship first because if the Bridge turns out to be the primary pattern there as well, I do not need to consider the Adapter–Facade relationship. (Remember, I am only trying to identify the seniormost pattern at this point.)

It should be readily apparent that the same logic that applied to Bridge and Adapter also applies to Bridge and Facade:

The Bridge–Facade relationship

- I will be using the Facade pattern to simplify the V1 system's interface.

- But what will be using the new interface I create? One of the implementations of the Bridge pattern.

Therefore, the Bridge pattern creates the context for the Facade. The Bridge is the seniormost pattern.

The Bridge is the winner

According to Alexander, I am supposed to start with the whole. Going back to the beginning, I find that I do not yet have the context for the Bridge.

Thinking in Patterns: Step 2b

So I retrace the design steps until I come to the context in which the Bridge pattern shows up. I want to build a system that translates CAD/CAM models into an NC set (the instructions to build the part) to give to a machine so that the part described by the model can be built (see Figure 13-3).

The problem stated as a whole

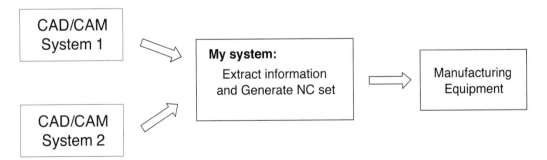

Figure 13-3 High-level view of system.

The expanded design   Of course, I had expanded this design by noting that I could use object-oriented design techniques to have the expert system use a **Model** class to get its information. **Model** would have two versions, one for each of the CAD/CAM systems, as shown in Figure 13-4.

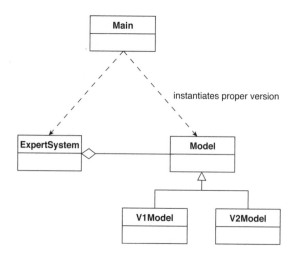

Figure 13-4 The classes to generate the NC set.

Expanding the design   Remember, I am not concerned about the design of the expert system. Although interesting (and, in many ways more challenging), that design had already been worked out. My focus is on the design of the **Model**. I know that **Model** consists of **Feature**s, as shown in Figure 13-5.[2]

Ready for the Bridge   Now I am ready for the Bridge pattern. It is apparent that I have multiple **Feature**s (the abstraction) with multiple CAD/CAM systems (the implementations). These are the objects that set the context for the Bridge pattern.

*How do we handle the **Model**?*   The Bridge pattern relates the **Feature**s to the different CAD/CAM system implementations. The **Feature** class is the **Abstraction** in

---

2. The differences between **V1Model** and **V2Model** present little difficulty. Therefore, I only discuss **Model** in general.

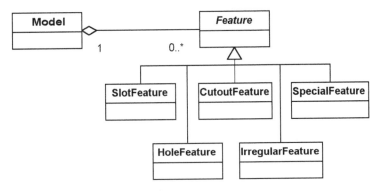

Figure 13-5 The Model design.

the Bridge pattern, whereas the V1 and V2 systems are the
Implementations. But what about the **Model**? Is there a Bridge
pattern present here as well? Not really. I can build the **Model** using
inheritance because the only thing about the **Model** that varies is the
implementation that is being used. In this case, I could make derivations of the **Model** for each CAD/CAM system, as in Figure 13-6.
If I tried using a Bridge pattern for the **Model**, I'd get the design
shown in Figure 13-7.

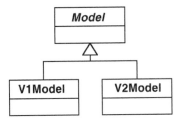

Figure 13-6 Using inheritance to handle the two model types.

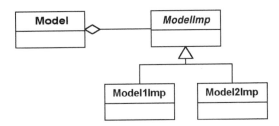

Figure 13-7 Using the Bridge pattern to handle the two model types.

Note that I do not really have a Bridge pattern in Figure 13-7 because **Model** is not varying except for the implementation. Or, at least, it is a degenerate sort of Bridge in that there is only one concrete **Model**. In the **Feature**, I have different types of **Feature**s that have different types of implementations—a Bridge pattern does exist here.

Start with the generic form

I start implementing the Bridge pattern by using **Feature** as the abstraction and using V1 and V2 as the basis for the implementations. To translate the problem into the Bridge pattern, I start with the standard example of the Bridge pattern and then substitute classes into it. Figure 13-8 shows the generic structure (sometimes called the *canonical form*).

…and map classes into it

In the problem, **Feature** maps to **Abstraction**. There are five different kinds of features: slot, hole, cutout, irregular, and special. The implementations are the V1 and V2 systems; I choose to name the classes responsible for these implementations **V1Imp** and **V2Imp**, respectively.

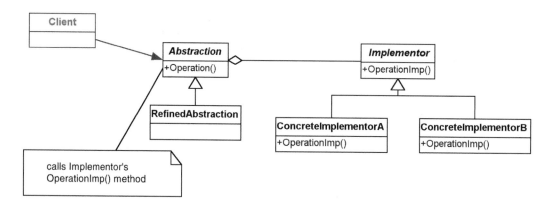

Figure 13-8 The generic structure of the Bridge pattern.

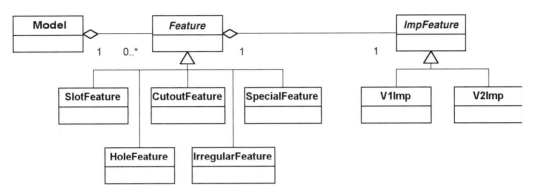

Figure 13-9 Applying the Bridge pattern to the problem.

Substituting the classes into the canonical Bridge pattern gives Figure 13-9.

In Figure 13-9, the **Feature**s are being implemented by an **ImpFeature**, which is either a **V1Imp** or a **V2Imp**. In this design, **ImpFeature** would have to have an interface that allowed for **Feature** to get whatever information it needed to give **Model** the information it requested. Thus, **ImpFeature** would have an interface including methods such as these:

- *getX* to get the X position of **Feature**

- *getY* to get the Y position of **Feature**

- *getLength* to get the length of **Feature**

It would also have methods used by only some **Feature**s:

- *getEdgeType* to get the type of edge of **Feature**

Note: Only features that need this information should call this method. Later I talk about how to use this contextual information to help debug the code.

Thinking in Patterns: Step 2c

Not done yet

Maybe I cannot see how to finish the implementation yet, but that is okay. I still have other patterns to apply.

Identifying any additional patterns

Looking at Figure 13-9, I should ask myself whether any other patterns show up that I had not previously identified. I do not see any additional patterns. There is only the challenge of hooking the V1 and V2 CAD/CAM systems into the design. That is what the Facade and Adapter patterns will do for me.

Patterns help me see possibilities

Here is another benefit from using patterns: I can start to see the possibilities for reuse and flexibility that would never have been apparent to me when I was enmeshed in the details. For example, using the Bridge pattern, I note that at some level, the V1 and V2 systems are now interchangeable—at least, they appear to be the same to the feature objects that use them. In my earlier, weaker design, it was probably still true, but I didn't see it. This flexibility was hidden by the details. The pattern approach helped me more clearly to see the potential.

Thinking in Patterns: Steps 2a and 2b Repeated (Facade)

Do the remaining patterns create a context for each other?

Next I need to verify whether any of the remaining patterns create a context for each other. In this case, Facade and Adapter now clearly relate to different pieces of the design and are independent of each other. Therefore, I can apply them in whatever order I choose. I will arbitrarily pick the Facade to apply next, which results in Figure 13-10.

The Facade

Applying the Facade pattern means that I insert a Facade between the V1 modules and the **V1Imp** object that is going to use them. **V1Facade** has simplified methods that relate to what **V1Imp** needs to do. Each method in **V1Facade** will look like a series of function calls on the V1 system.

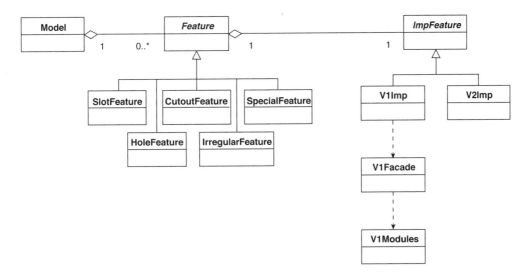

Figure 13-10 After applying the Bridge and Facade patterns.

The kind of information that I need to call these functions will determine how **V1Imp** is implemented. For example, when using V1, I need to tell it which model to use and what the **Feature**'s ID is. All **V1Imp** objects that use the **V1Facade** will therefore need to know this information. Because this is implementation-specific information, it will need to know it itself, instead of getting it from the calling **Feature**. Therefore, in a V1 system, each **Feature** will need its own **V1Imp** object (to remember system-specific information about the feature). I go over this in more detail after the general architecture has been completed.

Thinking in Patterns: Steps 2a and 2b Repeated (Adapter)

Having applied Facade, I can now apply Adapter. This results in Figure 13-11.

Pick Adapter next

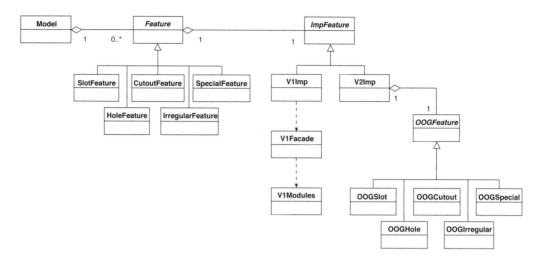

Figure 13-11 After applying the Bridge, Facade, and Adapter.

Thinking in Patterns: Steps 2a and 2b Repeated (Abstract Factory)

Finally, do Abstract Factory

All that is left is the Abstract Factory. As it turns out, this pattern is not needed. The rationale for using an Abstract Factory was to ensure that all the implementation objects were of type **V1** if I had a V1 system or of type **V2** if I had a V2 system. However, the **Model** object itself will know this. There is no point implementing a pattern if some other object can easily encapsulate the rules of creation. I left the Abstract Factory in the set of patterns because while I was first solving this problem I did think the Abstract Factory was present. It also illustrates how thinking that a pattern is present when it is not is not necessarily counterproductive.

Thinking in Patterns: Step 3

Finishing the rest

The details of the design may still take some work. However, I would continue with the design by following Alexander's mandate of designing by context. For example, when I see how I need to implement a **SlotFeature** class or the **V1Imp** class, I should remember how the patterns involved are used. In this case, I note that in the Bridge pattern, the methods involving the abstractions are independent of implementation. This means that the **Abstraction** class (**Feature**) and all of its derivations (**SlotFeature**, **HoleFeature**, and so forth) contain no implementation information. Implementation information is left to the **Implementation** classes.

This means the **Feature** subclasses will have methods such as *getLocation* and *getLength*, whereas the **Implementation**s will contain a way to access this required information. A **V1Imp** object, for example, would need to know the ID of the **Feature** in the V1 system. Because each **Feature** has a unique ID, this means there will be one **Implementation** object for each **Feature** object. The methods in the **V1Imp** object will use this ID to ask the **V1Facade** for information about the object.

Assigning responsibilities

A comparable solution will exist for the V2 implementations. In this case, the **V2Imp** objects will contain a reference to the **OOGFeature** in question.

Comparison with the Previous Solution

Compare this new solution, shown in Figure 13-11, with the earlier solution, which is shown again in Figure 13-12.

Comparing solutions

Another way to compare two solutions is to *read* them. In other words, the diagrams visually show inheritance (the *is-a* relationship) and composition (the *has-a* relationship). Read these diagrams using those words where the relationships are present.

A different way to compare solutions

In the original solution, I had a model that contains **Feature**s. **Feature**s are either slot features, hole features, cutout features, irregular features, or special features. Slot features are either V1 slots or V2 slots. V1 slots use the V1 system, whereas the V2 slots use **OOGSlot**. Hole features are either V1 hole features or V2 hole features.

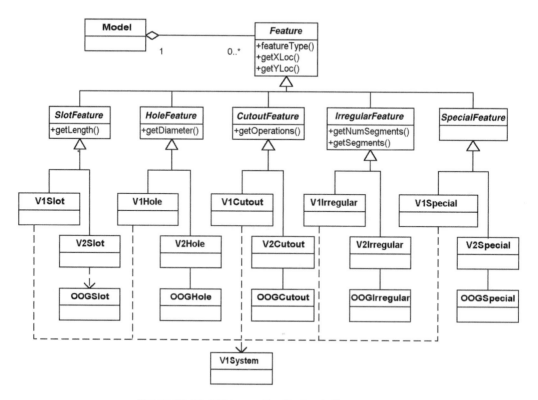

Figure 13-12 This was the first solution.

V1 hole features use the V1 system, whereas the V2 hole features use **OOGHole**. Getting tired of this already, aren't you?

Now read the latest solution. I have a model that contains **Feature**s. **Feature**s are either slot features, hole features, cutout features, irregular features, or special features. All features contain an implementation that is either a V1 implementation or a V2 implementation. V1 implementations use a V1 Facade to access the V1 system, whereas V2 implementations adapt an **OOGFeature**. That's it. It sounds much better than just a portion of the other solution.

And, of course, one has to compare what will happen in each design when the anticipated V3 system comes out. In the previous design,

I would have to derive a new slot, hole, and so on for the new system. In the current design, I just create a new adapter (assuming V3 will be object oriented, which is a fair bet).

Summary

In this chapter, I showed how the standard way of doing designs can often lock us into systems that are hard to maintain. Often it can be difficult to see the forest for the trees, because I become overly focused on the details of the system—the classes.

In this chapter

Christopher Alexander gives us a better way. By using patterns in the problem domain, I can look at the problem in a different way. I start with the big picture and add distinctions as I go. Each pattern gives me more information than what I had before I used it.

By selecting the pattern that creates the biggest picture—the context for the system—and then inserting the next significant pattern, I developed an application architecture that I could not have seen by looking at the classes alone. Thus I begin to learn to design by context instead of by putting together pieces that were identified locally.

Like the two carpenters in Chapter 5 who were trying to decide between a dovetail joint and a miter joint, it is the context that should shape the design. In design decisions, we often get bogged down by the details and forget about the larger context of the system. The details cast a cloud around the bigger picture by focusing us on small, local decisions. Patterns give you the language to rise above the details and bring the context into the discussion in practical ways. This makes it more likely that you will see the forces present in the problem domain. Patterns help us apply what other designers before us have learned about what does and does not work. In so doing, they help to create systems that are robust, maintainable, and alive.

Review Questions

Observations

1. What are the three steps of software design with patterns that the authors use?

2. Define *context*.

3. Define *seniormost pattern*.

4. When comparing two patterns, what are the two rules for discerning which pattern might be "seniormost"?

5. Define *generic structure* of a pattern. When is it used?

Interpretations

1. Can a problem always be defined in terms of patterns? If not, what else is needed?

2. In the CAD/CAM problem, the Abstract Factory was rejected as the "seniormost" pattern. What were the reasons for this?

3. In the CAD/CAM problem, what were the reasons for labeling Bridge as senior to Adapter?

Opinions and Applications

1. After all the patterns have been applied, there are still likely to be more details. Alexander's general rules (design by starting with the context) still apply. Does this ever stop? Is there ever a time when you should go ahead and dive into the details? Isn't that what "rapid prototyping" suggests? How can you avoid this temptation that all programmers have? Should you?

2. Compare the first solution to the CAD/CAM problem (Figure 13-12) with the new version (Figure 13-11). What do you like better about the new design?

PART V

Toward a New Paradigm of Design

Part Overview

Although patterns are useful in their own right, the lessons learned from them can be used to create a different approach to designing application architectures from one that focuses on specialization or identifying the nouns and verbs of the problem domain. In this part, I discuss the way I now design application architectures based on the lessons I have learned from design patterns.

In this part

Chapter	Discusses These Topics
14	**The Principles and Strategies of Design Patterns** We have learned enough about patterns now to formulate an approach that is consistent with the lessons of design patterns.
15	**Commonality and Variability Analysis** In this chapter, I put forward a strategy to design application architectures by identifying and encapsulating variation.
16	**The Analysis Matrix** How to perform CVA in the real world so that the relationships can be more easily identified and implemented.
17	**The Decorator Pattern** Illustration of how patterns should not be taken too literally. Implementation approaches of the past are not the pattern. The thought process that led to them is more useful.
18	**The Design Implications of Patterns** Designing our system to contain variations and relate only to the concepts in our problem domain has significant and useful implications. I discuss these here.

CHAPTER 14

The Principles and Strategies of Design Patterns

Overview

Previously I described how design patterns can be used at both the local and global levels. At the local level, patterns tell us how to solve particular problems for a given context. At the global level, patterns create a map of how the components of the application interrelate with one another.

In this chapter

One way to study design patterns is to learn how to apply them more effectively at both levels. They will indeed help you produce better, more maintainable code based on the experience of others.

Another way to study design patterns is to learn their essential mechanisms and the principles and strategies that underlie them. Learning these will improve your abilities as an analyst and designer. You will know what to do even in situations where a design pattern has not yet been discovered, because you will already have the underlying concepts needed to solve the problem in the way that a pattern would. In effect, you are trying to learn the mindset that the developers had when they solved the problems that were later identified as patterns.

This chapter

- Describes the open-closed principle, which underlies many design patterns.

- Discusses the principle of designing from context, which is the objective of Alexander's patterns. In doing so, I will describe the dependency inversion principle and the Liskov substitution principle,[1] two further cornerstones of design patterns.

• Discusses the principle of encapsulating variation.

• Discusses the difference between abstract classes and interfaces.

• Closes with a discussion about the need to maintain a healthy skepticism about patterns. They are very helpful guides, but are not "truth."

The Open-Closed Principle

Extend software's capabilities without changing it

Software clearly needs to be extensible. However, making changes to software runs the risk of introducing problems. This dilemma led Bertrand Meyer to propose the *open-closed principle* (OCP).[2] To paraphrase this principle, the modules, methods, and classes should be *open* for extension, while *closed* for modification.[3] In other words, design your software so that you can extend its capabilities without changing it.

As contradictory as this may sound at first, you have already seen examples of it. In the Bridge pattern, for instance, it is quite possible to add new implementations (that is, to extend the software) without changing any of the existing classes. In essence, the open-closed principle means to design our software so new functionality can be added in separate, distinct modules, with the integration cost being minimal.

It's usually not possible to follow the open-closed principle completely; but as a goal, it is the right thing to be aiming for. The more my code follows the OCP, the easier my life will be later on when I have to accommodate new (and perhaps unforeseen) requirements.

---

1. I did not name these principles, but believe me, they are easier to understand than they sound.

2. Meyer, B., *Object-Oriented Software Construction*, Upper Saddle River, NJ: Prentice Hall, 1997, p. 57.

3. See this book's Web site at *http://www.netobjectives.com/dpexplained* for a link to *The Open-Closed Principle*, an excellent article by Robert C. Martin.

The Principle of Designing from Context

Alexander tells us to design from context, to create the big picture before designing the details in which our pieces appear. Most design patterns follow this approach, some to a greater extent than others. Of the four patterns I have described so far, the Bridge pattern is the best example of this.

Patterns are microcosms of Alexander's philosophy

Refer to the Bridge pattern diagram in Chapter 10, "The Bridge Pattern" (see Figure 10-13). When deciding how to design the interface of the **Implementation** classes, I think about their context: the way that the classes derived from the **Abstraction** class will use them.

For example, if I were writing a system that needed to draw shapes on different types of hardware and that therefore required different implementations, I would use a Bridge pattern. The Bridge suggests that the shapes will use my implementations (that is, the drawing programs I will write) through a common interface. Designing from context, as Alexander would have me do, means that I should first look at the requirements of my shapes—that is, what am I going to have to draw? These shapes will determine the required behaviors for my implementations. For example, the implementations (the drawing programs) may have to draw lines, circles, and so forth. In other words, even though the concrete abstractions (the different shapes) *depend* upon the concrete implementations (the drawing programs), it is the shapes that define the drawing programs. I start with a service-orientation, asking "What kinds of services do we provide?" Because I am defining from the needs of the **Abstraction** class (and its derivations), I must define the services at an abstract level. When developing the interface for the implementation, I consider the needs of the concepts that are being expressed in the concrete abstractions, rather than just the specific cases in front of me.

*Dependency
inversion principle:
Depend on the
abstractions!*

This is called the "dependency inversion principle":

- High-level modules should not depend on low-level modules. Both high-level modules and low-level modules should depend upon abstractions.

- Abstractions should not depend on details. Details should depend upon abstractions.[4]

Christopher Alexander called this "complexification"—the process of starting at the simplest (conceptual) level and gradually adding details and features, making the design more complex as you go deeper. Complexification/dependency inversion is a central principle underlying the use of design patterns.

This principle implies that the coupling between the using objects and the used objects is done at a conceptual level, not at the implementation level, much as the Gang of Four was suggesting when they said we should "design to interfaces." This allows for new services and new client objects in the relationship with much greater ease than if detailed knowledge of how the services were provided were available.

*Advantages to
designing from
context*

I will spend some time trying to identify the general cases and the variations I am likely to encounter. I do this by considering the context within which my classes occur and using a technique called *commonality and variability analysis* (CVA). I describe this technique in detail in Chapter 15, "Commonality and Variability Analysis." This helps me decide how generalized I want to make the implementations based on the cost of extra generalization. This often leads to a more general implementation than I would have thought of otherwise, but with only marginally higher cost.

---

4. Martin, B. *Agile Software Development: Principles, Patterns, and Practices,* Upper Saddle River, N.J.: Prentice Hall, 2003, p. 127.

For example, when looking at my needs to draw shapes, I might readily identify lines and circles as requirements. If I ask myself, "What shapes do I not support with lines and circles?" I might notice that I would not be able to implement ellipses. Now I have a choice:

- Implement a way to draw ellipses in addition to the lines and circles.

- Realize that ellipses are a generalized case of circles and implement them instead of circles.

- Don't implement ellipses if the cost is greater than the perceived gain.

It is important when designing classes within a context that they present the same external behavior. This decouples the client classes from these implementations. It also promotes the encapsulation of type that design patterns suggest. Barbara Liskov presented a principle in 1988[5] that I will paraphrase here:

The flip side of designing by context

> *A class deriving from a base class should support all of the behavior of this base class.*

When possible, I like to extend this to make it so the using object cannot even tell that a derivation is present. In other words, given a reference to a base class (or interface), the using object cannot tell whether a derivation (or implementation) is present. This makes all such derivations (or implementations) interchangeable with each other. This would be an example of type encapsulation. In practice it means that subtypes should not add new public methods to the base type's public interface. It also means that the base type must be a complete specification of the concept being modeled.

The prior example illustrates another important concept in design:

---

5. Liskov, Barbara. *Data Abstraction and Hierarchy*, SIGPLAN Notices, 23.5 (May 1988).

Identifying opportunities doesn't mean having to follow them

Just because an opportunity exists doesn't mean it has to be pursued. My experience with design patterns is that they give me insights into my problem domains. However, I don't always (nor even usually) act on these insights by writing code for situations that have not yet arisen. However, by helping me design from context, the patterns themselves allow me to anticipate possible variation because I have divided my system into powerful, useful abstractions, thereby making changes easier to accommodate. Design patterns help me see where variations may occur, not so much which particular variations will occur. The well-defined interface I use to contain my current variations often limits the impact of new requirements just as well.[6]

The context of the Abstract Factory

The Abstract Factory is another good example of designing by context. I may understand early on that a factory object of some sort will be used to coordinate the instantiation of families (or sets) of objects. However, there are many different ways to implement it.

Implementation	Comments
Using derived classes	The classic Abstract Factory implementation suggests that I implement a derivation for each set that I need. This is a little cumbersome but has the advantage of allowing me to add new classes without changing any of my existing classes.
Using a single object with switches	If I am willing to change the Abstract Factory class as needed, I can simply have one object that contains all of the rules. Although this doesn't follow the open-closed principle fully, it does contain all of my rules in one place and is not hard to maintain.
Using a configuration file with switches	This is more flexible than the prior case, but still requires modifying the code at times.
Using a configuration file with dynamic class loading	Dynamic class loading is a way of instantiating objects based on the name of the object placed in a string. Implementations of this sort have great flexibility in that new classes and new combinations can be added without having to change any code.

6. For a deeper discussion of this issue, see Alan Shalloway's article "Can Patterns Be Harmful?" which can be found at the book's Web site *http://www.netobjectives. com/dpexplained*. This is also a good article to give to someone who wants an easy introduction to what design patterns are.

With all of these choices, how do you decide which one to use to implement the Abstract Factory? Decide from the context in which it appears. Each of the four cases just shown has advantages over the others, depending upon factors such as

How to decide? From the context

- The likelihood of future variation

- The importance of not modifying our current system

- Who controls the sets of objects to be created (us or another development group)

- The language in use (e.g., C++, C#, Java)

- The availability of a database or configuration file

This list of issues is not complete. Neither is the list of implementation possibilities. What should be evident, however, is that trying to decide how to implement an Abstract Factory without understanding how it will be used (that is, without understanding its context) is a fool's errand.

How to Make Design Decisions

When trying to decide between alternative implementations, many developers ask the question, "Which of these implementations is better?" This is not the best question to ask. The problem is that often one implementation is not inherently better than another. A better set of questions to ask is, for each alternative, "Under what circumstances would this alternative be better than the other alternative?" Then ask, "Which of these circumstances is most like my problem domain?" It is a small matter of stopping and stepping back. Using this approach tends to keep me more aware of the variation and scalability issues in my problem domain. It also doesn't stop the inquiry with the first, probably incomplete, answer.

The context of the Adapter

The Adapter pattern illustrates design from context because it almost always shows up within a context. By definition, an Adapter is used to convert an existing interface into another interface. The obvious question is, "How do I know what to convert the existing interface to?" You typically don't until the context is presented (that is, the class or abstraction to which you are adapting).

I have already shown that Adapters can be used to adapt a class to fit the role of a pattern that is present. This was the case in my CAD/CAM problem, where I had an existing implementation that needed to be adapted into my Bridge-driven implementation.

The context of the Facade

The Facade pattern is very similar to the Adapter pattern in terms of context. Typically, it is defined in the context of other patterns or classes. That is, I must wait until I can see who wants to use the Facade to design its interface. In fact, the interface of a Facade is often developed incrementally, as I build more and more of the system that uses it, and as each new part of the system establishes a richer context for the Facade.

A word of warning

Early on in my use of patterns I tended to think I could always find which patterns created context for others. In Alexander's *A Pattern Language*, he is able to do just that with patterns in architecture. Because many people are talking about pattern languages for software, I wondered, "Why can't I?" It seems pretty clear that Adapters and Facades would always be defined in the context of something else. Right?

Wrong.

One great advantage of being a software developer who also teaches is that I have the opportunity to get involved in many more projects than I could possibly be involved in as a developer only. Early in my teachings of design patterns I thought Adapters and Facades would always come after other noncreational patterns in the order of defining context. In fact, they usually do. However, some systems have the requirement of building to a particular interface. In this case, it is a Facade or an Adapter (just one of many in the system, of course) that may be the seniormost pattern.

The Principle of Encapsulating Variation

Several people have remarked about a certain similarity in all the designs they have seen me create: My inheritance hierarchies rarely go more than two levels of classes deep. Those that do go deeper typically fit into a design pattern structure that requires two levels as a base for the derived classes. (The Decorator pattern, discussed in Chapter 17, is an example that uses three levels.) Where I do have multiple levels of inheritance, it's almost always because I am trying to eliminate some kind of redundancy. (Again, with the Decorator pattern, the abstract **Decorator** class exists to keep the relationship from the decorators to the decorated in one place.)

A note on my designs

The reason for this is that one of my design goals is never to have a class contain two issues that are varying unless these variations are explicitly coupled to each other (e.g., implementation methods of a database). To do so would weaken cohesion and not allow loose coupling between the variations. The patterns I have described so far do illustrate different ways of encapsulating variation effectively.

The Bridge pattern is an excellent example of encapsulated variation. The implementations present in the Bridge pattern are all different but are accessed through a common interface. New implementations can be accommodated by implementing them within this interface.

Encapsulating variation in the Bridge pattern

The Abstract Factory encapsulates the variation of which sets or families of objects can be instantiated. There are many different ways of implementing this pattern. It is useful to note that even if one implementation is initially chosen and then it is determined another way would have been better, the implementation can be changed

Encapsulating variation in the Abstract Factory

without affecting any other part of the system (because the interface for the factory does not change, only the way it is implemented). Thus, the notion of the Abstract Factory itself (implementing to an interface) hides all the variations of how to create the objects.

Using the Adapter pattern to help encapsulate variation

The Adapter pattern is a tool to be used to take disparate objects and give them a common interface. This is often needed now that I am designing to interfaces as called for in many patterns.

Encapsulating variation in the Facade pattern

The Facade typically does not encapsulate variation. However, I have seen many cases where a Facade was used to work with a particular subsystem. Then, when another subsystem came along, a Facade for the new subsystem was built with the same interface. This new class was a combination Facade and Adapter in that the primary motivation was simplification, but now had the added constraint of being the same as the one used before so none of the client objects would need to change. Using a Facade this way hides variations in the subsystems being used.

Not just about encapsulating variation

Patterns are not just about encapsulating variation, however. They also help to identify relationships between objects and assist us in thinking about the essential concepts in the problem domain. Referring to the Bridge pattern again, note that the pattern not only defines and encapsulates the variations in the abstraction and implementation, but also defines the relationship between the two sets of variations.

Abstract Classes vs. Interfaces

Abstract classes and interfaces at a superficial level

One difference between abstract classes and interfaces is that abstract classes allow for common state and behavior. That is, if all the derived classes have some common state or behavior, this can be put in the abstract class. Making a distinction between these approaches is particularly important for languages such as Java and C# where you can derive from only one class. In other words, do not use an abstract class when you do not need to because you only get one shot at deriving from a class.

There is another way to think of the difference between these two mechanisms of getting polymorphism that is more useful to the designer. This exists within the context of the principles mentioned earlier in this chapter. Abstract classes can be viewed as a way to bring together related entities. The focus is on how these concrete items (the derived classes) should be designed to be used in the same way. In other words, how to take these implementations and encapsulate them. The focus here can still very much follow the dependency inversion principle: Look at the service objects (the implementations) and see how to abstract them so that the using object does not get coupled to any implementation-specific details.

Abstract classes compared to interfaces at a design level

To use interfaces in this way, during design you will want to ask, "What is the interface these things must have in common if they are going to be used in the same way?"

But there is another thought process you must include; it centers on the object(s) that will be using these derivations/implementations. That is, what interface should the service objects have to be able to work best with the contextual/controlling object? In the e-commerce example used earlier, the question would be, "What interface should the tax objects have to be able to work best with a **SalesOrder** object?" This goes one step beyond the dependency inversion principle.

By *starting* with the client object, you can differentiate the "used" objects into smaller, more cohesive pieces. In other words, if the using object requires many different types of objects (i.e., several abstractions), you can come up with an interface for each type. The result is more concise (thinner) interfaces than might result otherwise.[7]

---

7. I believe this approach is very much related to generic programming and aspect-oriented programming. However, these topics are beyond the scope of this book. See Chapter 25 for more information on these areas.

One is not better than the other

Interfaces are not better than abstract classes just because they appear to align more with the dependency inversion principle or because they might result in thinner interfaces.

- You might very well develop an interface this way and then use an abstract class because the objects you have defined have some common state/behavior that would otherwise be redundant in the implementing classes.

- You might also come up with an interface and have an abstract class implement that interface.

- An abstract class can establish default behavior, which can make the implementation classes simpler and easier to maintain.

This allows objects with the common state/behavior to derive from this abstract class while objects that don't share this state/behavior directly (or are required to derive from some other class for other reasons) implement the interface.

The Principle of Healthy Skepticism

Patterns are useful guides but dangerous crutches

Pattern-based analysis has been used in many disciplines. In my field of anthropology and knowledge engineering, analysts have developed some important lessons into problems that analysts can have with patterns. The patterns are useful as far as they go, but use them only as a help to your thinking and not as a prescription for a solution. I cannot stress this enough.

Meta-level patterns and models are not truth. They are abstractions of truth. They are distillations of experience and lessons learned. They must be instantiated with real-world data. The danger of patterns includes the following:

This Error	Happens When the Analyst
Superficiality	Is too quick to select a pattern based on a superficial understanding of the lower-level situation.
Bias	Assigns too much credibility to the pattern. He begins to interpret all of the data through the pattern/model that he has selected. He is unwilling to keep questioning his biases.
Selection	Doesn't understand the context and conditions that define when a pattern is appropriate (has a faulty understanding of the taxonomy of patterns). The wrong pattern can be selected.
Misdiagnosis	Is not familiar with the entire collection of patterns and so may make a misdiagnosis through ignorance.
Fit	Ignores exceptions in the behavior of actual, concrete instances because they don't seem to fit the theory expressed in the pattern. The analyst risks causing the objects/individuals being modeled to be stiffer than they really are.

It is also important to remember that the patterns are discoveries, not inventions. The pattern that is "right" for your problem is *in* the problem, not something to be imposed upon it. The specific way a pattern should be implemented, similarly, should be dictated by the nature of the problem, its constraints, requirements, etc., not based on an implementation you happened to have run across in a patterns book.

Summary

In this chapter, I have shown how patterns illustrate two powerful design strategies: *In this chapter*

- Design from context
- Encapsulate variations in classes

These strategies enable us to defer decisions until we can see the ramifications of these decisions. Looking at the context from which we are designing gives us better designs.

By encapsulating variation, I can accommodate many future variations that may arise but would not be accommodated when I do not try to make my designs more general purpose. This is critical for those projects that do not have all of the resources you would like to have (in other words, all projects). By encapsulating variation appropriately, I can implement only those features I need without sacrificing future quality. Trying to figure out and accommodate all possible variations typically does not lead to better systems, but often leads to no system at all. This is called paralysis by analysis.

Principle	Description
Open-closed principle	Modules, methods, and classes should be *open* for extension while closed for modification. In other words, design your software so that you can extend its capabilities without changing it.
Dependency inversion principle	Based on the idea that you should create the big picture before designing the details. High-modules should not depend on low-level modules. Instead, both of them should depend upon abstractions.
Healthy skepticism	Be careful of over-relying on patterns. Meta-level patterns and models are abstractions of truth. They are distillations of experience and lessons learned. Use them to help you think about the problem before you.

Review Questions

Observations

1. When it comes to choosing how to implement a design, what question should you ask?

2. What are five possible errors in using design patterns. Can you state them?

Interpretations

1. The "open-closed" principle says, "modules, methods, and classes should be open for extension while closed for modification." What does this mean?

2. In what way does the Bridge pattern illustrate the open-closed principle?

Opinions and Applications

1. Even though a design pattern might give you insights into what could happen, you do not have to build your code to handle those possibilities. How do you decide which possibilities to handle now and which to be ready for in the future?

2. Give a concrete example of the danger of misapplying a design pattern, based upon your current work

CHAPTER 15

Commonality and Variability Analysis

Overview

This chapter shows how to use *commonality and variability analysis* (CVA) to develop a high-level application design. Although design patterns can't be used in all designs, the lessons learned from them can. One of the most important of these lessons is that you can identify variation in your system using CVA. You can then follow the lessons of design patterns (program to interfaces, encapsulate variation using aggregation) to create designs that are flexible and easily testable.

In this chapter

Commonality and Variability Analysis and Application Design

Experienced developers know that when adding new function to an existing system, the major cost is often not in writing the new code, but in integrating it into the existing system. The reason for this is that the pieces in most existing systems are fairly tightly coupled. We must eliminate, or greatly limit, this coupling. One reason this occurs is that developers often consider how entities relate to each other before they are clear what the right entities are. From my experience of training people at all different levels of competency, I have come to the conclusion that more experienced developers do this even more than inexperienced developers. Developers need a way first to identify what they have before trying to find the relationships involved.

Isolating variation is a design pattern philosophy

I suggest that you design applications in the following way: First, use CVA to identify the concepts (commonalities) and concrete implementations (variabilities) that are present in the problem domain. At this point we are mostly interested in identifying the concepts here, but many variabilities will be identified as part of this process. Any entities in the problem domain that are not included in these concepts (e.g., there may be some one-of-a-kind objects present) should also be identified. Then, after the concept for the functionality you need has been identified, you go on to specify the interface for the abstraction that encapsulates this. Derive this interface by considering how the concrete implementations derived from this abstraction will be used.

This approach basically follows Alexander's contextual design approach, which is incorporated into the previously mentioned dependency inversion principle. By defining these interfaces, you are also determining which object uses which objects—completing the specification of the design.

Let's see this in action with the CAD/CAM problem.

Solving the CAD/CAM Problem with CVA

Finding the concepts (and therefore abstract classes)

When analyzing the problem domain with CVA, I want to see what concepts are there and then try to organize these pieces as cohesively as possible. Remembering the CAD/CAM system, there are

- **Different CAD/CAM systems**—V1, V2. In this situation, these are essentially read-only, proprietary databases that will provide the numeric control sets the expert system needs to do its work.

- **Different kinds of Features**—Slots, holes, cutouts, special and irregular.

- **Different kinds of Models**—V1-based and V2-based.

To say there are different CAD/CAM systems really means that the concept is "CAD/CAM system" and the variations of it are V1 and V2. CVA leads to the following commonalities and their corresponding variations.

Table 15-1 Commonality and Variability Analysis Table

This Commonality	Has These Variations
CAD/CAM system	V1
	V2
Features	slot
	hole
	cutout
	special
	irregular
Model	V1-based
	V2-based

An alternative approach is to pick any two items in the problem domain and ask the following questions:

Is one of these a variation of the other?

Are both of these a variation of something else?

For example, I might notice that there are features and slots. A slot is a kind of feature. I guess that "features" is a commonality and "slots" is a variation of it. Or, I might see that there are slots and holes. Within this problem domain, they do not seem to be variations of each other. They both seem to be variations of "features." Or I might compare the V1 CAD/CAM system and slots. There does not seem to be anything in common with them.

One issue per commonality

Of course, it is not always this simple. I may collapse concepts without realizing it. For example, suppose you think about the problem domain as having **V1Slot**s, **V1Hole**s, **V2Slot**s, **V2Hole**s, etc. The commonality would seem to be "CAD/CAM features." But this is commonality with two concepts: "CAD/CAM version" and "features." CVA says that commonalities should really be based on one issue per commonality. Otherwise I will not have strong cohesion in my design. Recognizing that I have two commonalities, CAD/CAM and features, should lead me to ask which variations of these commonalities do I have? When I do this I come up with the variations I listed in Table 15-1. This is one of the values of CVA: It results in cohesive concepts.

Representing the concepts

Figure 15-1 is a reproduction of Figure 6-5.

The information in Table 15-1 can be translated into three different class hierarchies by following the guidelines laid out in Figure 15-1. These are shown in Figure 15-2.

Relating the concepts

The next step involves determining how the concepts relate to each other. Models contain **Feature**s and **Feature**s are extracted from the CAD/CAM system. When I was designing this system, I thought

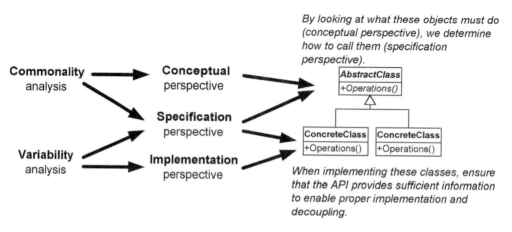

Figure 15-1 The relationship between commonality and variability analysis, perspectives, and abstract classes.

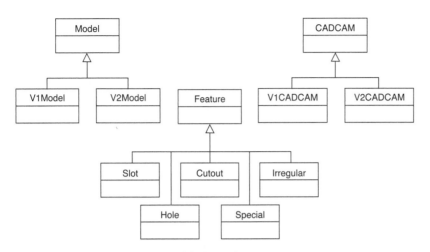

Figure 15-2 Translating CVA table into classes.

it would be simpler if I built standalone **Feature**s that contained all the information that had been in the CAD/CAM system that related to them. In other words, the CAD/CAM system was like a database to the Features; it contained the information about the **Feature**s. The **Feature**s presented the appropriate methods to make this information available, but the **Feature**s extracted this info from the CAD/CAM to get it. Models would also have to relate to the CAD/CAM system. Based on this analysis, the next level of detail is shown in Figure 15-3.

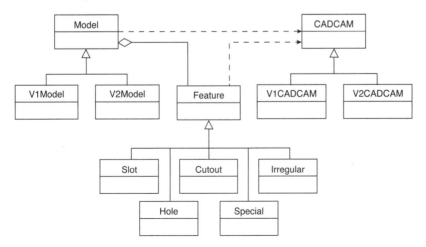

Figure 15-3 Our class diagram showing relationships between the classes.

I am faced with a design decision here. Do I want to have different types of models or have one type of model that uses the different CAD/CAM systems through the **CADCAM** interface? In other words, if I move the methods in **V1Model** and **V2Model** that are peculiar to the CAD/CAM system into the **CADCAM** class hierarchy, I can probably avoid having different types of **Model**s. This approach seems superior because **Model**s use the CAD/CAM systems to implement them, but the concepts in **Model** are not inherently part of the CAD/CAM system. I show this approach in Figure 15-4. Don't get hung up on this distinction: There is not a great difference in code quality between the two of them so long as you make sure you do not have any redundancy. Personally, I like the solution shown in Figure 15-4 better because it has classes that are more cohesive. Therefore, I will use that for the rest of the design.

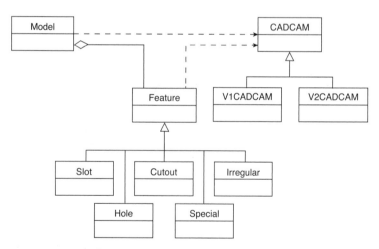

Figure 15-4 Handling variations in Models by using the CADCAM classes.

Expanding the design

I still need to expand the design to relate the **CADCAM** classes to the actual V1 and V2 implementations. Recalling what we know about the Facade and Adapter patterns, it should be clear that **V1CAD-CAM** should simply be a facade to the V1 system while **V2CAD-CAM** should wrap (adapt) the V2 system (**OOG_Part**). I show this in Figure 15-5.

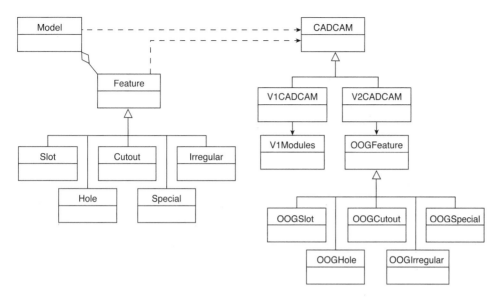

Figure 15-5 A completed design.

Contrast this with the solution arrived at using design patterns directly, shown in Figure 15-6.

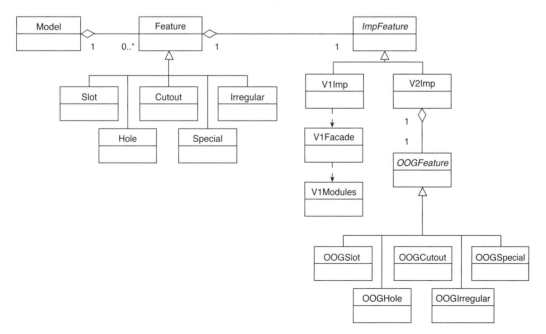

Figure 15-6 A solution using design patterns

The two look surprisingly similar. Or maybe not. The solution arrived at using design patterns was derived by using patterns in a contextual way. I applied one pattern at a time until the solution unfolded. This is very similar to the CVA approach:

1. Identify commonalities first.

2. Create abstractions from these.

3. Identify derivations with the variations of the commonalities.

4. See how the commonalities relate to each other.

This is another type of design by context. The interfaces of the classes are defined within the context of how they are used by other abstractions. The class definitions are similar in both approaches because CVA is just another way of finding what varies and encapsulating it in cohesive, loosely coupled classes (principles upon which the design patterns are based). The same principles and approaches therefore lead to remarkably similar solutions.

In truth, the two approaches are highly synergistic. CVA says to focus on abstractions early, which increases the probability that I will find the most useful ones. Design patterns focus on the relationships between those abstractions, but do not help identify those abstractions in the first place.

On the other hand design patterns allow me to apply specific insights from past successful designs, whereas CVA does not. For example, I know it is often desirable to keep Facades stateless due to the fact that they tend to be large, and so creating multiple instances can affect performance. Pulling the state needed by the features out of the Facade and placing it in the Adapter allows me to implement the Facade as a Singleton. CVA would not lead me to that conclusion.

Summary

I explained how CVA can be used to create high-level application designs. By defining our commonalities first, we eliminate coupling between our special cases. Because design patterns are really about isolating variations and commonality and variability analysis (used the way I described) does the same thing, we can get similar solutions with CVA that we get using design patterns. The advantage of the CVA approach, however, is that it can be used all the time. We can only design with patterns when we know the patterns involved. Something that my experience shows doesn't happen that often.

In this chapter

Review Questions

Observations

1. What are two approaches to identifying commonalities and variabilities?

Interpretations

1. CVA says you should have only one issue per commonality. Why is this important?

2. How do CVA and design patterns complement each other?

Opinions and Applications

1. Experienced developers, even more than inexperienced ones, often focus on entity relationships too early, before they are clear what the right entities are. Is that your experience? Give an example to confirm or refute this statement.

2. Relate the approach to design starting with CVA with Alexander's approach.

CHAPTER 16

The Analysis Matrix

Overview

This chapter concludes the e-commerce case study discussed earlier in Chapter 9, "The Strategy Pattern."

In this chapter

Now that I have discussed an entire set of individual patterns, it is time to step back to look at one of the biggest problems in software development: handling variation within the problem domain. Design patterns can help analysts identify and organize variations successfully.

This chapter

- Considers the problem of variation in the real world.

- Looks at a portion of the e-commerce case study that represents significant problems of variation. In the process of solving this problem, I develop the analysis matrix, a simple variant on decision tables that I have found helpful to understand and coordinate variation in concepts. There is a parallel between this and the concepts of Christopher Alexander and Jim Coplein.

- Describes my use of the analysis matrix in the real world.

In the Real World: Variations

In the real world, problems are not tidy or well behaved. Except in the most trivial problems, there always seem to be exceptions and variations that are not well organized. They are the "gotchas" that rise up to wreck our finely crafted models.

More variation in the real world

For example, patients coming to a hospital typically go to the admitting office first. But when there is a life-threatening situation, the patient goes directly to the emergency room before having to go to admitting. These are the variations in the real world, the different special cases that our system has to deal with.

And this is what creates headaches for us analysts. Can patterns help us deal with variation more efficiently?

I have used an approach to make explicit the variations in the system and then use this analysis to identify the patterns I should consider using in my design. The steps in my approach are as follows:

1. Identify the most important features in a particular scenario and organize them in a matrix. Label each feature with the concept that the feature represents.

2. Proceed through other scenarios, expanding the matrix as necessary. Handle each scenario independently of the others.

3. Expand the analysis matrix with new concepts.

4. Use the rows to identify rules.

5. Use the columns to identify specific situations.

6. Identify design patterns from this analysis.

7. Develop a high-level design.

The International E-Commerce System Case Study: Handling Variation

e-commerce: A case study about variation

I now return to the case study introduced in Chapter 9, a study of an order-processing system for an international e-commerce company in the United States. This system must be able to process sales orders in many different countries. In this chapter, I want to consider techniques for handling variation.

Initially, the requirements are easy: process orders only in the United States and Canada. Here is the initial list of features that the system must handle, in no particular order:

- Build a sales order system for Canada and the United States.

- Calculate freight based on the country we're in.

- Money will also be handled in the currency of the country we are in.

- In the United States, tax will be calculated by the locale.

- Use U.S. postal rules for verifying addresses.

- In Canada, use FedEx for Canada shipping and use Government Sales Tax (GST) and Provincial Sales Tax (PST) for tax.

The first thing I want to do is to separate the requirements into the two scenarios presented:

- When the customer is in the United States

- When the customer is in Canada

I note these in Table 16-1.

Table 16-1 Different Scenarios Depending Upon Residence of Customer

Case	Procedure
United States	Calculate freight based on UPS charges
	Use U.S. postal rules for verifying addresses
	Calculate tax based on sales and/or services depending upon locale
	Handle money in U.S. dollars
Canada	Handle money in Canadian dollars
	Use Canadian postal rules for verifying addresses
	Ship via FedEx to Canada
	Calculate tax based on sales and/or services depending upon Canadian province taxing rules (using GST and PST)

…to illustrate the analysis matrix technique

The variations presented in this problem are not too complicated. Just by looking, it seems obvious how to deal with them. A simple problem, yes. But it illustrates a technique for dealing with variation that I have used many times. It is a simple technique but it seems to scale well for many real-world problems. I call this the *analysis matrix*.

The Origins of the Analysis Matrix

Although the example I am describing here is pretty simple, I invented the analysis matrix in my need to solve a particularly large problem. In that problem, there were literally hundreds of cases and 50 or so variations present. I found myself not even talking to the project's analyst because I was so overwhelmed with information. Realizing that this wasn't a particularly good tack to take, I figured I needed to come up with a way to organize an overwhelming amount of data.

I created the analysis matrix as I describe it here in response to this need. At first I was just trying to organize the data. However, as you will see later in this chapter, after the problem domain has been organized around variation, it becomes easier to see how to use design patterns to create a high-level design of the application. In other words, the analysis matrix helps us both understand our problem domain, and then implement it.

---

1. Identify the most important features in one case and organize them in a matrix

At this stage, the objective is to find the *concepts* that are varying, to find points of commonality, and to uncover missing requirements. The concepts come from the specific requirements of each case. Design and implementation issues are handled in later stages.

Let's begin by looking at one case.

I look at each function that I must implement and label the concept it represents. Each function point will be put on its own line. I will put the concept it represents at the far left.

I will show this process step by step, starting with Table 16-2.

Table 16-2 Filling Out the Analysis Matrix: First Concept

	U.S. Sales
Calculate freight	Use UPS rates

Now I continue with the next piece of information, "use U.S. postal rules for verifying addresses," by adding another row to hold that piece of information, as shown in Table 16-3.

Table 16-3 Filling Out the Analysis Matrix: Second Concept

	U.S. Sales
Calculate freight	Use UPS rates
Verify address	Use U.S. postal rules

I continue through all of the concepts in the first case, as shown in Table 16-4.

Table 16-4 Filling Out the Analysis Matrix: Complete First Case—U.S. Sales

	U.S. Sales
Calculate freight	Use UPS rates
Verify address	Use U.S. postal rules
Calculate tax	Use state and local taxes
Money	U.S. dollars

Now I move to the next case and the other cases, one column per case, completing each cell with as much information as I have. I take each requirement in the order it was given to me. I do not compare one case with the other; rather, I compare the new case with the concept being handled. The important thing to remember is that I

2. Proceed through the other cases, expanding the matrix as necessary

am looking for this new cases way of handling the concept I have identified in the leftmost column.

The other thing to remember is that I am building this by first looking at relationships found with CVA. I am not looking for other relationships at this time. Let's try this out. I first add a Canadian column. See Table 16-5.

Table 16-5 The Analysis Matrix for the Next Case—Canadian Sales

	U.S. Sales	Canadian Sales
Calculate freight	Use UPS rates	
Verify address	Use U.S. postal rules	
Calculate tax	Use state and local taxes	
Money	U.S. dollars	

The first requirement I have is: *handle money in Canadian dollars.* I ask myself, what row should this go in? I realize I will use Canadian dollars in calculating freight, but Canadian dollars is not a kind of "Calculating freight," so it doesn't go on this row. I don't see any relationship between Canadian dollars and "Verify Address" so I go to the next row. "Calculate Tax" is the same as the "Calculate Freight" row; there is a relationship, but not a CVA relationship. Ah, "Money," Canadian dollars is a variation of the commonality "Money." It goes here. I show this in Table 16-6.

Table 16-6 The Analysis Matrix for the Next Case—Canadian Dollars

	U.S. Sales	Canadian Sales
Calculate freight	Use UPS rates	
Verify address	Use U.S. postal rules	
Calculate tax	Use state and local taxes	
Money	U.S. dollars	Canadian dollars

I repeat this process until I complete the table as shown in Table 16-7.

The completed matrix for the next case is in Table 16-7.

Table 16-7 The Analysis Matrix for the Next Case—Canadian Sales

	U.S. Sales	Canadian Sales
Calculate freight	Use UPS rates	Use Canadian shipper
Verify address	Use U.S. postal rules	Use Canadian postal rules
Calculate tax	Use state and local taxes	Use GST and PST
Money	U.S. dollars	Canadian dollars

Of course, it usually doesn't work out this nicely. Usually, new cases require new functionality. However, this is a good thing. It enables us to check for the completeness of our analysis. My experience with customers is that they do not give us complete requirements because they are used to thinking in terms of the normal cases, not the exceptional cases (which we have to handle).

…and look for incompleteness or inconsistencies as you go

As I build the matrix, I discover gaps in the requirements. I will use this information to expand my analysis. These inconsistencies give clues about incomplete information from the customer. That is, in one case a customer might mention some specific requirement whereas another customer did not. For example, in getting requirements for the United States, no maximum weight may have been mentioned, whereas 31.5 kilograms might have been stated for Canada. By comparing the requirements, I can fill in the holes by going back to my American contact and asking her specifically about weight limits (which, in fact, may not exist).

As time goes on we get new cases to handle (for example, we may expand into Germany). When you discover a new concept for one of the cases, add a new row even if it does not apply to any of the other cases. I illustrate this in Table 16-8.

3. Expand the analysis matrix with new concepts

Table 16-8 Expanding the Analysis Matrix

	U.S. Sales	Canadian Sales	German Sales
Calculate freight	Use UPS rates	Use Canadian shipper	Use German shipper
Verify address	Use U.S. postal rules	Use Canadian postal rules	Use German postal rules
Calculate tax	Use state and local taxes	Use GST and PST	Use German VAT
Money	U.S. dollars	Canadian dollars	German DM
Dates	mm/dd/yyyy	dd/mm/yyyy	dd/mm/yyyy
Maximum weight			30kg

Are there maximum weights in the United States and Canada? Maybe not. Maybe so, and the customer forgot to mention them. Now I have a good, specific question to ask. My customers are good at answering specific questions. They are not good at answering the question "Is there anything else?"

A Note About Customers

My experience with customers has taught me several things:

- They usually know their problem domain very well (most know it better than I ever will).

- In general, they do not express things on the conceptual level, as developers often do. Instead, they talk in specific cases.

- They often use the term *always* when they mean *usually*.

- They often use the term *never* when they mean *seldom*.

The bottom line is that I trust customers to tell me what happens when I ask specific questions, but I do not trust their generalized answers. I try to interact with them at a very concrete level. Even those customers who sound as if they think in a conceptual way often do not, but are trying to "help me out."

Now that the concepts are revealed, what should I do with what I know? How do I begin to move toward implementation?

4. Use the rows to identify rules

Look at the matrix in Table 16-8. The first row is labeled "Calculate freight," and includes "Use UPS rates," "Use Canadian shipper," and "Use German shipper." This row represents both

- A general rule to implement "Calculate freight rate."

- The specific set of rules that I must implement—that is, each shipper I may use in the different countries.

In fact, each row represents specific ways of implementing a generalized concept. Two of the rows (Money and Dates) may be handled at the object level. For example, money can be handled with objects containing a currency object. Many computer languages support different date formats for different nationalities in their libraries. Table 16-9 shows the conceptual way of handling each row.

Table 16-9 Concrete Implementation Rules: Rows

	U.S. Sales	Canadian Sales	German Sales
Calculate freight	The concrete implementations for the ways to calculate freight rates		
Verify address	The concrete implementations for the ways to verigy addresses		
Calculate tax	The concrete implementations for the ways to calculate taz due		
Money	Use Money objects that can contain Currency and Amount fields that convert currency automatically		
Dates	Use Date objects that can contain display as required for the country in which the customer lives		
Maximum weight	The concrete implementations for the ways to maximum weight		

5. Use the columns to identify implementation

What do the columns represent? They are the specific implementations we will use for the case the column represents. This is illustrated in Table 16-10.

Table 16-10 Concrete Implementation Rules: Columns

	U.S. Sales	Canadian Sales	German Sales
Calculate freight			
Verify address	These implementations are used when we have a U.S. customer	These implementations are used when we have a Canadian customer	These implementations are used when we have a German customer
Calculate tax			
Money			
Dates			
Maximum weight			

For example, the first column shows the concrete implementations to use to process a sales order in the United States.

6. Identify design patterns from this analysis: Look at rows

How should I translate these insights into patterns? Look at Table 16-9 again. Each row represents the specific way to implement the concept stated in the leftmost column. For example

- In the "Calculate freight" row, the "Use UPS rates," "Use Canadian shipper," entries really mean, "How should I calculate the freight?" The algorithm I am encapsulating is "freight rate calculation." My concrete rules will be "UPS rates," "Canadian rates," and "German rates."

- The next two rows are also organizations of different rules and their associated concrete implementations.

- The "Money" and "Dates" rows represent classes that may be consistent throughout the application, but which will behave differently depending upon the country involved.

Therefore, all but the "Money" and "Dates" rows can be thought of as a Strategy pattern. This is illustrated in Table 16-11. For example, the objects in the first row can be implemented as a strategy pattern encapsulating the "Calculate freight" rule.

Table 16-11 Implementing with the Strategy Pattern

	U.S. Sales	**Canadian Sales**	**German Sales**
Calculate freight	Objects in this row can be implemented as a Strategy pattern encapsulating the "Calculate freight" rule		
Verify address	Objects in this row can be implemented as a Strategy pattern encapsulating the "Verify address" rule		
Calculate tax	Objects in this row can be implemented as a Strategy pattern encapsulating the "Calculate tax" rule		
Money	We can use Money objects that contain Currency and Amount fields that convert currency automatically		
Dates	We can use data objects that can display as required for the country in which the customer lives		
Maximum weight	Objects in this row can be implemented as a Strategy pattern encapsulating the "Calculate maximum weight" rule		

In a similar vein, I can look at the columns. Each column describes which rules to use for each case. These entries represent the family of objects needed for that case. This sounds like the Abstract Factory pattern. This is shown in Table 16-12.

7. Identify design patterns from this analysis: Look at columns

Table 16-12 Implementing with the Abstract Factory Pattern

	U.S. Sales	Canadian Sales	German Sales
Calculate freight	These objects can be coordinated with the use of the Abstract Factory pattern	These objects can be coordinated with the use of the Abstract Factory pattern	These objects can be coordinated with the use of the Abstract Factory pattern
Verify address			
Calculate tax			
Money			
Dates			
Maximum weight			

8. Develop a high-level design

Armed with the information that some of the rows represent a Strategy pattern and each column represents a family in an Abstract Factory pattern, I can develop a high-level application design as shown in Figure 16-1.

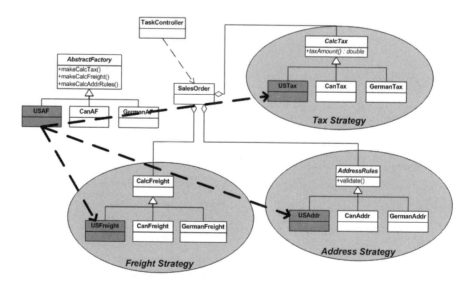

Figure 16.1 High-level application design

Field Notes

In practice, almost any kind of pattern that involves polymorphism *Other patterns* could be present in the Analysis Matrix. Other patterns I have used *present* in an Analysis Matrix are Bridge, Composite, Chain of Responsibility, Command, Decorator, Iterator, Mediator, Observer, Proxy, Template and Visitor.

A sequence diagram showing how this would work in the U.S. Case is shown in Figure 16-2

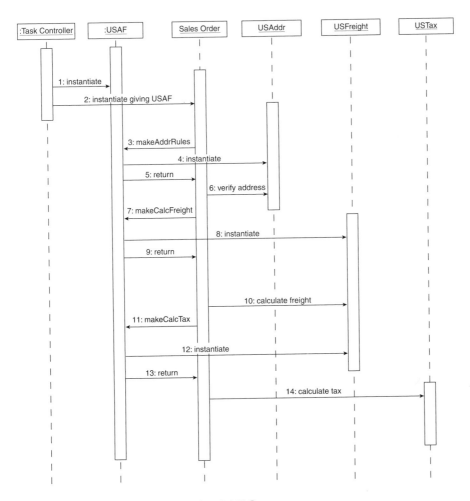

Figure 16-2 Sequence diagram for the U.S. case.

For example, if in our e-commerce system I included requirements on printing sales tickets and found the following variations:

- U.S. sales tickets need headers.

- Canadian sales tickets need headers and footers.

- German sales tickets need two different footers.

I would include this information in its own row, each entry relating to the format of sales tickets. I would implement this row's requirements with a Decorator pattern. This would allow for easily changing which footers and headers I used (as well as their order).

Applicability of the analysis matrix

Although the analysis matrix rarely captures all aspects of a particular problem domain, I have found it useful for at least part of most problem domains. I find it most useful when I am given so many special cases that I can't get my head around the big picture.

More useful as problems get bigger

It is usually worse than this. Rarely are different cases of requirements stated to analysts or developers in any coordinated fashion. This does not significantly complicate the analysis matrix process, however. In these situations, I take a feature and look in the leftmost column and see what concept it is a variant of. If I find the concept, I put the feature in that row. Not being able to find such a concept indicates I must create a new row.

In extreme situations, the analysis matrix may be the only way to get a handle on things. I once had a client that literally had dozens of special cases. Each case was a separately developed document control system. The problem was to integrate all of these document control systems together. So many special cases were present (there were also dozens of rows) that it was impossible to think about the entire problem all at once. The analysts did not have a good conceptual grasp of what was involved. They just talked about general rules and exception cases. By considering each case individually, I was able to abstract out the common data and behavior (which showed up in the leftmost columns) and then implement them with design patterns.

In practice, a simple matrix is usually not sufficient. Even in our simple case, it is easy to imagine more than one way to ship in one country. It is sometimes advisable to have matrices within the master matrix. Figure 16-3 shows such an example.

Often get sub-matrices

	US Sales	Canadian Sales
Calculate freight	Use US Carrier Rates	Use Canadian shipper
Verify address	Use US Carrier Rules	Use Canadian Postal Rul es
Calculate tax	Use state and local taxes	Use GST and PST
Money	US $	Canadian $

Calculate freight	Use US Postal	Use UPS	Use FedEx
Verify Address	Use US Postal Rules	Use US Postal Rules no PO Boxes	Use US Postal Rules
Pick-up charge	N/A	$5.00	$4.00
Max weight	50 lbs	70 lbs	No maximum

Figure 16-3   A matrix within a matrix.

I actually just use the matrix within a matrix when I can't go straight to what I call "commonality and variability tables." I show the table for this embedded matrix in Table 16-13.

Table 16-13 The Commonalities and Variabilities Defined by the Embedded Matrix

Calculate Freight Commonality	Pick-Up Charge Commonality
UPS Rates	None
USPS Rates	$5
FedEx Rates	$4
Verify Address Commonality	**Max Weight Commonality**
US Postal Rates	50 lbs
US Postal Rules with no PO Boxes	70 lbs
	No Maximum

Summary

In this chapter

Variation in concepts can be one of the greatest challenges that an analyst can face. In this chapter, I presented a simple analysis tool that I have found helpful in making sense of such variation. I call this tool the analysis matrix, and it is based on the concepts of Christopher Alexander and Jim Coplein. I applied this tool to a sample problem to show how it might reveal the types of patterns that are inherent in the problem. Although this tool is very useful in containing variation and helping me think about my problem domain, I do not pretend it captures all aspects of a design.

Review Questions

Observations

1. What goes in the far left column of the analysis matrix?

2. What do the rows of the analysis matrix represent?

3. What do the columns of the analysis matrix represent?

4. Which patterns described in this book might be present in an analysis matrix?

Interpretations

1. At what level of perspective does the analysis matrix operate?

2. In what way is the analysis matrix similar to commonality/variability analysis?

Opinions and Applications

1. Can patterns help handle variation more efficiently?

2. Do you agree with the observations about users made in this chapter? Can you give examples from your own experience?

3. Do you believe that the analysis matrix is generally useful for most problem domains?

CHAPTER 17

The Decorator Pattern

Overview

This chapter concludes the e-commerce case study introduced in Chapter 9, "The Strategy Pattern."

In this chapter

This chapter

- Describes a new requirement for the case study: Add header and footer information to the printed sales ticket.

- Shows how the Decorator pattern handles the requirement flexibly.

- Discusses how the Decorator pattern can be used to handle input/output (especially Java I/O).

- Describes the key features of the Decorator pattern.

- Describes some of my experience using the Decorator pattern in practice.

- Describes how the essence of the Decorator pattern is not a linked list, but a collection of optional, decorating objects.

A Little More Detail

Figure 9-2 showed the basic structure of the case study. Figure 17-1 shows this structure in more detail. Here, I show that the **SalesOrder** object uses a **SalesTicket** object to print a sales ticket.

Expanding the diagram

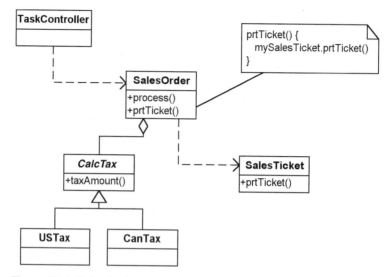

Figure 17-1 SalesOrder using SalesTicket.

As you saw in Chapter 9, **SalesOrder** uses a **CalcTax** object to cal-culate the tax on the order. To implement the printing function, **SalesOrder** calls the **SalesTicket** object, requesting that it print the ticket. This is a fine, reasonably modular design.

New requirement: Add a header

In the process of writing the application, suppose I get a new re-quirement to add header information to the **SalesTicket**.

One approach: Use switches in SalesTicket

How can I handle this new requirement? If I am writing the system to be used by just one company, it may be easiest simply to add the control of headers and footers in the **SalesTicket** class. This is shown in Figure 17-2.

The approach is not flexible

In this solution, I have put the control in **SalesTicket**, with flags saying whether it is to print the headers or the footers.

This works quite well if I do not have to deal with a lot of options or if the sales orders using these headers do not change.

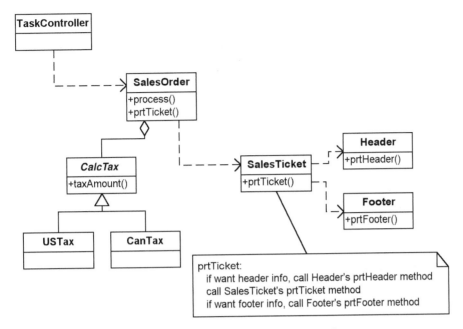

Figure 17-2 SalesOrder using SalesTicket with different options.

If I have to deal with many different types of headers and footers, printing only one each time, then I might consider using one Strategy pattern implementation for the header and another Strategy pattern implementation for the footer.

What happens if I have to print more than one header and/or footer at a time? Or what if the order of the headers and/or footers needs to change? The number of combinations can quickly overwhelm.

In situations like this, the Decorator pattern can prove very useful. Instead of controlling added functionality by having a control method, the Decorator pattern says to control it by chaining together the functions desired in the correct order needed. The Decorator pattern separates the dynamic building of this chain of functionality from the client that uses it (in this case, the **SalesOrder**). It also separates the building of the chain from the chain components (e.g., the headers, the footer, the **SalesTicket**). This allows for flexible use of these components.

The Decorator pattern helps

The Decorator Pattern

The intent, according to the Gang of Four

According to Gang of Four, the Decorator pattern's intent is to

> *Attach additional responsibilities to an object dynamically. Decorators provide a flexible alternative to subclassing for extending functionality.*[1]

How it works

The Decorator pattern works by allowing me to create a chain of objects that starts with the **decorator** objects—the objects responsible for the new function—and ends with the original object. Figure 17-3 illustrates this.

Figure 17-3 The Decorator chain.

The Decorator pattern is a chain of objects

The class diagram of the Decorator pattern in Figure 17-4 implies the chain of objects shown in Figure 17-3. Each chain starts with a **Component** (a **ConcreteComponent** or a **Decorator**). Each **Decorator** is followed either by another **Decorator** or by the

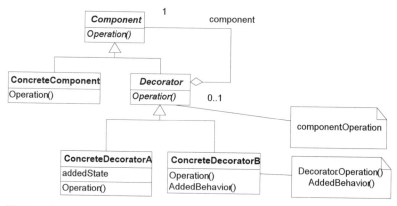

Figure 17-4 The Decorator pattern class diagram.

---

1. Gamma, E. Helm, R., Johnson, R. Vlissides, J., *Design Patterns: Eelements of Reusable Object-Oriented Software*, Boston, Mass.: Addison-Wesley, 1995, p. 175.

original **ConcreteComponent**. A **ConcreteComponent** always ends the chain.

For example, in Figure 17-4, **ConcreteDecoratorB** performs its *Operation* and then calls the *Operation* method in **Decorator**. This calls **ConcreteDecoratorB**'s trailing **Component**'s *Operation*.

Applying the Decorator Pattern to the Case Study

In the case study, the **SalesTicket** is the **ConcreteComponent**. The concrete decorators are the headers and footers. Figure 17-5 shows the application of the Decorator pattern to the case study.

In this case

Figure 17-6 shows the application of Decorator to one header and one footer.

The pattern instantiated

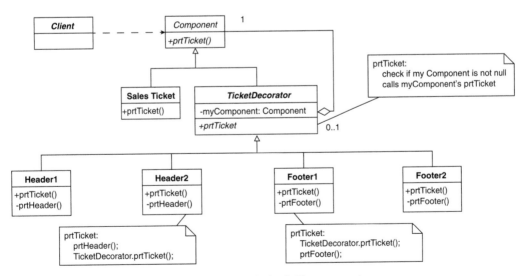

Figure 17-5 Setting up headers and footers to look like a report.

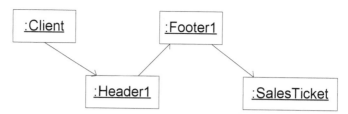

Figure 17-6 An example Decorator object diagram.

How it works:
Decorators wrap
their trailing object

Each **Decorator** object wraps its new function around its trailing object. Each **Decorator** performs its added function either before its decorated function (for headers) or after it (for footers) or both. The easiest way to see how it works is to look at code for a specific example and walk through it. See Example 17-1.

Example 17-1 Java Code Fragment: Decorator

```java
public class Client {
  public static void main( String[] args) {
      Factory myFactory;
          myFactory= new Factory();
          Component myComponent=
              myFactory.getComponent();
    }
}
abstract public class Component {
    abstract public void prtTicket();
}
public class SalesTicket extends Component {
    public void prtTicket() {
       // place sales ticket printing code here
    }
}
abstract public class TicketDecorator extends
Component {
    private Component myTrailer;
    public TicketDecorator (Component myComponent) {
      myTrailer= myComponent;
    }
    public void callTrailer () {
       if (myTrailer != null) myTrailer.prtTicket();
    }
}
```

```java
public class Header1 extends TicketDecorator {
   public Header1 (Component myComponent) {
      super( myComponent);
   }
   public void prtTicket () {
      // place printing header 1 code here
      super.callTrailer();
   }
}
public class Header2 extends TicketDecorator {
   public Header2 (Component myComponent) {
      super( myComponent);
   }
   public void prtTicket () {
      // place printing header 2 code here
      super.callTrailer();
   }
}
public class Footer1 extends TicketDecorator {
   public Footer1 ( Component myComponent) {
      super( myComponent);
   }
   public void prtTicket() {
      super.callTrailer();
      // place printing footer 1 code here
   }
}
public class Footer2 extends TicketDecorator {
   public Footer2 ( Component myComponent) {
      super( myComponent);
   }
   public void prtTicket() {
      super.callTrailer();
      // place printing footer 2 code here
   }
}

public class Factory {
   public Component getComponent () {
      Component myComponent;
      myComponent= new SalesTicket();
      myComponent= new Footer1( myComponent);
      myComponent= new Header1( myComponent);
      return myComponent;
   }
}
```

What happens in the code

If I want the sales ticket to look like:

> HEADER 1
>
> SALES TICKET
>
> FOOTER 1

Then *myFactory.getComponent* returns

```
return( new Header1( new Footer1 ( new
SalesTicket())));
```

This creates a **Header1** object trailed by a **Footer1** object trailed by a **SalesTicket** object.

If I want the sales ticket to look like

> HEADER 1
>
> HEADER 2
>
> SALES TICKET
>
> FOOTER 1

Then *myFactory.getComponent* returns

```
return( new Header1( new Header2 (new Footer1(
                    new SalesTicket())))));
```

This creates a **Header1** object trailed by a **Header2** object trailed by a **Footer1** object trailed by a **SalesTicket** object.

Decomposing by responsibilities

The Decorator pattern helps to decompose the problem into two parts:

- How to implement the objects that give the new functionality

- How to organize the objects for each special case

This enables me to separate implementing the **Decorator**s from the object that determines how they are used. This increases cohesion because each of the **Decorator**s is only concerned with the function it adds—not in how it is added to the chain. It also enables me to arbitrarily reorder the **Decorator**s without changing any of their code.

Another Example: Input/Output

A common use for the Decorator pattern is in stream I/O. Let's look at stream I/O a little before seeing how the pattern can be used here. I will limit the discussion to input since output works in an analogous way. (If you see how it works in one direction, it should be clear how it works in the other direction.) For any particular stream input, there is exactly one source, but there can be any number (including zero) of actions to perform on the input stream. For example, I can read from

Stream I/O

- A file.

- A socket and then decrypt the incoming stream.

- A file and then decompress the incoming data.

- A string.

- A file, decompress the input, and then decrypt it.

Depending upon how the data was sent (or stored) any combination of behaviors is possible. Think of it this way: Any source can be decorated with any combination of behaviors. Some of the possibilities available for stream input are shown in Table 17-1.

Developers in object-oriented languages can take advantage of this by having source and behavior objects derive from a common abstract class. Each behavior object can be given its source or prior behavior in its constructor. A chain of actions is then built as the objects themselves are instantiated. (Each is given a reference to its trailing

Languages reflect this

Table 17-1 Kinds of Sources and Behaviors

Sources	Behaviors
String	Buffered input
File	Run checksum
Socket (TCP/IP)	Unzip
Serial port	Decrypt (any number of ways)
Parallel port	Selection filters (any number of ways)
Keyboard	

object.) The sources derive from **ConcreteComponent** (see Figure 17-4), whereas the behaviors are decorators. Note that **ConcreteComponent** is now a misnomer because it is now abstract.

For example, to get the behavior "read from a file, decompress the input, and then decrypt it," do the following:

1. Build the decorator chain by doing the following:

    a. Instantiate a file object.

    b. Pass a reference to it to the constructor of a decompression object.

    c. Pass a reference to that to the constructor of a decryption object.

2. Read, decompress, and decrypt the data—all transparently to the client object that is using it. The client merely knows it has some sort of input stream object.

If this client needs to get its input from a different source, the chain is created by instantiating a different source object using the same behavior objects.

Understanding "The Complete Stream Zoo"[*]

Java is notorious for its confusing array of I/O streams and associated classes. It is much easier to understand these classes in the context of the Decorator pattern. The classes directly derived from java.io.InputStream **(ByteArrayInputStream, FileInputStream, FilterInputStream, InputStream, ObjectInputStream, SequenceInputStream, and StringBufferInputStream)** all play the role of the decorated object. All of the decorators derive from **FilterInputStream** (either directly or indirectly).

Keeping the Decorator pattern in mind explains why the Java language requires wrapping these objects inside one another—this gives programmers the ability to pick any number of combinations from the different behaviors available.

---

[*] Horstmann, C., *Core Java—Volume 1—Fundamentals*, Palo Alto, CA: Pearson Education, 1999, p. 627.

Field Notes: Using the Decorator Pattern

The power of the Decorator pattern requires that the instantiation of the chains of objects be completely decoupled from the **Client** objects that use it. This is most typically accomplished through the use of factory objects that instantiate the chains based upon some configuration information.

Instantiating the chains

I have used the Decorator pattern to wrap precondition and postcondition tests on an object to be tested with nice results. During testing, the first object in the chain can do an extensive test of preconditions prior to calling its trailing object. Immediately after the trailing object call, the same object calls an extensive test of postconditions. If I have different tests I want to run at different times, I can keep each test in a different Decorator and then chain them together according to the battery of tests I want to run.

Decorators in testing

The Decorator Pattern: Key Features

Intent
: Attach additional responsibilities to an object dynamically.

Problem
: The object that you want to use does the basic functions you require. However, you may need to add some additional functionality to the object, occurring before or after the object's base functionality. Note that the Java foundation classes use the Decorator pattern extensively for I/O handling.

Solution
: Allows for extending the functionality of an object without resorting to subclassing.

Participants and collaborators
: The **ConcreteComponent** is the class having function added to it by the **Decorator**s. Sometimes classes derived from **ConcreteComponent** are used to provide the core functionality, in which case **Concrete-Component** is no longer concrete, but rather abstract. The **Component** defines the interface for all of these classes to use.

Consequences
: Functionality that is to be added resides in small objects. The advantage is the ability to dynamically add this function before or after the functionality in the **ConcreteComponent**. Note: Although a decorator may add its functionality before or after that which it decorates, the chain of instantiation always ends with the **ConcreteComponent**.

Implementation
: Create an abstract class that represents both the original class and the new functions to be added to the class. In the decorators, place the new function calls before or after the trailing calls to get the correct order.

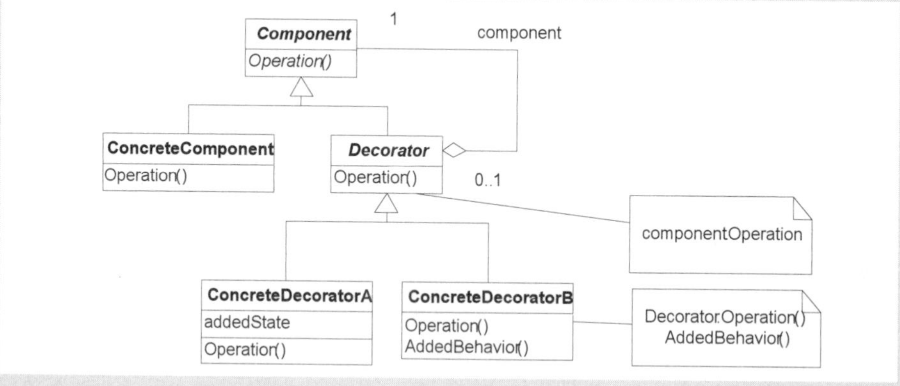

Figure 17-7 Generic structure of the Decorator pattern.

The Essence of the Decorator Pattern

The Decorator pattern comes into play when there are a variety of optional functions that can precede or follow another function that is always executed. For example, prior to sending a transmission (which is always done), it may be that you want to encrypt, compress, translate data check, or any number of other things in any order. How would you best do this? The Decorator pattern's implementation tells you to make a linked list of the optional functions ending with the Transmission object. The "decorating" objects should all have the same interface as the Transmission object.

The Structure is not the pattern

This implementation can actually be a very bad design. For example, suppose that these "decorators" (i.e., the optional functionality) are created by different development groups. Let's further state that certain exceptions may be thrown by the system and need to be handled by each of the decorators. In a perfect world, you could have confidence that each of these groups will do what they are supposed to do—catch these exceptions properly. However, what if they do not? What if an exception is thrown and the group writing the code doesn't catch it? The entire system may crash at this point.

Another solution is to have the Client object catch the exception. However, this loses some of the value of the Decorator pattern in that your Client class now needs to do more than it did before.

A more robust solution is to implement a collection object that has the same interface as the Transmission object. This calls the "decorators" and catches any required exceptions in case they don't. In fact, this might have the added advantage of making it so the decorating objects no longer needed to have the same interface.

The point is that you can view the Decorator pattern as having the following forces:

- Several optional functions exist.

- These decorators may or may not be following all of the rules they should.

- You need some way to invoke these decorating objects, in different orders as needed, without encumbering the Client object.

- You don't want to encumber your application with knowing which of these to use (or even that they exist).

Thinking of the Decorator pattern in this light makes a distinction between the *purpose* of the Decorator pattern and the *implementation* of the Decorator pattern.

Summary

In this chapter

The Decorator pattern is a way to add additional function(s) to an existing function dynamically. In practice, it requires building a chain of objects that give the desired behaviors. The first object in this chain is called by a **Client** that had nothing to do with the building of it. By keeping the creation of the chain independent from its use, the **Client** object is not affected by new requirements to add functionality.

Review Questions

Observations

1. What does each Decorator object wrap?

2. What are two classic examples of decorators?

Interpretations

1. How does the Decorator pattern help to decompose the problem?

2. "The structure is not the pattern." This statement is made
    during the discussion of the essence of the Decorator pattern.
    What does this mean? Why is this important?

Opinions and Applications

1. Why do you think the Gang of Four call this pattern
    "Decorator"? Is it an appropriate name for what it is doing?
    Why or why not?

2. Sometimes people think of patterns as recipes. What is
    wrong with this?

PART VI

Other Values of Patterns

Part Overview

This part extends the notion of patterns containing variation by illustrating different types of variation that can occur besides functionality.

In this part

Chapter	Discusses These Topics
18	**The Observer Pattern** How to contain variation in both which object wants to be notified and under what circumstances.
19	**The Template Method** How to both eliminate redundancy and encapsulate a procedure to be followed. Alternatively, how to have variations in the implementations of the steps you must take.

CHAPTER 18

The Observer Pattern

Overview

This chapter continues the international e-commerce case study start-ed in Chapter 9, "The Strategy Pattern," and continued in Chapter 16, "The Analysis Matrix."

In this chapter

This chapter

- Introduces the categorization scheme of patterns.

- Introduces the Observer pattern by discussing additional re-quirements for the case study.

- Applies the Observer pattern to the case study.

- Describes the Observer pattern.

- Describes the key features of the Observer pattern.

- Describes some of my experiences using the Observer pattern in practice.

Categories of Patterns

There are many patterns to keep track of. To help sort this out, the Gang of Four has grouped patterns into three general categories, as shown in Table 18-1.[1]

The GoF has three categories

---

1. Gamma, E., Helm, R., Johnson, R., Vlissides, J., *Design Patterns: Elements of Reusable Object-Oriented Software*, Boston: Addison-Wesley, 1995, p. 10.

Table 18-1 Categories of Patterns

Category	Purpose	Examples in This Book	Use For
Creational	Create or instantiate objects	Abstract Factory (Chapter 11)	Instantiating objects
		Singleton (Chapter 21)	
		Double-Checked Locking (Chapter 21)	
		Factory Method (Chapter 23)	
Structural	Bring together existing objects	Facade (Chapter 6)	Handling interfaces
		Adapter (Chapter 7)	
		Bridge (Chapter 10)	Relating implementations to abstractions
		Decorator (Chapter 17)	
Behavioral	Give a way to manifest flexible (varying) behavior	Strategy (Chapter 9)	Containing variation

A note on the classification of the Bridge and Decorator patterns

When I first started studying design patterns, I was surprised to see that the Gang of Four had classified the Bridge and Decorator patterns as structural patterns rather than as behavioral patterns. After all, they seemed to be used to implement different behaviors. As it turns out, I simply did not understand the Gang of Four's classification system. For them, structural patterns are used for tying together existing functionality. In the Bridge pattern, we typically start with abstractions and implementations and then bind them together with the bridge. In the Decorator pattern, we have an original functional class, and want to decorate it with additional functions. They tie together functions and therefore are structural.

In practice, the objects used by structural patterns are in fact separate to begin with. I have found, however, that many times the pattern could be used when the way I was thinking about the pattern had them combined. The CAD/CAM problem earlier in this book is an example of this. In that situation, the value of the Bridge pattern was useful in identifying the fact that I had two implementations separate from the features that used them. I have found the Bridge useful to remind myself to separate things that are entwined in my classes.

I have found it valuable to think of a fourth category of patterns, one whose primary purpose is to decouple objects from each other. One motivation for these is to allow for scalability or increased flexibility. I call this category of patterns *decoupling patterns*. Because most of the patterns in the decoupling category belong to the Gang of Four's behavioral category, I could almost call them a subset of the behavioral category. I chose to make a fourth category simply because my intent in this book is to reflect how I look at patterns, focusing on their motivations—in this case, decoupling.

My "fourth" category: Decoupling

I would not get too hung up on the whys and wherefores of the classifications. They are meant to give insights into what the patterns are doing. In fact, most patterns have a combination of all four characteristics.

This chapter discusses the Observer pattern, which is the best example of a decoupling pattern I can think of. The Gang of Four classifies the Observer pattern as a behavioral pattern.

Observer is a decoupling (behavioral) pattern

More Requirements for the International E-Commerce Case Study

In the process of writing the application, suppose I get a new requirement to take the following actions whenever a new customer is entered into the system:

New requirement: Take actions for new customers

- Send a welcome e-mail to the customer.

- Verify the customer's address with the post office.

Are these all of the requirements? Will things change in the future?

One approach

If I am reasonably certain that I know every requirement, then I could solve the problem by hard coding the notification behavior into the **Customer** class, such as shown in Figure 18-1.

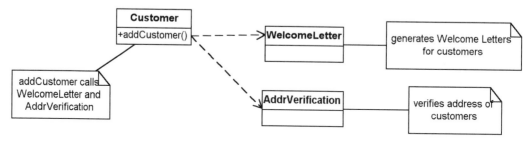

Figure 18-1 Hard coding the behaviors.

For example, using the same method that adds a new customer into the database, I will also make calls to the objects that generate welcome letters and verify post office addresses.

These classes have the following responsibilities.

Class	Responsibility
Customer	When a customer is added, this object will make calls to the other objects to have the corresponding actions take place.
WelcomeLetter	Creates welcome letters for customers that let them know they were added to the system.
AddrVerification	This object will verify the address of any customer that asks it to.

The problem?
Requirements
always change

The hard-coding approach works fine—the first time. But requirements *always* change. I know that another requirement will come that will require another change to **Customer**'s behavior. For example, I might have to support different companies' welcome letters, which would require a different **Customer** object for each company. Surely, I can do better.

The Observer Pattern

According to the Gang of Four, the intent of the Observer pattern is to "define a one-to-many dependency between objects so that when one object changes state, all its dependents are notified and updated automatically."[2]

The intent, according to the Gang of Four

Often, I have a set of objects that need to be notified whenever an event occurs. I want this notification to occur automatically. However, I do not want to change the broadcasting object every time there is a change to the set of objects listening to the broadcast. (That would be like having to change a radio transmitter every time a new car radio comes to town.) I want to decouple the notify-ers and the notify-ees.

What this means: handling notification automatically

This pattern is a very common one. It also goes by the names **Dependents** and **Publish-Subscribe**,[3] and is analogous to the notify process in COM. It is implemented in Java with the **Observer** interface and the **Observable** class (more on these later). In rule-based, expert systems, they are often implemented with daemon rules.

A common pattern

Applying the Observer to the Case Study

My approach is to look in the problem for clues as to what is varying. Then I attempt to encapsulate the variation. In the current case, I find

Two things are varying

- **Different kinds of objects**—There is a list of objects that need to be notified of a change in state. These objects tend to belong to different classes.

- **Different interfaces**—Because they belong to different classes, they tend to have different interfaces.

---

2. Gamma, E., Helm, R., Johnson, R., Vlissides, J., *Design Patterns: Elements of Reusable Object-Oriented Software*, Boston: Addison-Wesley, 1995, p. 293.

3. Ibid, p. 293.

Step 1: Make the Observers behave in the same way

First, I must identify all of the objects that want to be notified. I will call these the *Observers* because they are waiting for an event to occur.[4]

I want all of the observers to have the same interface. If they do not have the same interface, then I would have to modify the *subject*—that is, the object that is triggering the event (for example, **Customer**) —to handle each different type of observer. I don't want to do this because that would complicate the *subject*.

By having all the observers be of the same type, the subject can easily notify all of them. To get all of the observers to *be* of the same type

- In C# and Java, I would probably implement this with an interface (either for flexibility or out of necessity).

- In C++, I would use single inheritance or multiple inheritance, as required.

Step 2: Have the observers register themselves

In most situations, I want the observers to be responsible for knowing what they are to watch for and I want the subject to be free from knowing which observers depend on it. To do this, I need to have a way for the observers to register themselves with the subject. Because all of the observers are of the same type, I must add two methods to the subject:

- *attach(Observer)*—adds the given **observer** to its list of observers

- *detach(Observer)*—removes the given **observer** from its list of observers

Step 3: Notify the observers when the event occurs

Now that the **Subject** has its **Observer**s registered, it is a simple matter for the **Subject** to notify the **Observer**s when the event occurs. To do this, each **Observer** implements a method called *update*.

---

4. Actually, I call them this because that's what objects in the Observer pattern that wait for events to occur are called. I just figure this is the reason they got that name.

The **Subject** implements a *notify* method that goes through its list
of **Observer**s and calls this *update* method for each of them. The
update method should contain the code to handle the event.

But notifying each **Observer** is not enough. An **Observer** may need
more information about the event beyond the simple fact that it has
occurred. Therefore, I must also add method(s) to the **Subject** that
allow the **Observer**s to get whatever information they need. Figure
18-2 shows this solution.

*Step 4: Get the
information from the
subject*

In Figure 18-2, the classes relate to each other as follows:

How this works

1. The **Observer**s attach themselves to the **Customer** class
   when they are instantiated. If the **Observer**s need more information from the subject (**Customer**), the *update* method
   must be passed a reference to the calling object.

2. When a new **Customer** is added, the *notify* method calls
   these **Observer**s.

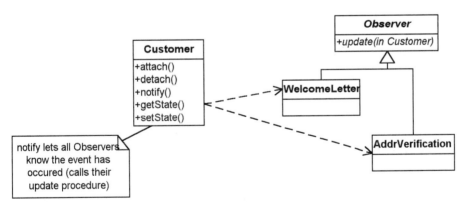

Figure 18-2 Implementing Customer with Observer.

Each **Observer** calls **getState** for information on the newly added
Customer to see what it needs to do. Note: Typically, there would be
several methods to get the needed information.

Note in this case, we use static methods for attach and detach because observers want to be notified for all new **Customer**s. When notified, they are passed the reference to the **Customer** created.

Example 18-1 shows some of the code required to implement this.

The Observer pattern aids flexibility and keeps things decoupled

This approach enables me to add new observers without affecting any existing classes. It also keeps everything loosely coupled. This organization works if I have kept all of the objects responsible for themselves.

New requirement: Send coupons, too

How well does this work if I get a new requirement? For example, what if I need to send a letter with coupons to customers located within 20 miles of one of the company's "brick and mortar" stores.

Example 18-1 Java Code Fragment: Observer Implemented

```java
// Note: I don't use the Java Observer or Observable.
// In practice they give me little assistance and I
// don't like their interfaces.

import java.util.*;

public class Customer {
   static private Vector myObs;
   static {
      myObs= new Vector();
   }
   public static void attach(MyObserver o){
      myObs.addElement(o);
   }
   public static void detach(MyObserver o){
      myObs.remove(o);
   }
   public String getState () {
      // have other methods that will give the
      // required information
      // Here, just return null so this will compile
      return null;
```

```
    }

    public void notifyObs () {
        // set arg to something that helps
        // tell the Observers what happened
        for (Enumeration e = myObs.elements();
            e.hasMoreElements() ;) {
                ((MyObserver) e).update(this);
        }
    }
}

interface MyObserver {
    void update (Customer myCust);
}

class AddrVerification implements MyObserver {
    public AddrVerification () {
    }
    public void update ( Customer myCust) {

        // do Address verification stuff here
        // can get more information about customer
        // in question by using myCust

    }
}

class WelcomeLetter implements MyObserver {
    public WelcomeLetter () {
    }
    public void update (Customer myCust) {
    // do Welcome Letter stuff
    // here can get more
    // information about customer
    // in question by using myCust
    }
}
```

To accomplish this, I would just add a new observer that sends the coupon. It only does this for new customers living within the specified distance. I could name this observer **BrickAndMortar** and make it an observer to the **Customer** class. Figure 18-3 shows this solution.

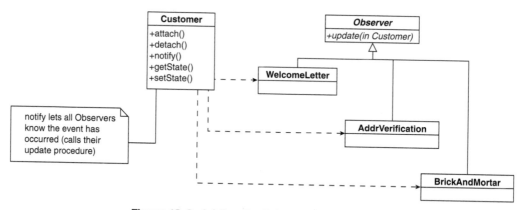

Figure 18-3 Adding the BrickAndMortar observer.

The Observer pattern in the real world   Sometimes, a class that will become an observer may already exist. In this case, I may not want to modify it. If so, I can easily adapt it with the Adapter pattern. Figure 18-4 shows an example of this.

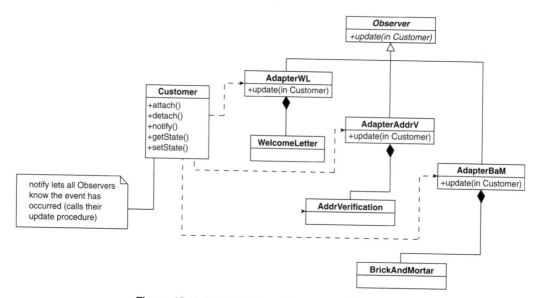

Figure 18-4 Implementing Observer with Adapters.

The Observable Class:
A Note to Java Developers

The Observer pattern is so useful that Java contains an implementation of it in its packages. The Observable class and the Observer interface make up the pattern. The Observable class plays the role of the subject in the Gang of Four's description of the pattern. Instead of the methods attach, detach, and notify, Java uses addObserver, deleteObserver, and notifyObservers, respectively (Java also uses update). Java also gives you a few more methods to make life easier.*

---

* See http://java.sun.com/j2se/1.3/docs/api/index.html for information on the Java API for **Observer** and **Observable**.

Field Notes: Using the Observer Pattern

The Observer pattern is not meant to be used every time there is a dependency between objects. For example, suppose in a ticket-processing system, a tax object handles taxes. It is clear that when items are added to the ticket, the tax object must be notified so the tax can be recalculated. This would not be a good place for an Observer pattern because this notification is known up front and others are not likely to be added. When the dependencies are fixed (or virtually so), adding an Observer pattern probably just adds complexity.

Not for all dependencies

If the list of objects that need to be notified of an event changes, or is somehow conditional, the Observer pattern has greater value. These changes can occur either because the requirements are changing or because the list of objects that need to be notified are changing. The Observer pattern can also prove useful if the system is run under different conditions or by different customers, each having a different list of required observers.

…but for changing or dynamic dependencies

The Observer Pattern: Key Features

Intent
: Define a one-to-many dependency between objects so that when one object changes state, all its dependents are notified and updated automatically.

Problem
: You need to notify a varying list of objects that an event has occurred.

Solution
: Observers delegate the responsibility for monitoring for an event to a central object: the **Subject**.

Participants and collaborators
: The **Subject** knows its **Observer**s because the **Observer**s register with it. The **Subject** must notify the **Observer**s when the event in question occurs. The **Observer**s are responsible both for registering with the **Subject** and for getting the information from the **Subject** when notified.

Consequences
: **Subject**s may tell **Observer**s about events they do not need to know if some **Observer**s are interested in only a subset of events (See "Field Notes: Using the Observer Pattern" on page 325). Extra communication may be required if **Subject**s notify **Observer**s which then go back and request additional information.

Implementation
: Have objects (**Observer**s) that want to know when an event happens attach themselves to another object (**Subject**) that is watching for the event to occur or that triggers the event itself.

: When the event occurs, the **Subject** tells the **Observer**s that it has occurred.

: The Adapter pattern is sometimes needed to be able to implement the **Observer** interface for all of the **Observer**-type objects.

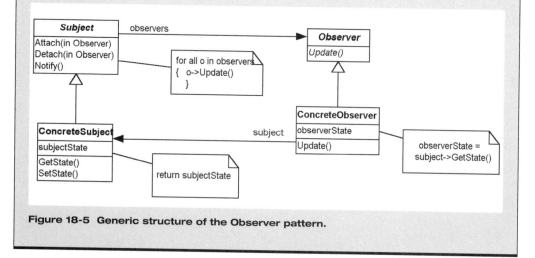

Figure 18-5 Generic structure of the Observer pattern.

An observer may only need to handle certain cases of an event. The Brick and Mortar case was an example. In such situations, the observer must filter out extra notifications.

Whether to process an event

Extraneous notifications can be eliminated by shifting the responsibility for filtering out these notifications to the **Subject**. The best way to do this is for the **Subject** to use a Strategy pattern to test whether notification should occur. Each observer gives the **Subject** the correct strategy to use when it registers.

Sometimes, **Subject**s will call the observers' *update* method, passing along information. This can save the need for callbacks from the observers to the **Subject**. However, it is often the case that different observers have different information requirements. In this case, a Strategy pattern can again be used. This time, the **Strategy** object is used for calling the observers' *update* procedure. Again, the observers must supply the **Subject** with the appropriate **Strategy** object to use.

How to process an event

Summary

In learning the Observer pattern, I looked at which object is best able to handle future variation. In the case of the Observer pattern, the object that is triggering the event—the **Subject**—cannot anticipate every object that might need to know about the event. To solve this, I create an **Observer** interface and require that all Observers be responsible for registering themselves with this **Subject**.

In this chapter

While I focused on the Observer pattern during the chapter, it is worth pointing out several object-oriented principles that are used in the Observer pattern.

Summary of object-oriented principles used

Concept	Discussion
Objects are responsible for themselves	There were different kinds of **Observer**s, but all gathered the information they needed from the **Subject** and took the action appropriate for them on their own.
Abstract class	The **Observer** class represents the concept of objects that needed to be notified. It gave a common interface for the subject to notify the **Observer**s.
Polymorphic encapsulation	The subject did not know what kind of observer it was communicating with. Essentially, the **Observer** class encapsulated the particular **Observer**s present. This means that if I get new **Observer**s in the future, the **Subject** does not need to change.

Review Questions

Observation

1. According to the Gang of Four, what are structural patterns responsible for?

2. What are the three classifications of patterns, according to the Gang of Four? What is the fourth classification that the authors suggest?

3. What is the one true thing about requirements?

4. What is the intent of the Observer pattern?

Interpretation

1. Why are the Bridge and Decorator patterns more correctly classified as structural rather than behavioral patterns?

2. One example of the Observer pattern from outside of software is a radio station: It broadcasts its signal; anyone who is interested can tune in and listen when they want to. What is another example from "real life"?

3. Under what conditions should an Observer pattern not be used?

Opinion and Application

1. The "fourth category" of patterns somewhat includes patterns from other categories. Is this a good idea? Why or why not?

CHAPTER 19

The Template Method Pattern

Overview

This chapter continues the e-commerce case study discussed thus far in Chapters 9, 16, and 18.

In this chapter

This chapter

- Introduces the Template Method pattern by discussing additional requirements for the case study.

- Presents the intent of the Template Method pattern.

- Describes the key features of the Template Method pattern.

- Describes how the Template Method pattern can eliminate redundancy.

- Describes some of my experiences using the Template Method pattern in practice.

More Requirements for the International E-Commerce Case Study

In the process of writing the international e-commerce application, suppose I get a new requirement to support both Oracle and SQL Server databases. Both of these systems are based on SQL (Structured Query Language), the common standard that makes it easier to use databases. Even though this is a common standard at the general level, however, there are still differences in the details.

New requirement: Access multiple SQL database systems

This steps are the same at the general level...

For example, I know that in general, when executing queries on these databases, I will use the following steps:

1. Format the **CONNECT** command.

2. Send the database the **CONNECT** command.

3. Format the **SELECT** command.

4. Send the database the **SELECT** command.

5. Return the selected dataset.

...but the details differ

The specific implementations of the databases differ, however, requiring slightly different formatting procedures.

The Template Method Pattern

Standardizing on the steps

The Template Method is a pattern intended to help us generalize a common process, at an abstract level, from a set of different procedures. According to the Gang of Four, the intent of the Template Method pattern is as follows:

> *Define the skeleton of an algorithm in an operation, deferring some steps to subclasses. Redefine the steps in an algorithm without changing the algorithm's structure.*[1]

In other words, although there are different methods for connecting and querying Oracle databases and SQL Server databases, they share the same conceptual process. The Template Method pattern gives us a way to capture this common ground in an abstract class while encapsulating the differences in derived classes. The Template Method pattern is about controlling a sequence common to different processes.

---

1. Gamma, E., Helm, R., Johnson, R., Vlissides, J., *Design Patterns: Elements of Reusable Object-Oriented Software*, Boston: Addison-Wesley, 1995, p. 325.

Applying the Template Method to the International E-Commerce Case Study

In the international e-commerce case study, the variations in database access occur in the particular implementations of the steps involved. Figure 19-1 illustrates this.

The details are varying

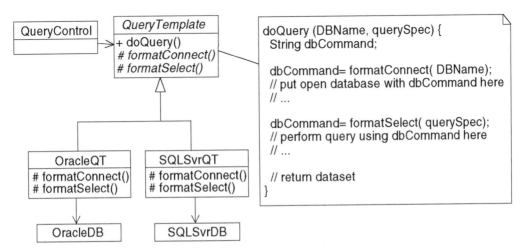

Figure 19-1 Using the Template Method pattern to perform a query.

I have created a method called ***doQuery*** that handles the query I need to perform. I pass it the name of the database and the query specification. The ***doQuery*** method follows the five general steps above, providing virtual methods for the steps (such as ***formatConnect*** and ***formatSelect***) that must be implemented differently.

How this works: Virtual methods for the steps that vary

The ***doQuery*** method is implemented as follows. As shown in Figure 19-1, it first needs to format the **CONNECT** command required to connect to the database. Although the abstract class (**QueryTemplate**) knows this format needs to take place, it doesn't know how to do it. The exact formatting code is supplied by the derived classes. This is true for formatting the **SELECT** command as well.

The Template Method pattern manages to do this because the method call is made via a reference pointing to one of the derived classes. That is, although **QueryControl** has a reference of type **QueryTemplate**, it is actually referring to an **OracleQT** or an **SQLSvrQT** object. Thus, when the *doQuery* method is called on either of these objects, the methods resolved will first look for methods of the appropriate derived class. Suppose our **QueryControl** is referring to an **Oracle-QT** object. Because **OracleQT** does not override **QueryTemplate**, the **QueryTemplate**'s *doQuery* method is invoked. This starts executing until it calls the *formatConnect* method. Because the **OracleQT** object was requested to perform *doQuery*, the **OracleQT**'s *formatConnect* method is called. After this, control is returned to the **QueryTemplate**'s *doQuery* method. The code common to all queries is now executed until the next variation is needed—the *formatSelect* method. Again, this method is located in the object that **QueryControl** is referring to (**OracleQT** in this example).

When a new database is encountered, the Template Method provides us with a boilerplate (or template) to fill out. We create a new derived class and implement the specific steps required for the new database in it.

Using the Template Method Pattern to Reduce Redundancy

Eliminating redundancy can lead to abstractions

Many times in my consulting practice, I work with teams of people who are very sharp but who do not yet have strong backgrounds in object orientation. They are transitioning to agile methods, and they appreciate the need for concepts such as eliminating redundancy, having strong cohesion, and having loose coupling; however, they do not know how to go about getting there.

On one occasion, I was asking the team lead to describe a typical problem they had. He related to me how they had to support systems for different partner companies. The rules were pretty much the same, but there were always subtle differences. The code was be-coming increasingly hard to maintain because it had so many "if-then-else" statements scattered throughout to check which situation was current and how to handle it. He could only see two alternatives, neither of them very good:

- Continue putting in more "if-then-else" statements, further de-grading the code

- Copy and paste the code for each case, resulting in duplication

Using "if-then-else" statements or switches is the common approach taken here. The difficulty with this is switch creep. At first, a few "if-then-else" statements or switches is not bad. But at some point (around 57 of them?) the code is really difficult to understand. The advantage of the copy-and-past approach is that although it doesn't seem particularly elegant, at least each section is clear because it only relates to one situation.

Because I knew the Template Method pattern, I could offer a third alternative. I will illustrate the alternative in two steps. First I will show what happens when people copy and paste and then update the code. It turns out that even if all of the code is changed, there is still a process common to both; if not there wouldn't be a reason to do the copy and paste. Second, I'll show how after this duplication of process is recognized, one can refactor the code to eliminate it.

Figure 19-2 shows an example of some "code" that I will use to show the shortcomings of copy and paste. Note that I am just showing the "code" as a sequence of letters, because the details of the code do not matter. I am trying to help you see the problems of copy and paste more easily.

Copy and paste and changing code leaves redundancy

After I use copy and paste to change the code, I might end up with a new sequence of code, as shown in Figure 19-3. Note that in this copy-and-paste operation, some of the a's have been converted to A's,

Figure 19-2 The original code.

b's to B's, etc. Where a letter has changed to a capital, this indicates code that was changed after the copy and paste. Where it remains lowercase, this is code that was simply duplicated. The new row of X's is code that was added to the new case, but did not exist at all in the original.

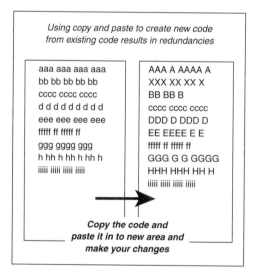

Figure 19-3 The original code and the new code.

There are at least two types of duplication here. The first is the more obvious: the lines with c's, f's, and i's, are duplicated code. I copied and pasted the original code, and then changed most, but not all of it. The part I didn't change is obviously redundant. However, there is another duplication. There is a sequence of operations that is common to both code fragments. In other words, this type of copy and paste is mostly employed when there is a well-defined sequence of steps but the implementation of some of the steps has changed. I illustrate this in Figure 19-4.

Different types of duplication

Figure 19-4 Comparing the code to identify redundancies.

The steps point out those things that are conceptually the same, but that are implemented in different ways (the difference illustrated here by the use of capital and lowercase letters, and by the addition of new code in some cases, shown as X's). So, for example, in the original class Step 1 consisted of lowercase a's and b's, but in the new (second) class, it consisted of capital A's, X's, and B's. The step exists in both classes, and so that fact is redundant, even though the implementation is not.

Eliminating the duplication

The Template Method pattern could be used to eliminate duplication here. It prescribes a base class that implements the step sequence. Each case then has its own derivative class to implement the specific steps, as shown in Figure 19-5.

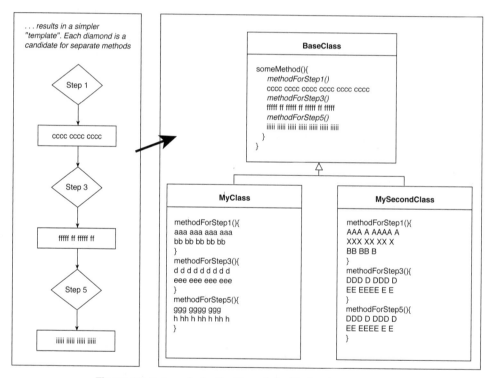

Figure 19-5 Leads to the Template Method pattern .

Some details missing

To actually implement this takes filling in several details. First of all, the steps in the derived classes need to be declared as abstract and/or protected methods in the base class. Second, there may have been local method variables used between the steps. These either need to be passed in and returned or made as data members of the class. Those common to both steps should be put in the base class.

Of course, refactoring to fix a bad situation after it is identified is preferable to just leaving it alone. However, refactoring to avoid the bad situation in the first place is preferable even more. In this situation, if we recognized the Template Method pattern approach's viability when the second system became a requirement, we could take the following approach:

An approach to avoid the duplication in the first place

1. First, refactor the first solution (using the **Extract** method) to pull out the code that will change. This is shown in Figure 19-6. By the way, "pull out the code that will change" should sound a little similar to the Gang of Four's advice, "find what varies and encapsulate it." Instead of specializing the method, I have the **someMethod** method contain other methods that will change.

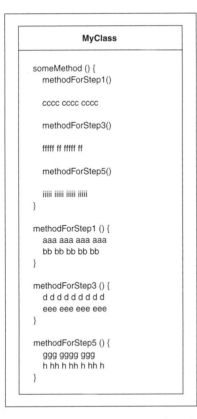

Figure 19-6 Refactoring out the steps that will change.

2. Second, create a base class that contains the method (*someMethod*) that will not change. The code now looks like the code in Figure 19-5 for **BaseClass** and **MyClass**. (I have not yet written **MySecondClass**.)

3. Write **MySecondClass**. Note that adding the new function now will not affect any other code except for the factory (and possibly not that).

Of course, wherever I indicate that I should "extract method," you might notice that this would not have been necessary if I'd been programming by intention in the first place. Good practices like this one tend to show up again and again, which is why they're good practices in the first place.

Knowing patterns helps guide refactoring

This is a generally good approach for refactoring. When a new requirement needs to be handled, take this two-step approach:

1. Refactor your code without adding any function so the new function can go in following the open-closed principle.

2. Add your new code, touching only the factory and the new code.

Knowing patterns will help you follow this approach in many different situations.

Field Notes: Using the Template Method Pattern

The Template Method is not coupled Strategies

Sometimes a class will use several different Strategy patterns. When I first looked at the class diagram for the Template Method pattern, I thought, "Oh, the Template Method pattern is simply a collection of Strategies that work together." This is dangerous (and usually incorrect) thinking. Although it is not uncommon for several Strategies to appear to be connected to each other, designing for this can lead to inflexibility.

> ## Knowing Patterns Can Help Code Quality Without Causing Extra Work
>
> The story I just related is an example about how knowing patterns can help one follow the practices of *eXtreme Programming* (XP). A skilled XP designer would know to consider (and do if appropriate) something like the Template Method pattern in the case described. If this were the best way to handle avoiding redundancy, the pattern would be implemented. The XP designer may not think of himself as "following the pattern," but knowledge of the pattern gives one an option he may not think of otherwise. Unfortunately, a designer not yet experienced in XP may just never recognize that such a solution is available. He may not even recognize that by copying and pasting, he is creating a redundant procedure even if he changes *all* of the code. This again confirms my point that patterns are guides. They can be used as effectively in an XP-style coding project as they can in an upfront design one.

The Template Method pattern is applicable when there are different, but conceptually similar processes. The variations for each process are coupled together because they are associated with a particular process. In the example I presented, when I need a format a **Connect** command for an Oracle database, if I need a format a **Query** command, it'll be for an Oracle database as well.

Summary

Sometimes, I have a set of procedures that I must follow. The procedures are common at a high level, but implementing some of the steps can vary. For example, querying a SQL database is fairly routine at a high level, but some of the details—say, how to connect to the database—can vary based on details such as the platform.

In this chapter

The Template Method Pattern: Key Features

Intent
Define the skeleton of an algorithm in an operation, deferring some steps to subclasses. Redefine the steps in an algorithm without changing the algorithm's structure.

Problem
There is a procedure or set of steps to follow that is consistent at one level of detail, but individual steps may have different implementations at a lower level of detail.

Solution
Allows for definition of substeps that vary while maintaining a consistent basic process.

Participants and collaborators
The Template Method consists of an abstract class that defines the basic **TemplateMethod** (see figure below) classes that need to be overridden. Each concrete class derived from the abstract class implements a new method for the Template.

Consequences
Templates provide a good platform for code reuse. They also are helpful in ensuring the required steps are implemented. They bind the overridden steps together for each **Concrete** class, and so should only be used when these variations always and only occur together.

Implementation
Create an abstract class that implements a procedure using abstract methods. These abstract methods must be implemented in subclasses to perform each step of the procedure. If the steps vary independently, each step may be implemented with a Strategy pattern.

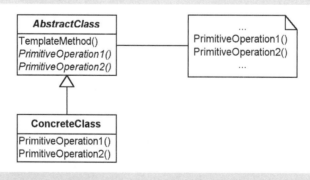

Figure 19-7 Generic structure of the Template Method pattern.

The Template Method pattern enables me to define the sequence of steps and then override those steps that need to change.

The Template Method pattern also enables me to avoid introducing redundancy when I need to support multiple systems that behave conceptually the same but have different implementations for each of their steps.

Review Questions

Observation

1. The Template Method pattern makes the method call in a special way. What is that?

Interpretation

1. According to the Gang of Four, the intent of the Template Method pattern is to "define the skeleton of an algorithm in an operation, deferring some steps to subclasses. Redefine the steps in an algorithm without changing the algorithm's structure." What does this mean?

2. The Gang of Four calls this a "Template Method." Why do they do this?

3. What is the difference between the Strategy pattern (Chapter 9) and the Template Method pattern?

PART VII

Factories

Part Overview

Factory patterns help with the creation of objects. But that may not be their most important use. Seen from the new perspective, they are much more.

In this part

CHAPTER 20

Lessons from Design Patterns: Factories

Overview

This chapter discusses the use of factories—objects that make other objects. Although factories are presented in the Gang of Four book, their use in design is not discussed fully.

In this chapter

This chapter

- Discusses why the use of factories can greatly simplify your design and code.

- Explains the proper steps of seeing first what your objects are and then deciding how to create and/or manage them.

Factories

Usually, when I am designing objects, I am concerned with their behavior: what the objects do and how other objects tell them to do it. But I also need to be concerned about figuring out when a particular object is needed and making sure it is ready when I need it. I need to be sure the rules for object creation get followed.

Factories encapsulate business rules for creating objects

Developers who are new to object-oriented programming often lump the management of object creation in with object instantiation. I believe this stems from the fact that when using procedural languages developers know the specific case at hand. They are thinking at the implementation level. Object-oriented languages present both a new problem and a new opportunity. In object-oriented programming, objects come into being at various times and for various reasons. If the code that uses the objects also is responsible for instantiating the objects (which is often the case), the code can become complicated. It has to keep track of many things: which objects to create, which construction parameters are needed, and how to use the object after construction—often even how to manage a pool of objects. This reduces cohesion, which is not what we want. It also often leads the developer to choosing an instantiation scheme too early, before you know what needs to be instantiated. I much prefer not getting locked into an approach until I know what the most appropriate approach to use is.

Factories address these issues. They help to keep objects cohesive, decoupled, and testable. They help to keep my design flexible. They enable me to split my problem up into smaller, more manageable pieces.

What are factories?   But first, let me define what I mean by a "factory." A factory is a method (static or otherwise), an object, or anything else that is used to instantiate other objects. I have already shown one example of a factory in the Abstract Factory pattern in Chapter 11, "The Abstract Factory Pattern." This was a particularly sophisticated factory because it did not simply instantiate *one* object but rather controlled the instantiation of a *set* (family) of objects. The Gang of Four describes several patterns involving factories in their book. They call these creation patterns and are as follows:

- The Abstract Factory pattern
- The Builder pattern
- The Factory Method pattern
- The Prototype pattern
- The Singleton pattern

The Gang of Four defines patterns by general purpose   The Gang of Four has built their general classification around the conceptual motivations of the patterns:

- The **behavioral** patterns are used to contain variation of behavior.

- The **structural** patterns are useful to integrate existing code into new object-oriented designs.

- The **factory** patterns are useful to manage the creation of objects.

This makes sense within the context of us handling variation in new ways. When I define new objects, I define them how I want to, using the behavioral patterns to guide me. However, when I have to incorporate existing objects into new design paradigms, it makes more sense to use structural patterns to guide me.

The use of factories is a natural result of hiding variation. Consider the Strategy pattern. If the Context object in the pattern (the **SalesOrder** class in the example in Chapter 9, "The Strategy Pattern") does not know which **Tax** object it is using, who does? The easiest answer is — *someone else*. This "someone else" can be a factory.

The Universal Context Revisited

In Chapter 13, "Solving the CAD/CAM Problem," I discussed the "universal context for software development."

Factories— a universal context

> *Rule: Consider what you need to have in your system before you concern yourself with how to create it…. That is, we define our factories after we decide what our objects are.*

First, decide what your objects are and how they work, *and then* decide on how to instantiate them. To see the value of this, try this little mind experiment.

Imagine a project you worked on where there were many different cases to handle—lots of variations, lots of ifs, and switches. Now imagine a time before all of this code was written. Suppose your team lead said, "We are going to break into two groups. Group A will decide what our objects are and how they will work together. Group B will have the task of instantiating the correct objects under various circumstances."

That is, Group A will design the objects according to the rules we've outlined in this book, but *only how they will work.* This means that the client objects will not need to worry about all of the different variations present. In fact, we are going to make sure Group A does not have to worry about this because Group B will write classes and objects that will instantiate the correct objects needed for each case involved. Actually, Group B's code may do more than instantiate objects. Sometimes objects are shared or reused. Therefore, their "factories" will really be "managing factory" (a factory that does more than simply instantiate objects), but I will keep calling them factories anyway.

Now I would like you to consider two things. First, which group has the harder task? The one defining the objects and seeing how to use them? Or the one which just knows which objects are needed and how to create and manage them? Almost every student I have asked says that Group B has the easier task: They have a lot of reasonably straightforward rules that are mostly decoupled from each other. It is relatively easy to implement the rules about when to create objects according to which case you have.

Second, think about this. How much does the work of Group B simplify the work of Group A? I would suggest the answer on a typical project is, "quite a bit." The reason for this is that complex code is usually difficult because it has to attend to the particular case at hand *and* which particular objects are used in that case. Taking this approach makes it so Group A now just needs to design to interfaces and abstract classes. Group B figures out which implementations and derivations to actually use. The job of both groups is simpler. By making the creation and management of the objects easier, it is also possible that you can manage them better with the same effort.

The relatively simple problem of organizing the rules for which objects you have for a given circumstance greatly simplifies the code that uses these objects. This approach, illustrated in Figure 20-1, is the one I recommend.

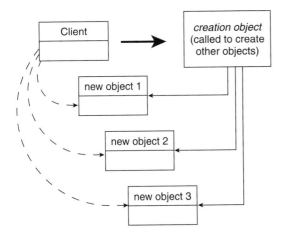

Figure 20-1 Client using a factory to make objects and then using the objects.

Factories Follow Our Guidelines

Consider this approach of splitting up development into these two steps:

Factories increase cohesion, loosen coupling, assist in testing,....

1. Define the objects and how they work together.

2. Write factories that instantiate the correct objects for the right situation and manage existing objects if they are shared.

The code generated in Step 1 does not concern itself with which objects get instantiated, whereas the code in Step 2 does not concern itself with how the objects work together. In other words, the code for both steps is more cohesive. Why? If you were not following this approach, you would have code that dealt with both the functionality and the rules that determine which objects should be built and/or managed under different circumstances. By separating these issues, you only deal with one or the other of these in a given class.

Rule: Objects should either make other objects or use other objects, but never both

When it comes to object creation and management, here is a good, general rule to follow: An object should either *make and/or manage* other objects, or it should *use* other objects *but it should never do both.*

If you conform to this constraint, you will end up with less coupling because there is a clear division of labor. The "using objects" are de-coupled from the objects they are using. They do not know which objects they have—nor even what they possibly *could* have—as collaborating objects. That job belongs to the factories. At the same time, the factories only know which objects they are creating or managing; they do not know how those objects are being used. This distinction is illustrated in Figures 20-2 and 20-3.

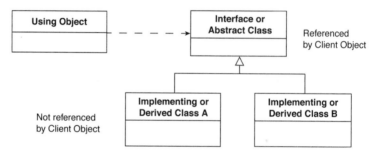

Figure 20-2 The perspective of the "using object."

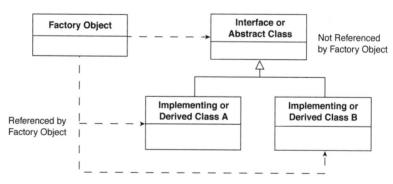

Figure 20-3 The perspective of the "creating object."

Look at Figure 20-2. The "using object" only knows how to use the objects it is pointing to. It doesn't know which particular object it has. On the other hand, looking at Figure 20-3, you can see that Factory objects know which objects they have, but don't know how to use them. This separation of concerns both strengthens cohesion and decreases coupling.

Furthermore, it creates more opportunities for encapsulation, which I've said before is something we should value highly. The implementing classes are totally hidden from the "using object." I can add new implementations or take away one or more of the existing ones without changing the "using object" at all.

This also improves testing because the "using objects" should behave in the same way with any set of derivatives present. I should not need to test every possible combination, because I can test each piece individually. No matter how I combine them, the system will work in the same manner.

Limiting the Vectors of Change

One of the major issues that patterns help us focus on is making future maintenance easier and more economical. Generally, they help me to follow the open-closed principle, which means that, when changes are needed, I am adding new code rather than changing old code. This tends to reduce the costs of maintenance.

Factories are a major player here:

1. Although there are often many "users" of an object, there is usually only one factory to build and/or manage it. Therefore, the more I can restrict my code modification to factories, the less work there will be for the main system— which is typically where the change of cost is highest.

2. When a change is needed, usually it is either a change in which objects are required or it is a change in the way in which some objects are used. Factories help to limit maintenance to the users of the object or the builder of the object. I will have to modify both much less frequently.

3. The knowledge that I can "worry about instantiation later" enables me to focus on the "pluggable" aspects of the design. It frees me to see opportunities for flexibility.

Another Way to Think About It

Making integration easier

When I discussed commonality and variability analysis in Chapter 15, "The Commonality and Variability Analysis," I mentioned that it is usually more expensive to integrate new code into a system than it is to develop it in the first place. Separating use from construction makes integration costs lower. This occurs because I only have to deal with the new case I have. I have already created the framework for adding in new cases.

When you encounter code that is difficult to understand and/or integrate, you'll often find some major piece of it that has to continuously track the particular situation it is currently in. This no longer happens when the factories handle this. Essentially, all the situational information is placed in a few objects. This makes it much easier to figure out how the cases interact with each other. In other words, the factories aren't eliminating work, but they contain it in such a way that the more complex code does not have to become even more complex when new cases must be handled.

Factories enable us to capitalize on the advantages of doing things in an object-oriented way, as opposed to using lots of procedural logic. Instead of using a switch to vary a behavior, just vary which object is in play. Factories make this easier to do and to control.

Different Roles of Factories

Chapter 16, "The Analysis Matrix," illustrated the way the proper use of the Abstract Factory pattern enabled the **SalesOrder** object to deal only with the concepts of taxes, freight charges, etc. Adding new implementations often involved only creating the new cases and updating the factory. However, as mentioned, factories can also manage our objects. Sometimes we want to share objects, have only one or a limited number of these. Database connections fall into this category. Factories should therefore be concerned about the rules of *which* objects as well as how to manage them, which may include how many objects are instantiated and how they are shared. This enables us to encapsulate all of the rules of which objects are being used in our factories.

More than which objects

In Chapter 17, "The Decorator Pattern," you saw how chains of objects can be placed in front of the object that the code thinks it is using. In this, and other Gang of Four patterns, the construction of objects and inserting them into a design can be fairly complex. Factories can hide this complexity, leaving the "using object" to believe it is dealing with just a simple object. This enables encapsulation of design.

Factories can encapsulate design

You might say that factories are solving a problem that patterns have created. The approach of patterns is to add layers of indirection in the code because it allows for more maintainable objects. However, this can put a burden on the client code, forcing it to know about all of these objects, and that can complicate the code. Factories hide the fact that these extra objects exist, and this results in less-complex code

Field Notes

As you attempt to follow the guidelines of this chapter, you will see that similar recurring problems will happen in different situations. Many of these have resulted in particular solutions that have been

Common problems in making objects

identified as design patterns. You have already seen one of these—the Abstract Factory. I will review a few more of these in the following chapters.

Going one step beyond this, complex creation problems are often solved by incorporating behavioral and structural patterns into the factory logic. For example, I have created factories using the Bridge pattern and other factories that used the Decorator pattern. Patterns not described in this book that I've used in creating factories include the Chain of Responsibility pattern to determine which object to instantiate to handle a given protocol object.

Summary

In this chapter   This chapter explained why having factories should make our life easier. Factories encapsulate the rules of which objects we have under which circumstances. This allows the rest of the system to use the objects without regard to the particular implementations present.

Review Questions

Observation

1. Define a "factory."

2. Name one factory pattern that was shown in a previous chapter. Name the factory patterns mentioned in this chapter

3. When it comes to managing object creation, what is a good, universal rule to use?

Interpretation

1. Developers who are new to object-oriented programming often lump the management of object creation in with object instantiation. What is wrong with doing this?

2. Factories increase cohesion. What is the reason for this?

3. Factories also help in testing. In what ways is this true?

Opinion and Application

1. Factories are useful for more than just deciding which object to create or use. They also help with encapsulating design by solving a problem created by patterns? Evaluate this argument.

CHAPTER 21

The Singleton Pattern
and the Double-Checked
Locking Pattern

Overview

This chapter continues the e-commerce case study introduced in Chapter 9, "The Strategy Pattern."

In this chapter

This chapter

- Illustrates how a factory can control the number of instances of an object that can ever exist, using the Singleton pattern.

- Describes the key features of the Singleton pattern.

- Introduces a variant to the Singleton called the Double-Checked Locking pattern.

- Describes some of my experiences using the Singleton pattern in practice.

The Singleton pattern and the Double-Checked Locking pattern are very simple and very common. Both are used to ensure that only one object of a particular class is instantiated. The distinction between the patterns is that the Singleton pattern is used in single-threaded applications, whereas the Double-Checked Locking pattern is used in multithreaded applications.[1]

While reading this chapter, keep in mind the ideas about factories that I discussed in the previous chapter. In this chapter, the focus of the factory is on encapsulating the rule that controls the number of ob-

---

1. If you do not know what a multithreaded application is, don't worry; to understand the basic principles, you only need to concern yourself with the Singleton pattern.

jects present—in this case, there can be only *one* object present. The patterns help to separate use from construction.

Introducing the Singleton Pattern

The intent, according to the Gang of Four

According to the Gang of Four, the Singleton's intent is to

> *Ensure a class only has one instance, and provide a global point of access to it.*[2]

How the Singleton pattern works: A special method

The Singleton pattern works by having a special method that is used to instantiate the desired object. Here is what is most interesting about this special method:

- When this method is called, it checks to see whether the object has already been instantiated. If it has, the method just returns a reference to the object. If not, the method instantiates it and returns a reference to the new instance.

- To ensure that this is the only way to instantiate an object of this type, I define the constructor of this class to be protected or private.

...and all collaborating objects use the same instance

The essence of the Singleton pattern is that every object in the application uses the same instance of the Singleton. I do not want to have to be responsible for passing the instance around to all the objects that want to use it. This is especially important when a change made to the instance by one collaborating object needs to be visible to another collaborating object.

---

2. Gamma, E., Helm, R., Johnson, R., Vlissides, J., Design Patterns: *Elements of Reusable Object-Oriented Software*, Boston: Addison-Wesley, 1995, p. 127.

Applying the Singleton Pattern to the Case Study

In Chapter 9, I encapsulated the rules about taxes within strategy objects. I have to derive a **CalcTax** class for each possible tax calculation rule. This means that I need to use the same objects over and over again, just alternating between their uses.

A motivating example: Instantiate tax calculation strategies only once and only when needed

For performance reasons, I might not want to keep instantiating them and throwing them away again and again. And, although I could instantiate all of the possible strategies at the start, this could become inefficient if the number of strategies grew large. (Remember, I may have many other strategies throughout my application.) Instead, it would be best to instantiate them as needed, but only do the instantiation once.

The problem is that I do not want to create a separate object to keep track of what I have already instantiated. Instead, I would like the objects themselves (that is, the strategies) to be responsible for handling their own single instantiation.

Singleton makes objects responsible for themselves

This is the purpose of the Singleton pattern. It enables me to instantiate an object only once, without requiring the client objects to be concerned with whether it already exists.

The Singleton could be implemented in code as shown in Example 21-1. In this example, I create a method (*getInstance*) that will instantiate at most one **USTax** object. The Singleton protects against someone else instantiating the **USTax** object directly by making the constructor private, which means that no other object can access it.

Example 21-1 Java Code Fragment: Singleton Pattern

```
public class USTax extends Tax {
   private static USTax instance;
   private USTax() { }
```

```
      public static USTax getInstance() {
         if (instance== null) instance= new USTax();
         return instance;
      }
   }
}
```

Singleton with
polymorphism

In this case study, however, I actually need the **SalesOrder** to ask the **Tax** object which **Tax** object to use. The reason for this is that the **SalesOrder** does not want to know which particular tax object is present. There are two notions being combined here:

1. Hide which concrete class I use (the factory in a method in the **Tax** class)

2. Hide how many instantiations of each class I have (the Singleton in the **USTax** and other **Tax** concrete classes).

I show this in Example 21-2.

Example 21-2 Java Code Fragment: Singleton Pattern in the Context of the E-Commerce System

```
abstract public class Tax {
   static private Tax instance;
   protected Tax() { };

   abstract double calcTax(
      double qty, double price);

   public static Tax getInstance() {
      // use whatever rule you use to determine
      // which tax object to use.  For now,
      // let's create a USTax object.
      instance= USTax.getInstance();

      return instance;
   }
}
public class USTax extends Tax {
   private static USTax instance;
   private USTax() { }
   // Note in the following, I had to change USTax
```

```
    // to Tax since I used the same "getInstance"
    // name.
    public static Tax getInstance() {
        if (instance== null) instance= new USTax();
        return instance;
    }
}
```

The Singleton Pattern: Key Features

Intent	You want to have only *one* of an object, but there is no global object that controls the instantiation of this object. You also want to ensure that all entities are using the same instance of this object, without passing a reference to all of them.
Problem	Several different client objects need to refer to the same thing, and you want to ensure that you do not have more than one of them.
Solution	Guarantees one instance.
Participants and collaborators	**Clients** create an instance of the **Singleton** solely through the *getInstance* method.
Consequences	**Clients** need not concern themselves whether an instance of the **Singleton** exists. This can be controlled from within the **Singleton**.
Implementation	• Add a private static member of the class that refers to the desired object. (Initially, it is null.)
	• Add a public static method that instantiates this class if this member is null (and sets this member's value) and then returns the value of this member.
	• Set the constructor's status to protected or private so that no one can directly instantiate this class and bypass the static constructor mechanism.

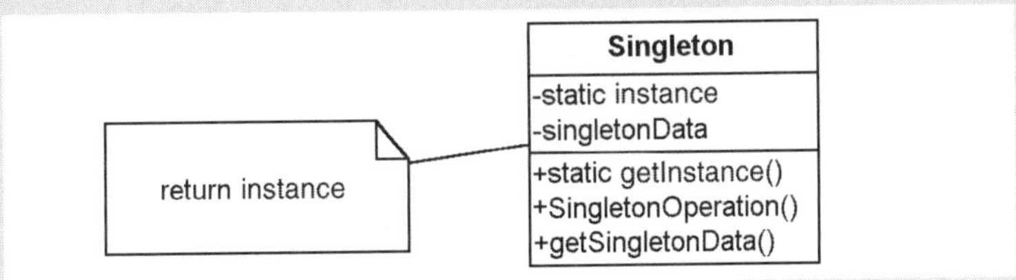

Figure 21-1 Generic structure of the Singleton pattern.

A Variant: The Double-Checked Locking Pattern

Only for multithreaded applications

This pattern *only* applies to multithreaded applications. If you are not involved with multithreaded applications, you might want to skip this section. This section assumes that you have a basic understanding of multithreaded issues, including synchronization.

In a multithreaded mode, Singleton does not always work properly

A problem with the Singleton pattern may arise in multithreaded applications.

Suppose two calls to *getInstance ()* are made at virtually the same time. This can be very bad. Consider what can happen in this case:

1. The first thread checks to see whether the instance exists. It does not, it goes into the part of the code that will create the first instance.

2. However, before it has done that, suppose a second thread also looks to see whether the instance member is null. Because the first thread hasn't created anything yet, the instance is still equal to null, so the second thread also goes into the code that will create an object.

3. Both threads now perform a *new* on the Singleton object, thereby creating two objects.

Is this a problem? It may or may not be.

None, small, bad, or worse

- If the Singleton is absolutely stateless, this may not be a problem.

- If the Singleton has state, and if you expect that when one object changes the state, all other objects should see the change, then this could become a serious problem. The first thread will be interacting with a different object than all other threads do. Examples of problems likely to occur:

  – Inconsistent state between threads using the different Singleton objects.

– If the object creates a connection, there will actually be two connections (one for each object).

– If a counter is used, there will be two counters.

• In C++, regardless of state, the program may create a memory leak, because it may only delete one of the objects when I have actually created two of them.

It may be very difficult to find these problems. First of all, the dual creation is very intermittent—it usually won't happen. Second, it may not be obvious why the counts are off, because only one client object will contain one of the Singleton objects while all the other client objects will refer to the other Singleton.

At first, it appears that all I need to do is synchronize the test for whether the Singleton object has been created. The only problem is that this synchronization may end up being a severe bottleneck, because all the threads will have to wait for the check on whether the object already exists.

Synchronizing the creation of the Singleton object

Perhaps instead I could put some synchronization code in after the **if (instance== null)** test. This will not work either. Because it would be possible that both calls could meet the null test and then attempt to synchronize, I could still end up making two Singleton objects, making them one at a time.

The solution is to do a "sync" after the test for null and then check again to make sure the instance member has not yet been created. I show this in Example 21-3. This is called ***double-checked locking***.[3] The intent is to optimize away unnecessary locking. This synchronization check happens at most one time, so it will not be a bottleneck.

A simple solution: Double-checked locking

The features of double-checked locking are as follows:

---

3. Martin, R., Riehle, D., Buschmann, F., *Pattern Language of Program Design,* Boston: Addison-Wesley, 1998, p. 363.

• Unnecessary locking is avoided by by adding another test before creating the object

Support for multithreaded environments.

Example 21-3 Java Code Fragment: Instantiation Only

```
public class USTax extends Tax {
    private static USTax instance;
    private USTax() { }
    public static Tax getInstance() {
        if (instance== null) {
            synchronized(this) {
                if (instance == null)
                    instance = new USTax();
            }
        }
        return instance;
    }
    private synchronized static void doSync() {
        if (instance == null)instance = new USTax();
    }
}
```

Unfortunately, this doesn't work either

When the Double-Checked Locking pattern was converted from C++ to Java, it was soon discovered that it did not work for Java.[4] The reason is that the Java compiler, in its optimization efforts, may return the reference to an object from a constructor before the constructor is through instantiating the object. Thus, **dosync** may complete before **USTax** is actually completely built. This may cause a problem. Also an optimizing compiler may "notice" that there is "no way" for the "instance" member to change state between the two "if" statements, and optimize the second one out. You can avoid this problem in C# by using the keyword **volatile**.

---

4. See the book's Web site at *http://www.netobjectives.com/dpexplained* for more information on this.

It is not all that hard to fix this—not that I figured it out on my own. One solution is to take advantage of the class loader, as shown in Example 21-4.

A Solution for Java

Example 21-4 Java Code Fragment: Instantiation Only

```
public class USTax extends Tax {
    private static class Instance {
        static final Tax instance= new USTax();
    }
    private static USTax instance;
    private USTax() { }
    public static Tax getInstance() {
        return Instance.instance;
    }
}
```

This works because the inner class (**Instance**) will get loaded only once; therefore, only one **USTax** object is built.

Reflections

When it was discovered that the Double-Checked Locking pattern as initially described did not work in Java, many people saw it as evidence that patterns were overhyped. I drew exactly the opposite conclusion. The mistake made was in viewing the pattern from the wrong perspective. Critics looked at the pattern from the implementation perspective and were surprised that techniques were not universally applicable. They seemed surprised that one could not apply an idiom in one language directly into another language. The descriptions at the conceptual and specification level still held true; the implementation level required differences.

What works in one language may not work in another

In fact, even at the implementation level, having patterns was more of a help than a hurt. Because this idiom was defined in a pattern, developers had a common frame of reference, a common jargon they

could use to talk about the problem. They learned quickly and succinctly that it did not work in Java in the same way as it did in C++.
Then they worked out solutions that did work that were true to the
requirements of the pattern. Furthermore, alternative solutions have
been worked out in other languages. Evidence of this is the quick
adoption of the "volatile" solution in C#.

Field Notes: Using the Singleton and Double-Checked Locking Patterns

Only use when needed

If you know you are going to need an object and no performance
issue requires you to defer instantiation of the object until it's needed, it is usually simpler to have a static member contain a reference
to the object.

Typically stateless

In multithreaded applications, Singletons typically have to be thread-
safe (because the single object may be shared by multiple objects).
This means either using synchronization between the threads or having no data members (i.e., having only variables whose scope is no
larger than a method).

Stateful Singletons are essentially globals

Stateful Singletons should be used sparingly as a result because global data like this can potentially couple disparate parts of the system.

Used to instantiate objects used in other patterns

Stateless Facades can be instantiated with a Singleton to avoid having more than one of them. The concrete strategies of the Strategy
pattern (when stateless), the concrete implementations of the Bridge
(again, if stateless) can also be instantiated this way. This is true for
the objects in many other patterns as well.

Can be modified to contain more than one object

Although they would no longer be "Singletons," of course, static
public methods could be modified to contain more than one element
if a particular number of instances were needed. I explore this more
in Chapter 22, "The Object Pool Pattern."

Summary

The Singleton and Double-Checked Locking patterns are common patterns to use when you want to ensure that there is only one instance of an object. The Singleton is used in single-threaded applications, whereas the Double-Checked Locking pattern is used in multithreaded applications.

In this chapter

These patterns illustrate that factories may be separate objects or methods that contain the rules of object creation. They also illustrate that factories are not about just which objects are present, but also how many.

Review Questions

Observations

1. What type of pattern is the Singleton? What general category of pattern does it belong to?

2. What is the intent of the Singleton pattern?

3. How many objects is the Singleton responsible for creating?

4. The Singleton uses a special method to instantiate objects. What is special about this method?

5. What is the difference in when to use the Singleton and Double-Checked Locking patterns?

Interpretations

1. Is it better to have objects be responsible for handling their own single instantiation than to do it globally for the objects? Why or why not?

Opinions and Applications

1. Why do you think the Gang of Four call this pattern "Singleton"? Is it an appropriate name for what it is doing? Why or why not?

2. When it was discovered that the Double-Checked Locking pattern as initially described did not work in Java, many people saw it as evidence that patterns were overhyped. I drew exactly the opposite conclusion. Do you agree with this logic? Why or why not?

CHAPTER 22

The Object Pool Pattern

Overview

This chapter discusses the Object Pool pattern. Rather than using the international e-commerce case study, I illustrate this pattern with an actual project I worked on several years ago. This project gives evidence of the proposal I made in Chapter 10, "The Bridge Pattern." That was that if you understand the principles of patterns and work on a project where a pattern that is unknown to you applies, you are likely to derive it yourself. In particular, on this project, I ended up deriving the Object Pool pattern from the basic principles of design patterns. Later I discovered that what I had written had been written by others as well, and named the Object Pool pattern. The point I want to reinforce for you is that it is more important for you to understand the basic principles of design patterns than it is to memorize a bunch of diagrams and patterns or to have a giant reference book. Knowing how to think with patterns will make you more likely to find the solutions or derive the patterns that are right for your situation.

In this chapter

This chapter

- Describes the Object Pool pattern.

- Shows how patterns can be used to focus on the most important aspects of the project—deferring things that cause no risk.

- Shows how factories can not only manage objects but can also be the best place to describe the logic about their proper functioning.

- Shows how patterns and knowing how to encapsulate issues facilitates agile coding practices.

A Problem Requiring the Management of Objects

A pool of connections   Several years ago, I was contracting for a company that was making a Web-based, personal investment system. Although such systems are common today, back then this was new territory. The general intent for this application was to enable users to look at their personal investments over the Web and enter orders to buy and sell the stocks, bonds, and so on that they had in their accounts. The information about the user accounts was kept on a mainframe computer. The physical architecture is shown in Figure 22-1.

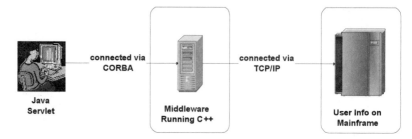

Figure 22-1 n-Tier architecture of the personal investment system.

The front end that we were using was written with Java servlets; this fed the middle layer that I was writing in C++. My tier communicated with the mainframe to retrieve information about the user's investments or to submit orders. The only way to communicate with the mainframe was through TCP/IP connections using a special messaging protocol that was specified by the company that supported the mainframe. The middleware code that I was writing had the responsibility of taking the input from the user and verifying its validity. It did this by checking with the mainframe computer, which had all the information. The servlet front end essentially just did formatting and basic checking.

A typical user session would look like this:

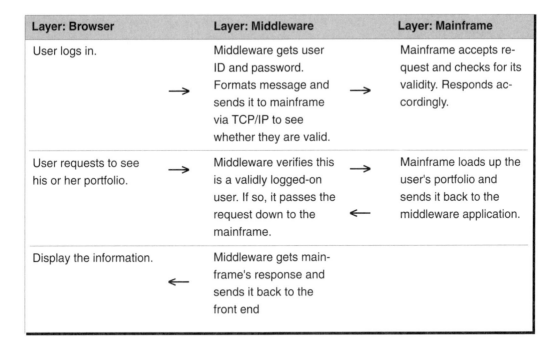

Layer: Browser	Layer: Middleware	Layer: Mainframe
User logs in. →	Middleware gets user ID and password. Formats message and sends it to mainframe via TCP/IP to see whether they are valid. →	Mainframe accepts request and checks for its validity. Responds accordingly.
User requests to see his or her portfolio. →	Middleware verifies this is a validly logged-on user. If so, it passes the request down to the mainframe. → ←	Mainframe loads up the user's portfolio and sends it back to the middleware application.
Display the information. ←	Middleware gets mainframe's response and sends it back to the front end	

There was some concern about the performance of this system. I was told to be more interested in throughput and not to worry about response time. Because my middleware application was taking requests from many, many people, this requirement meant that I wanted to handle as many transactions as possible, but that I did not need to worry about any particular thread's time through the system.

Throughput was the primary concern

I had never written an application like this before. I had no good ideas for how to balance this load. I knew it would require more than one TCP/IP connection to the mainframe, but how many? I was pretty sure that the right number was somewhere between 2 and 100—one was too few, and more than 100 would not do me any good because the available bandwidth could not handle more than 20 anyway.

So how many TCP/IP connections should I use? Although I knew I did not know the answer right at the start, I would have to figure it out before the end of the project. This was a dilemma for me. I didn't know how to start and did not have the time to do a lot of testing or emulation. And at that time, I did not really know that much about TCP/IP. This meant that the TCP/IP connection was a high risk for the project, even more so because no one on the project knew all that was entailed in it.

I prefer to tackle high-risk issues quickly. If they cannot be addressed, I try to isolate them, to try to turn them into lower-risk items. To solve the TCP/IP connection issue, I knew what I needed was an end-to-end solution as soon as possible, something that could take a request from the browser, perform some logic, pass it through to the mainframe, get a response, and send that information back to the browser. After that had been accomplished, this risk would be reduced because I would have demonstrated the ability to communicate through a TCP/IP connection.

To implement this end-to-end solution with the TCP/IP connection, I had to do the following:

1. Establish a robust TCP/IP connection.

2. Determine the number of TCP/IP connections to be used.

3. Establish methods to load balance the connections.

4. Handle errors on the TCP/IP connections. (These were known to sometimes fail.)

All four of these items were important. The risk issues I considered were as follows:

1. How much time would I need to become competent with TCP/IP?

2. If I changed the number of connections, would that affect the using code?

3. Would load balancing affect the using code?

4. Would error handling affect the using code?

There was not much I could do about Issue 1. I had to enhance my TCP/IP skills quickly. Issues 2 through 4, however, could be mitigated by encapsulating them from the using code. In other words, my main business logic really just needed to deal with *one* TCP/IP connection. How it functioned, how many connections there were, and how it handled errors, were issues for the connection-to-connection code to handle. If I could isolate these issues from my business logic—if my business logic could ignore them—then I could change them later, *after* I had solved Issue 1 without affecting the rest of the code. This told me I had to hide (encapsulate) them all.

This is a general approach for me: I try to look for ways to insulate myself from the impacts of changes to my system. I know I am going to have to change things as I figure out what to do because I rarely get it right the first time. And in this case, I had to be fast, which meant it was even more important to reduce debugging and rework.

With this approach in mind, and armed with a general understanding of patterns, I was ready to begin.

I figured because I didn't have any hope of guessing what the right solution was, I had to make my system so that I could *change* the number of TCP/IP connections without affecting my code (except maybe in the smallest way). This meant that my client code (the code that used the TCP/IP connections) should not be required to change when the number of connections changed. To me, this implied that these client objects *could not even know* how many TCP/IP objects there were. Who would know? *Someone else!*

Don't rely on hope

That "someone else" would be the manager of my TCP/IP objects. The result was that I had two main functions going on here:

Create a TCP/IP Manager

1. The TCP/IP objects that would communicate with the mainframe

2. The management of these objects

Although I could have put all of this logic in the TCP/IP object itself, the principle of cohesion prescribed using two separate objects. I called the object that controlled one TCP/IP object a "Port." I did this because TCP/IP is just one implementation of how a program communicates with the mainframe. Although I was using TCP/IP at the moment (and probably always would), in my mind the object was a port to the mainframe. I really thought of this connection as a port to the user's information. Naturally enough, I decided to name my port manager, **PortManager**.

Although there would be many ports, there would be only one **PortManager**. This one object would handle all of my **Port**s. What is the pattern to use if you need to ensure that there is at most one object? The Singleton pattern. That is what I decided to use.

Singleton ensured that I had only one **PortManager**; I also wanted ed this **PortManager** to be the only one that could create **Port**s.[1] Encapsulating the management of **Port**s enabled me to be arbitrary in picking the number of **Port**s to use. I reached up and pulled the number five out of the air. That seemed to be as good a number as any to start with.

I implemented the **PortManager** as follows[2]:

Data Members

I gave it a private array of five **Port** references, using a constant to define this number. I instantiated these in the **PortManager**'s constructor. If any of them did not instantiate, I threw an exception

---

1. Because I was using C++, I made the Port constructor protected and made the PortManager a friend of it. Had I been using C#, I could have used delegates to handle this restriction. See this book's Web site at *http://www.netobjectives.com/ dpexplained* to see how to do this. It is not obvious, but is easily doable. In Java, I would have put the PortManager and the Port classes in a package.

2. Note that although I used C++ on this project, the code I show here is in Java, to be consistent with the rest of the book.

because this was a bad start: not being able to get five connections did not bode well for keeping communications up!

Methods

I had a method that could be called to ask for a **Port**, called *getInstanceOfPort()*

I had another method that was called (with the **Port** reference) that said the port was no longer active: *returnInstanceOfPort (Port portToRelease)*.

Implementing each of these was very simple:

> *getInstanceOfPort()* The first one just looped through the **Port** array and found the first available port. (Each port had a status as to whether it was in use.) If one was found, its status was updated to active and it was returned. If one wasn't found, I put the thread to sleep for one second and tried again.

> *returnInstanceOfPort(Port portToRelease)* This one wasn't much harder. I just looped through my ports until I found the reference given and updated its status to inactive. I threw an exception if I could not find it, because that should not happen.

The client code was very straightforward. When a message needed to be handled, the client would

1. Ask the **PortManager** for a port.

2. Use the port as needed.

3. Release the port.

The client code did not have to concern itself with creating ports or how many of them would ever be used.

Patterns help with agile

The important thing to note here is that not only did this make the client code decoupled from the **Port** code, it also meant I could defer much of my work until later in the project. I have already shown how I could ignore the port handling. Even better, in the client code, I could also ignore error handling, which is one of the tougher problems with TCP/IP in C++. Why could I do this? Because I was confident that the **Port** and **PortManager** either could handle errors completely or handle them to such an extent that the client code would be virtually unaffected when I did implement it. I was free to focus on the more important aspects of the problem: the client code.

Focusing on what is most important is essential to agile development. In XP, they even have a slogan for it: YAGNI (ya ain't gonna need it). It reflects the idea that you should build what you need now while ignoring the rest. You should work on the most important things early, when solving them can make the greatest impact. It also means you avoid working on things that are at a minimum distracting, and typically never used (and therefore building is a waste of resources).

The most important thing I needed to do was to get the communication between my middleware application and the mainframe going. Things like load balancing and error handling, although extremely important, would have delayed me from building the system. By focusing on the communication first in a way that decoupled it from the rest of the system, I could get others working on responding to my needs. I could handle these other needs later.

What I had was the Object Pool pattern

Without knowing it at the time, I ended up with the Object Pool pattern. I had achieved this quality design just by following the principles of design patterns. This is what the Object Pool pattern enables you to do. Although you could say that my derivation implies that the pattern isn't needed, I feel that knowing it would ensure its use when that would be applicable. Also a less-experienced designer may not have taken my approach. It takes less effort to learn from others than to break new ground yourself. In addition, now that I know this pattern, I can easily communicate my chosen approach to others who know it, with a high degree of confidence that we will be talking about the same thing.

After I got the communications working, I decided I had better turn my focus to handling errors. This meant different things to different parts of my code:

Handling the errors

1. To the **Client**, it meant being able to get another **Port** to use and to resend the message.

2. To the **Port** that experienced the error, it meant disabling itself and not trying to use it anymore.

3. To the **PortManager**, it meant to remember the **Port** is bad and to get a new one to replace it.

The decoupling I had already achieved made this very straightforward as well. Here is what I had to do:

1. Throw an exception when an error occurred on the **Port**.

2. Catch the exception in the **Client** at the point the transmission of the messages began. It was relatively easy to see if anything needed to be backed out (typically not). After this, just return the **Port** to the **PortManager** indicating it was bad, and ask for another one.

3. Add a new method to the **PortManager** called *returnBadPort (Port badPort)*. This would identify the **Port** as bad (in much the *same* way that *returnInstanceOfPort* worked). It would then remove that **Port** from the array and insert a new **Port** where it was. If I couldn't get a new **Port**

(which is highly unlikely), I would send a message via e-mail to a system administrator—this was the preferred method to use if things looked as if they were going to crash and burn. I would then service any other requests with my remaining **Port**s (if I had any).

Going deeper

This should have been enough. But it wasn't. As the system moved forward and it looked as if it would actually go into production, I started having difficulty sleeping. Something was nagging me and would not go away. Another design principle I use is to pay attention to your instincts: You often know more than you think you do!

What was bothering me was that hundreds of millions of dollars were going to go through *my* pipeline, unsupervised. Although I had written a lot of software systems before, some of which were very mission critical, the pressure here seemed greater. If something went wrong on this system at midnight, it would not be acceptable to find out about this the next morning and restart the system. Hundreds of millions of dollars in trades might not get executed. This was not a pleasant thought! Some sort of supervision was needed.

I knew I had to solve this problem. In fact, I felt I had to solve it twice. I had to make sure I had a robust system and then I had to be sure it stayed robust. I remembered reading something in Steve Maguire's book, *Writing Solid Code,*[3] about having dual checking methods for mission-critical parts of the code. It made me think that if I had a separate, independent mechanism of checking the communications, I wouldn't have to worry.

Dual checking

The answer was relatively easy. The **PortManager** was already responsible for creating the **Port**s. I just gave it the additional responsibility for verifying the integrity of those **Port**s. To do this, I chose to have it start a thread that ran a check every 15 minutes; this check would do the following:

---

3. Maguire, S. *Writing Solid Code*, Redmond, WA: Microsoft Press, 1993, p. 33.

- See how many outstanding requests there were for **Port**s (and do something if the number were exceedingly large).

- Query the **Port**s about their status (active or not) and contrast this with the number of requests outstanding to see if something was wrong.

- See how many **Port**s were in an error condition (should be at most 1 or 2).

Basically, I could put anything I wanted to in this code, expanding these ideas if needed. It would provide a higher perspective, one that I could refine as I learned more about the failures possible. I could do this with affecting the rest of the code in any significant way.

Thanks to dual checking, I started sleeping again!

The Object Pool Pattern

Although I used the Object Pool pattern to illustrate how factories can be used and how patterns assist agility, the Object Pool pattern is a useful pattern in and of itself. Typically this pattern is useful whenever there is a shared resource and a single point of contact to that resource would be beneficial. This point of contact (the pool) can also perform other responsibilities (such as error handling). By encapsulating these responsibilities, the client code using these objects is both freed up from concerning itself from them and isolated from any changes to them.

Observation: Factories Can Do Much More Than Instantiation

I started out my discourse on factories to illustrate how I can separate the issues of use from construction. I have now illustrated how you can separate the issues of use from construction and from

Instantiation, management, error handling

object management. I even extended this to include error handling because bad **Port**s meant I needed new ones.

The point is, when you start thinking about objects as things with responsibilities, it becomes clearer how to separate these responsibilities. After the responsibilities have been identified, it is often easy to see the correct structure for the system to have. This results in code that is clearer, more robust, more manageable, and easier to change. And you can sleep at night.

The Object Pool Pattern: Key Features

Intent	Manage the reuse of objects when it is either expensive to create an object or there is a limit on the number objects of a particular type that can be created.
Problem	The creation and/or management of objects must follow a well-defined set of rules. Typically these rules relate to how to make an object, how many objects can be created and how to reuse existing objects once they have finished their current tasks.
Solution	The **Client** calls **ReusablePool**'s *acquireReusable* method when it needs a **Reusable** object. If the pool is empty, then the *acquireReusable* method creates a **Reusable** object if it can; otherwise, it waits until a **Reusable** object is returned to the collection.
Participants and collaborators	The **ReusablePool** manages the availability of **Reusable** objects for use by the **Client**. **Client** then uses instances of **Reusable** objects for a limited amount of time. **ReusablePool** contains all the **Reusable** objects so that they can be managed in a unified way.
Consequences	Works best when the demand for objects is fairly consistent over time; large variations in demand can lead to performance problems. To address this issue in the Object Pool pattern, limit the number of objects that can be created. Keeping the logic to manage the creation of instances separate from the class whose instances are being managed results in a more cohesive design.

Implementation

If there is a limit on the number of objects that may be created or if there is a limit on the size of the pool, use a simple array to implement the pool. Otherwise use a vector object. The object responsible for managing the object pool must be the only object able to create those objects. The **ReusablePool** is implemented with a Singleton pattern. Another variant is to put a release method on the Reusable object—and let it return itself to the pool

Reference

This pattern is not in the Gang of Four book. It is described in Mark Grand's book, *Patterns in Java, Volume 1,*[*] pages 135–142. Clifton Nock's book, *Data Access Patterns,*[**] covers this in a good amount of detail in the context of database resources; he refers to it as Resource Pool.

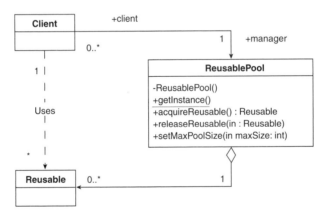

Figure 22-2 Generic structure of the Object Pool.

---

[*] Grand, Mark. *Patterns in Java—Volume 1, A Catalog of Reusable Design Patterns Illustrated with UML*, New York: John Wiley & Sons, Inc., 1998, p. 135–142.

[**] Nock, Clifton. *Data Access Patterns*. Boston: Addison-Wesley, 2003.

Summary

Creation, management, error handling

I illustrated in this chapter how factories can be used for much more than just creating and managing the reuse of objects. The Object Pool pattern is useful for two major reasons:

- It shows how a factory can be used to both instantiate and manage objects.

- It illustrates how encapsulation of responsibility assists developers in focusing on what they most need to.

Review Questions

Observations

1. What are three general strategies to follow when designing?

2. What two patterns does the Object Pool pattern incorporate?

3. What is the intent of the Object Pool pattern?

Interpretations

1. What does the XP community mean by YAGNI?

Opinions and Applications

1. Reading widely is an important discipline. You never know when you will find something you can use, such as the example from Steve Maguire's book, *Writing Solid Code*. Give at least one example from your own experienced where this has been true for you.

CHAPTER 23

The Factory Method Pattern

Overview

This chapter continues the international e-commerce case study that was introduced in Chapter 9, "The Strategy Pattern."

In this chapter

This chapter

- Introduces the Factory Method pattern by discussing additional requirements for the case study.

- Presents the intent of the Factory Method pattern.

- Describes the key features of the Factory Method pattern.

- Describes how the Factory Method pattern has been incorporated into most current object-oriented languages.

- Describes some of my experiences using the Factory Method pattern in practice.

More Requirements for the Case Study

In Chapter 19, "The Template Method Pattern," I ignored the issue of how to instantiate the database object required by the current context. I may not want to make the **Client** responsible for instantiating the database object. Instead, I might want to give that responsibility to the **QueryTemplate** class itself.

New requirement: Responsibility for instantiating database objects

In Chapter 19, each derivation of the **QueryTemplate** was specialized for a particular database. Thus, I might want to make each derivation responsible for instantiating the database to which it corresponds. This would be true whether the **QueryTemplate** (and its derivations) was the only class using the database or not. Figure 23-1 shows this solution.

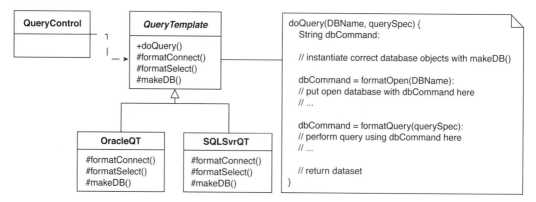

Figure 23-1 The Template Method (doQuery) using the Factory Method pattern (makeDB).

Template Method using Factory Method

In Figure 23-1, the *doQuery* method in the Template Method is using *makeDB* to instantiate the appropriate database object. **QueryTemplate** does not know which database object to instantiate; it only knows that one *must* be instantiated and provides an interface for its instantiation. The derived classes from **QueryTemplate** will be responsible for knowing which ones to instantiate. Therefore, at this level, I can defer the decisions on how to instantiate the database to a method in the derived class.

Because there is a method involved in making an object, this approach is called a Factory Method.

The Factory Method Pattern

Standardizing on the steps

The Factory Method pattern is a pattern intended to help assign responsibility for creation. According to the Gang of Four, the intent of the Factory Method is to

Public or Protected Methods?

Note that the *makeDB* methods are protected (as indicated by the # signs). In this case, only the **QueryTemplate** class and its derivations can access these methods. If I want objects other than **QueryTemplate** to be able to access these methods, they should be public. This is another, quite common way to use the Factory Method. In this case I still have a derived class making the decision about which object to instantiate.

Define an interface for creating an object, but let subclasses decide which class to instantiate. Factory Method lets a class defer instantiation to subclasses.[1]

Factory Method Pattern and Object-Oriented Languages

The Factory Method pattern has been implemented in all the major object-oriented languages:

Has been incorporated into the Java, C#, and C++ libraries

- In Java, the *iterator* method on collections is a Factory method. This method returns the right type of iterator for the collection being asked for it.

- In C#, collections implement the IEnumerable interface. This interface defines the *GetEnumerator,* which is a Factory method to get an iterator for the collection.

- In C++, the Factory methods used include *begin()* and *end()*.

In all of these cases, the methods used to get the appropriate iterator are Factory Method patterns.

---

1. Gamma, E., Helm, R., Johnson, R., Vlissides, J., *Design Patterns: Elements of Reusable Object-Oriented Software*, Boston: Addison-Wesley, 1995, p. 107.

Field Notes: Using the Factory Method Pattern

Abstract Factory can be implemented as a family of Factory Methods

In the classic implementation of the Abstract Factory, I had an abstract class define the methods to create a family of objects. I derived a class for each different family I could have. Each of the methods defined in the abstract class and then overridden in the derived classes was following the Factory Method pattern.

Useful to bind parallel class hierarchies

Sometimes it is useful to create a hierarchical class structure that is parallel to an existing class structure, with the new hierarchy containing some delegated responsibilities. In this case, it is important for each object in the original hierarchy to be able to instantiate the proper object in the parallel hierarchy. A Factory Method can be used for this purpose. In the languages example mentioned previously, the Factory Method patterns bind the different collections with the different iterators associated with the collections, as shown in Figure 23-2.

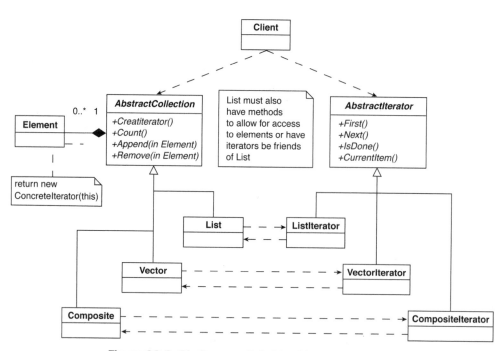

Figure 23-2 Binding parallel class hierarchies.

The Factory Method Pattern: Key Features

Intent	Define an interface for creating an object, but let subclasses decide which class to instantiate. Defer instantiation to subclasses.
Problem	A class needs to instantiate a derivation of another class, but doesn't know which one. Factory Method allows a derived class to make this decision.
Solution	A derived class makes the decision on which class to instantiate and how to instantiate it.
Participants and collaborators	**Product** is the interface for the type of object that the Factory Method creates. **Creator** is the interface that defines the Factory Method.
Consequences	Clients will need to subclass the **Creator** class to make a particular **ConcreteProduct**.
Implementation	Use a method in the abstract class that is abstract (pure virtual in C++). The abstract class' code refers to this method when it needs to instantiate a contained object but does not know which particular object it needs.

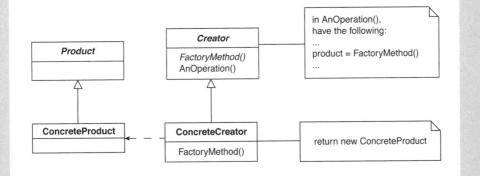

Figure 23-3 Generic structure of the Factory Method pattern.

Factory Method is used in frameworks

The Factory Method pattern is commonly used when defining frameworks. This is because frameworks exist at an abstract level. Usually they do not know and should not be concerned about instantiating specific objects. They need to defer the decisions about specific objects to the users of the framework.

Summary

In this chapter

The Factory Method pattern is a straightforward pattern that you will use again and again. It is used in those cases where you want to defer the rules about instantiating an object to some derived class. In such cases, it is most natural to put the implementation of the method in the object that is responsible for that behavior.

Review Questions

Observation

1. What are factories responsible for?

2. What is the essential reason to use the Factory Method?

3. The Factory Method pattern has been implemented in all of the major object-oriented languages. How has it been provided for in Java, C#, and C++?

Interpretation

1. Why is this pattern called the "Factory Method"?

2. How does the Factory Method pattern fit in with other factories?

3. The Gang of Four says that the intent of the Factory Method is to "define an interface for creating an object, but let subclasses decide which class to instantiate." Why is this important?

Opinion and Application

1. How should you go about deciding whether a method should be public, private, or protected?

2. This is a short chapter but this is not a trivial pattern. Think of one example where this pattern could be used.

CHAPTER 24

Summary of Factories

Overview

I summarize the lessons you've learned in this section. I also put into perspective the three main tasks of creating and using objects:

In this chapter

1. Identifying your objects based on the responsibilities they have to fulfill. Commonality and variability analysis prove extremely useful here.

2. Deciding how to use these objects. This is primarily about object relationships, which is what many of the patterns are about.

3. Deciding how to manage these objects. This is where factories come in.

I summarize the advantages of dividing your software development tasks into separate steps that deal with only one of these issues.

Steps in the Software Process

When developing software, it has long been recognized that breaking code into modules greatly benefits the quality of the code produced. Modules are easier to manage and, when properly designed, can be easier to modify or extend. In functionally decomposed systems, however, modules can pretty much just be used to modularize different functions. In object-oriented systems, a new possibility emerges. Chapter 1, "The Object-Oriented Paradigm," talked about three different perspectives: conceptual, specification, and implementation. This chapter discusses another set of perspectives that

Divide and Conquer

can be used in designing our applications: the perspective of use and the perspective of creation/management.

The power of doing this comes from the fact that conceptually similar objects can be dealt with the same way from the perspective of use. However, when creating objects, the creating entity typically needs to know which specific object it is making, and the rules about when to make one rather than another. This becomes particularly useful when you design systems such that their most complex parts use other objects at a conceptual level. This means following the open-closed principle, the dependency inversion principle, the Liskov substitution principle and others. However, to do all of this, the using code *cannot know which particular objects it is using*. Hence, someone else does—the Factories.

It might be better to call Factories "object managers" because creating the objects is only one of their responsibilities. By encapsulating the creation and subsequent management of objects, the more complex using code does not have to deal with these issues. This means that when the need for new functions arises, we can develop this new function by dealing with it under the context of the existing system. If there isn't already a conceptual place for it, we refactor one in. We then add the new code.

This is a two-step approach. First, you refactor a place for the new code to live in, and then you put it into the system. This approach assists in the following ways:

- It means we always have a working system.

- Moving in smaller steps means less debugging.

- The costs for integrating in new code (what most people consider to be the greatest cost of extending code) stays low.

- Code quality does not degrade, and the design does not decay.

Parallels in Factories and XP Practices

Refactoring can be used to fix up poor code or as a means to extend good code. The proper way of using refactoring to add new function is the process:

The right way to refactor

- Refactor the existing code so the new code can just fit in. (This does not add any new function.) In other words, take an approach that was not open-closed in the area of concern and refactor until it is.

- Plug the new function in.

In the context of factories, this means write your system so the using code doesn't know which particular implementation it is using. If you haven't already done this in an area that now has more than one way to do things, refactor your code to allow for this. After this has been done, adding new functionality is nothing more than writing it (something that typically can't be avoided) and modifying the factory/manager object responsible for these types of objects.

Scaling Systems

The beauty of this approach is that it works pretty much at all scales in the system. At the beginning, where we have few (if any) alternatives, the factories can take the shape of methods on the classes themselves that encapsulate their construction. Later, as things get more involved, we can write specialized factory/management objects that have the rules in question hard coded. Eventually, we may need to soft code our rules using databases or configuration tables.

The beauty of it all

However this is done, our factory/management logic is encapsulated behind methods and objects that decouple these rules from the using software. If this logic gets complicated (as it often does), it still remains loosely coupled to the system and can therefore remain flexible and easily expanded.

There will always be changes in software. However any given change will usually effect *either* the users of an object or service *or* the factories that instantiate it. By keeping these separate, we reduce the maintenance to one of these entities or the other, but seldom both.

This boils down to a fundamental principle: Given any two entities A and B in a system, the relationship should be limited such that A *uses* B or A *creates/manages* B, *but never both*!

Part VIII

Endings and Beginnings

Part Overview

This part continues with the new perspective on object-oriented design. In particular, this part describes how design patterns use this perspective in their design and implementation. I close this part with recommendations for further reading.

In this part

Chapter	Discusses These Topics
25	**Design Patterns Reviewed** Looks at the motivations and relationships of design patterns within the context of this new perspective on object-oriented design
26	**Bibliography** Suggests books and other resources for future study

CHAPTER 25

Design Patterns Reviewed:
A Summation and a Beginning

Overview

At the end of any book, it is always nice to step back and see what *In this chapter* we have gained. In this book, I have tried to give you a better understanding of object-oriented principles by using an approach that may have been new to you. I taught you design patterns and used them to show you how design patterns explain the object-oriented paradigm. Design patterns answer the fundamental question "why do you do it that way?"

This chapter reviews the following:

- The new perspective of object-oriented principles, based on an understanding of design patterns

- How design patterns help us encapsulate implementations

- How commonality and variability analysis, along with design patterns, helps us understand abstract classes

- Decomposing a problem domain by the responsibilities involved

- Design patterns and contextual design

- Relationships within patterns

- Design patterns and agile coding practices

Finally, I offer some field notes from my own practice.

A Summary of Object-Oriented Principles

Objects from the new perspective

In the course of the discussion on design patterns, I have stated a number of the principles of the object-oriented paradigm. These principles can be summarized as follows:

- Objects are things with well-defined responsibilities.

- Objects are responsible for themselves.

- Encapsulation means any kind of hiding

  - Data hiding

  - Implementation hiding

  - Class hiding (behind an abstract class or interface)

  - Design hiding

  - Instantiation hiding

- Abstract out variations in behavior and data with commonality and variability analysis.

- Design to interfaces.

- Think of inheritance as a method of conceptualizing variation, not for making special cases of existing objects.

- Keep variations in a class decoupled from other variations in the class.

- Strive for loose coupling.

- Strive for strong cohesion.

- Separate the code that uses an object from the code that creates the object.

- Be absolutely meticulous in applying the "once and only once" rule.

- Ensure your code is readable by "programming by intention" and by using intention-revealing names.

- Consider the testability of your code before coding it.

How Design Patterns Encapsulate Implementations

Several of the design patterns I have presented have the character-istic that they shield implementation details from a client object. For example, the Bridge pattern hides from the client how the classes derived from the **Abstraction** are implemented. Additionally, the **Implementation** interface hides the family of implementations from the **Abstraction** and its derivations as well. In the Strategy pattern, the implementations of each **ConcreteStrategy** are hid-den. This is true of most of the patterns described by the Gang of Four: They give ways to hide specific implementations.

Hiding variations in detail

The value of hiding the implementations is that the patterns allow for easily adding new implementations, because the client objects do not know how the current implementation works.

Commonality and Variability Analysis and Design Patterns

Chapter 10, "The Bridge Pattern," showed how the Bridge pattern can be derived using commonality and variability analysis. Many other pat-terns can be derived this way as well, including the Strategy, Iterator, Proxy, State, Visitor, Template Method, Decorator, Composite, and Abstract Factory patterns. What is more important, however, is that looking for commonalities—using commonality and variability analy-sis—helps us discover patterns that are present in the problem domain.

Commonality and variability analysis

For example, in the Bridge pattern, I may start with several special cases:

- Draw a square with drawing program one.

- Draw a circle with drawing program two.

- Draw a rectangle with drawing program one.

Knowing the Bridge helps me see these as special cases of two commonalities:

- Drawing programs

- Shapes to draw

The Strategy pattern is similar in that when I see several different rules, I know to look for a commonality among the rules so I can encapsulate them.

Although we can derive many patterns just from the use of commonality and variability analysis, it is important to keep learning patterns and reading the literature. Patterns provide the backdrop for discussions about lessons learned in analysis and design. They give a team of developers a common vocabulary for discussing a problem. They enable you to incorporate best-practice approaches into your code.

Decomposing a Problem Domain into Responsibilities

The next step in commonality and variability analysis

Commonality and variability analysis identifies my conceptual view (the commonality) and my implementation view (each particular variation). If I consider just the commonalities and the objects that use them, I can think about my problem space in a different way— a decomposition of responsibilities.

In the Bridge pattern, for example, the pattern says to look at my problem domain as being composed of two different types of entities (abstractions and implementations). Therefore, I am not limited to doing only object-oriented decomposition (that is, decomposing my problem domain into objects); I can also try decomposing my problem domain into responsibilities, if that is easier for me to do. I can then define the objects that I require to implement these responsibilities (ending up with object decomposition).

A broader extension of this approach is the rule I stated earlier that designers should not worry about how to instantiate objects until after they know all of the objects they need. That rule can be viewed as a decomposing the problem domain into two parts:

- Which objects are needed

- How these objects are instantiated and managed

Specific patterns often give us assistance in thinking about how to decompose responsibilities. For example, the Decorator pattern gives me a way to combine objects flexibly if I decompose my problem domain into the main set of responsibilities I always use (which is the **ConcreteComponent**) and the variations I optionally have (which are the **Decorator**s). Strategies decompose my problem into an object that uses rules (without regard as to which rule is being used) and the rules themselves.

Patterns and Contextual Design

In the CAD/CAM problem earlier in this book, I showed how design patterns can be used by focusing on their context with each other. Contextual design is another way of describing the dependency inversion principle discussed in Chapter 14, "Principles and Strategies of Design Patterns." Design patterns working together can assist in the development of an application's architecture. It is also useful to distinguish how many of the patterns are microcosmic examples of design by context. For example

Patterns are microcosmic examples of contextual design

- The Bridge pattern tells me to define my **Implementation**s within the context of the derivations of my **Abstraction**.

- The Decorator pattern has me design my **Decorator**s within the context of my original component.

- The Abstract Factory has me define my families within the context of my overall problem so that I can see which particular objects need to be implemented.

Designing to an interface is designing within a context

In fact, designing to interfaces and polymorphism in general is a kind of design by context. Look at Figure 25-1, which is a reprint of Figure 8-4. Notice how the abstract class' interface defines the context within which all of its derived classes must be implemented.

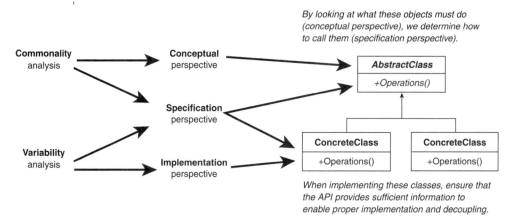

Figure 25-1 The relationships between commonality and variability analysis, perspectives, and abstract classes.

Relationships Within a Pattern

Patterns aren't really the important thing

I must admit that in my design pattern courses, I have some fun with a certain quote from Alexander. After I have been talking about how great patterns are for two thirds of a day, I pick up Alexander's *Timeless Way of Building*, turn to the end, and say:

> *This book is 549 pages long. On page 545, which, I think you will agree, is pretty close to the end, Alexander says, "At this final stage, the patterns are no longer important."*[1]

1. Alexander, C., *The Timeless Way of Building*, New York: Oxford University Press, 1979, p. 545.

I pause to say, "I wish he'd have told me this at the beginning and I could have saved myself some time!" Before my students start to revolt, I continue to quote from his book, "The patterns have taught you to be receptive to what is real."[2]

I finish with, "If you read Alexander's book, you will know what is real—the relationships and forces described by the patterns."

The patterns give us a way to talk about these. However, it is not the patterns themselves that are most important. This is true for software patterns as well.

A pattern describes the forces, motivations, and relationships about a particular problem in a particular context and provides us with an approach to addressing these issues. The Bridge pattern, for example, is about the relationship between the derived classes of an abstraction and their possible implementations. A Strategy pattern is about the relationships between

Software patterns are multi-dimensional descriptions

- A class that uses one of a set of algorithms (the **Context**).

- The members of this set of algorithms (the **Strategies**).

- The **Client**, which uses the context and specifies which of the algorithms to use.

I illustrate the parts of a pattern in Figure 25-2.

Design Patterns and Agile Coding Practices

Some people look at patterns and misconstrue their true nature. They believe they are canned solutions that you apply in different situations. As such, they do seem to run against agile coding techniques. However, I hope I have shown that patterns are much more

Different sides of the same coin

---

2. Ibid, p, 545.

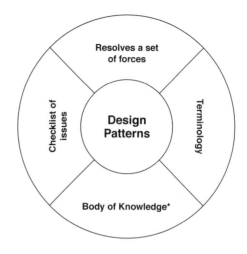

*Body of knowledge is not really part of the pattern. It is based on the pattern, on the language used, on the particular environment, and so forth

Figure 25-2 A diagram of the parts of a pattern.

than that. If you look at the philosophy and principles behind patterns you will see that they are very useful with agile coding techniques (including eXtreme Programming and Test-Driven Development).

I showed how patterns could help guide us in how to do refactoring. I also discussed how patterns are consistent with the issues of testability of code. Good coding and design techniques are typically not contrary to each other. If they first appear to be so, dig deeper and find their common ground.

Field Notes

Approaches to take Truly learning patterns from a book is not possible. You have to write them and use them in your designs. Writing them is easy. Even conjuring up an example and implementing the design of the pattern is a good first step. However, remember this isn't really the pattern; it is just one aspect of it. Nevertheless, it will help you understand the others.

As you learn patterns, it is useful to look for the following forces and concepts:

- **What implementations does this pattern hide?** Thereby allowing me to change them.

- **What commonalities are present in this pattern?** This helps me identify them.

- **What are the responsibilities of the objects in this pattern?** As it may be easier to do my decomposition by responsibility.

- **What are the relationships between these objects?** This will give me information about the forces present with these objects.

- **How may the pattern itself be a microcosmic example of designing by context?** This affords me a better understanding of why the pattern is good design.

When developing software, try to see whether any of these answers to the prior questions relate to the problem domain you are working on. If they do, look to see whether there is something in the pattern you are reminded of that would be useful there.

Summary

In this chapter, I summarized the new perspective on object-oriented design. I described how design patterns manifest this. I suggested that it is useful to look at patterns by seeing

In this chapter

- What they encapsulate.

- How they use commonality/variability analysis.

- How they decompose a problem domain into responsibilities.

- How they specify relationships between objects.

- How they illustrate contextual design.

Review Questions

Observations

1. Several of the patterns have the characteristic of shielding implementations from what? What is this called? Give examples.

2. What is one example of a pattern helping to think about decomposing responsibilities?

3. As you learn patterns, what five forces and concepts should you to look for?

Interpretations

1. What is the value of hiding implementations?

Opinions and Applications

1. In the course of this book, you have read many of the essential concepts of object orientation. This chapter reviews all of these concepts. What was the most interesting or useful insight you gained?

2. At the end of his book, Christopher Alexander says, "At this final stage, the patterns are no longer important...The patterns have taught you to be receptive to what is real." What is real, are the relationships and forces described by the patterns. Do you feel that you have new ways to analyze the problem domains you are responsible for?

CHAPTER 26

Bibliography

This book has been an introduction—an introduction to design patterns, object orientation, and to a more powerful way to design computer systems. Hopefully, it has given you some tools to get started in this rich and rewarding way of thinking.

In this chapter

Where should you turn next in your study? I conclude this book with an annotated list of my current recommendations.

This chapter

- Gives the address of the Web site companion for this book.

- Offers my recommendations for

  - Further reading in design patterns.

  - Java developers.

  - C++ developers.

  - COBOL programmers who want to learn object orientation.

  - Learning the powerful development methodology called XP (eXtreme Programming).

- Concludes with a list of the books that have been influential to me personally, in the belief that life is more than programming, and that more rounded individuals make better programmers.

Design Patterns Explained:
The Web Site Companion

The Web site

Learning anything is an evolutionary process. My understanding, just like yours, changes over time. To enable me to give you my current understanding of software development issues in design patterns and other areas of software development, I've set up a Web site related to this book. This is located at *http://www.netobjectives.com/dpexplained.*

At this site you will find all information mentioned to be on the site earlier in this book, as well as the following:

- A summary of design patterns in a nice reference format

- A considerable amount of information on agile development and the relationship of design patterns to eXtreme Programming

- A description of the courses my company offers on design patterns, agile software development, use cases, refactoring, test-driven development, and many other software development related topics

Electronic magazine

I also publish articles on software development on various topics on a monthly basis in an electronic format. To subscribe, go to *http://www.netobjectives.com/subscribe.htm.*

Recommended Reading

This is a partial list of books I like. See this book's Web site, *http://www.netobjectives.com/dpexplained*, for a full bibliography.

I recommend the following books on the UML:

The UML

- Fowler, M., Scott, K., *UML Distilled Second Edition: A Brief Guide to the Standard Object Modeling Language*, Boston: Addison-Wesley, 2000. This is by far my favorite source for learning the UML. It is both approachable to begin with and useful as a reference.

I recommend the following books and references on object-oriented programming:

*Object-oriented
programming*

- Fowler, M., *Refactoring: Improving the Design of Existing Code*,
  Boston: Addison-Wesley, 2000. The most extensive treatment
  of refactoring available.

- Martin, R, *Agile Software Development: Principles, Patterns and
  Practices*, Upper Saddle River, NJ: Prentice Hall, 2002. A well-
  written book both on how to write object-oriented code and
  how to do it in an agile manner.

- Meyer, B., *Object-Oriented Software Construction*, Upper Saddle
  River, NJ: Prentice Hall, 1997. An incredibly thorough book by
  one of the brilliant minds in our industry.

The field of design patterns continues to evolve and deepen. One
can study the field on a variety of levels and from many perspectives. I recommend the following books and references to help you
on your journey:

Design patterns

- Alexander, C., Ishikawa, S., Silverstein, M., *The Timeless Way of
  Building*, New York: Oxford University Press, 1979. Both a personal and professional favorite. It is both entertaining and in-
  sightful. If you read only one book from this list, have it be this one.

- Alur, D., Malks, D., Crupi, J. *Core J2EE Patterns: Best Practices and
  Design Strategies, Second Edition*, Upper Saddle River, NJ: Prentice
  Hall, 2003. Useful for J2EE developers as well as anyone work-
  ing on distributed applications in general.

- Coplein, J., *Multi-Paradigm Design for C++*, Boston: Addison-
  Wesley, 1998. Chapters 2 through 5 are a must-read even for
  non-C++ developers. This is the book that inspired our understanding of commonality and variability analysis. See our book's
  Web site for an online version of Jim's doctoral dissertation,
  which is equivalent to his book.

- Fowler, M., *Patterns of Enterprise Architecture*, Boston: Addison-Wesley, 2002.

- Gamma, E., Helm, R., Johnson, R., Vlissides, J., *Design Patterns: Elements of Reusable Object-Oriented Software*, Boston: Addison-Wesley, 1995. Now dated, but incredibly useful.

- Gardner, K., *Cognitive Patterns: Problem-Solving Frameworks for Object Technology*, New York: Cambridge University Press, 1998. This approaches patterns from the perspective of cognitive science and artificial intelligence. Dr. Gardner was also heavily influenced by Alexander's work.

- Metsker, S., *Design Patterns Java Workbook,* Boston: Addison-Wesley, 2002. A good book to learn patterns from.

- Nock, C., *Data Access Patterns: Database Interactions in Object-Oriented Applications,* Boston: Addison-Wesley, 2004. A good book for patterns in the database arena.

- Schmidt, D., Stal, M., Rohnert, H., Busehmann, F., *Pattern-Oriented Software Architecture, Volume 2,* New York: John Wiley, 2000. The book to use for multithreaded and distributed environments.

Recommended Reading for Java Programmers

Learning Java

When it comes to learning Java, my favorite books are as follows:

- Eckel, B., *Thinking in Java, Second Edition*, Upper Saddle River, NJ: Prentice Hall, 2000. Good both for learning and reference. See our Web site, *http://www.netobjectives.com*, for a bibliography for a downloadable version of this book.

- Horstmann, C., *Core Java 2—Volume 1—Fundamentals, Sixth Edition*, Palo Alto, CA: Pearson Education, 2002. Another good book for learning Java.

After you've learned Java, here are a few other books to read:

Programming in Java

- Bloch, P., *Effective Java Programming Language Guide*, Boston: Addison-Wesley, 2001. This is a great book. It inspired us in our understanding of separating use from construction.

- Coad, P., *Java Design*, Upper Saddle River, NJ: Prentice Hall, 2000. If you are a Java developer, this book is a must-read. It discusses most of the principles and strategies we have found useful in using design patterns even though it doesn't mention design patterns specifically.

- Grand, M., *Patterns in Java, Volume 1, Second Edition*, New York: John Wiley, 2002. If you are a Java developer, you may find this book useful. It has its examples in Java and it uses the UML. However, we believe the discussions on forces and motivations in the GoF book are more useful than those presented in Grand's book. However, there is a lot of value by getting another set of examples, particularly when in the language of use (Java).

There are special considerations when it comes to dealing with threads in Java. I recommend the following resources to help learn about this area:

Threads in Java

- Hollub, A., *Taming Java Threads*, Berkeley, CA: APress, 2000.

- Hyde, P., *Java Thread Programming: The Authoritative Solution*, Indianapolis, IN: SAMS, 1999.

- Lea, D., *Concurrent Programming in Java: Design Principles and Patterns, Second Edition*, Boston: Addison-Wesley, 2000.

Recommended Reading for C++ Programmers

I have found the following essential for using C++ for UNIX:

C++ and UNIX

- Eckel, B., *Thinking in C++, Volume 1: Introduction to Standard C++, Second Edition*, Upper Saddle River, NJ: Prentice Hall,2000. One of the best books to use to learn C++. Useful even after you know the language. You can also get this book in an electronic format for free at his Web site.

- Koenig, A., Moo, B., *Accelerated C++: Practical Programming by Example*, Boston: Addison-Wesley, 2000. This book approaches learning C++ by starting to write complete programs using the Standard Library. A very useful way to learn. It is both a great book to learn C++ with and to teach it with. Not strong on object orientation, unfortunately.

- Stevens, W., *Advanced Programming in the UNIX Environment*, Boston: Addison-Wesley, 1992. This is a must resource for anyone doing C/C++ development on UNIX (and yes, I know it is not about object orientation or patterns).

Recommended Reading for COBOL Programmers

Learning OO

I have found the following helpful for COBOL programmers who want to learn object-oriented design:

- Levey, R., *Reengineering Cobol with Objects*, New York: McGraw-Hill, 1995. A useful book for COBOL programmers who are trying to learn object-oriented design.

Recommended Reading on eXtreme Programming

Learning Agile and eXtreme Programming

When it comes to gaining proficiency in eXtreme Programming (XP), my best recommendations are as follows:

- Beck, K., *Extreme Programming Explained: Embrace Change*, Boston: Addison-Wesley, 2000. This is worthwhile reading for anyone involved in software development, even if you are not planning on using XP. I have selected 30 or so pages I consider essential reading and list them in the Resources section of the NetObjectives web site: *http://www.netobjectives.com.*

- Cockburn, A., *Agile Software Development.* Boston: Addison-Wesley, 2001. This is a great book to understand the issues of agile software development.

- Schwaber, K., Beedle, M., *Agile Software Development with Scrum.* Upper Saddle River, NJ: Prentice Hall, 2001. This is a book you can read and put to use immediately.

Recommended Reading on General Programming

This book mirrors my philosophy of being introspective and always looking to see how I can improve myself and my work:

Being a better programmer

- Hunt, A., Thomas, D., *The Pragmatic Programmer: From Journeyman to Master*, Boston: Addison-Wesley, 2000. This is one of those lovely books that I read a few pages of each day. When I come across things I already do, I take the opportunity to acknowledge myself. When I find things I'm not doing, I take the opportunity to learn.

Personal Favorites

It is my belief that the best designers are not those who live and breathe programming and nothing else. Rather, being able to think and to listen, having a more complete and deep personality, and knowing ideas are what make for great designers. You can connect better with other people. You can glean ideas from other disciplines (for example, as we did from architecture and from anthropology). You will create systems that better take into account human beings, for whom our systems exist anyway.

Beyond programming

Many of my students ask about what I like to read, what has shaped how I think and helped me in my journey. The following are my recommendations.

Alan's list

Alan recommends the following:

- Grieve, B., *The Blue Day Book: A Lesson in Cheering You Up*, Kansas City: Andrews McMeel Publishing, 2000. This is a fun and delightful book. Read it whenever you are feeling down (it's short).

- Hill, N., *Think and Grow Rich*, New York: Ballantine Books, 1960. "Rich" doesn't only mean in money—it means in whatever form you want to be rich in. This book has had a profound impact on both my personal and business success.

- Kundtz, D., *Stopping: How to Be Still When You Have to Keep Going*, Berkeley, CA: Conari Press, 1998. As a recovering workaholic, this book is a beautiful reminder of how to slow down and enjoy life, but still get things done.

- Mandino, O., *The Greatest Salesman in the World*, New York: Bantam Press, 1968. I read and "practiced" this book a few years ago. It has helped me live my life the way I've always wanted to. If you read it, I strongly suggest doing what the scrolls tell Hafid to do—not just read about it. (You'll know what I mean when you read the book.)

- Pilzer, P., *Unlimited Wealth: The Theory and Practice of Economic Alchemy*, Crown Publishers, 1990. This book presents both a new paradigm for resources and wealth, and how to take advantage of it. A must-read in the information age.

- Remen, R., *My Grandfather's Blessings: Stories of Strength, Refuge, and Belonging*, New York: Riverhead Books, 2000. A lovely book to reflect on one's blessings.

Jim recommends the following: *Jim's list*

- Buzan, T., and Buzan, B., *The Mind Map Book: How to Use Radiant Thinking to Maximize Your Brain's Untapped Potential*, New York: Dutton Books, 1994. This has revolutionized how I teach, communicate, think, and take notes. An incredibly powerful technique. I use this daily.

- Cahill, T., *How the Irish Saved Civilization*, New York: Doubleday, 1995. If you have any Irish blood in you, this will make you proud. Cannibals turned to the greatest force for civilization and rescue Europe.

- Dawson, C., *Religion and the Rise of Western Culture*, New York: Doubleday, 1950. How religion shaped the development of Western civilization and kept at bay the "barbarianism that is always lurking just below the surface." Important insights into scientific thought.

- Gerber, Michael E., *The E-Myth Revisited: Why Most Small Businesses Don't Work and What to Do About It*. New York: HarperBusiness, 1995. If you are involved in running your own business or are thinking about it, this book is essential reading. It applies equally well for for-profit and not-for-profit enterprises. (Note from Alan: As a small business owner, I couldn't agree with Jim more).

- Jensen, B., *Simplicity: The New Competitive Advantage in a World of More, Better, Faster*, Cambridge, MA: Perseus Books, 2000. A revolution in thought and knowledge management. Designing systems that are simpler for people to use, taking humans into account in our processes and technologies.

- Lingenfelter, S., *Transforming Culture*, Grand Rapids, MI: Baker Book House, 1998. A model for understanding cultures through social game theory.

- Spradely, J. P., *The Ethnographic Interview*, New York: Harcourt Brace Jovanovich College Publishers, 1979. A must-read for anyone who wants to become a better interviewer. The classic text used by all students of anthropology.

- Wiig, K., *Knowledge Management Methods*, Dallas: Schema Press, 1995. A virtual encyclopedia of techniques for helping organizations exploit their knowledge resources more effectively.

Index